The Economics of Industrial Development

The spread of the manufacturing industry is an important part of economic development, creating jobs, new products and trade and investment links between countries. Understanding this process is an important part of understanding how countries develop and how they are affected by current globalisation. The economic geography of the world has been changing significantly in the last few decades, with old and established industrial centres in the developed countries in decline, and new centres emerging in countries that were once thought of as poor and developing. However, this process has been very uneven, with some parts of the developing world still largely non-industrial.

This book aims to explain this process from the perspective of developing countries. It charts current trends in industrial development, drawing on available statistics and explores different perspectives on the role that the manufacturing industry can play.

The book covers topics including:

- Aspects of trade policy as they affect industry.
- The international rules of the World Trade Organisation.
- The network of links between firms in different parts of the world economy.

Separate chapters examine:

- The special role of small firms and of technology in industrialisation.
- Government policy towards the encouragement of industry, drawing particularly on the experience of economies in East Asia (the original Asian Tigers).
- Recent developments in China and India and their implications for other countries.

The book draws on simple concepts of economic theory but avoids a technical mathematical approach and should be accessible to a wide audience. It extends and updates the author's earlier work on industrialisation published by Routledge (*Industry in Developing Countries*, 1990, and *Industrialisation and Globalisation*, 2002) and aims to present a comprehensive overview of these important contemporary issues. The book is suitable for both undergraduate- and graduate-level courses, but will also be invaluable to professionals working in development.

John Weiss is Professor of Development Economics and Associate Dean for Research in the Bradford Centre for International Development, the University of Bradford, United Kingdom. He has worked as a consultant for many international organisations including the Asian Development Bank, the World Bank and the United Nations Industrial Development Organisation.

The Economics of Industrial Development

John Weiss

Routledge
Taylor & Francis Group
LONDON AND NEW YORK

First published 2011
by Routledge
2 Park Square, Milton Park, Abingdon, Oxon, OX14 4RN

Simultaneously published in the USA and Canada
by Routledge
270 Madison Avenue, New York, NY 10016

Routledge is an imprint of the Taylor & Francis Group, an informa business

Typeset in Times New Roman by Glyph International
Printed and bound in Great Britain by CPI Antony Rowe, Chippenham

British Library Cataloguing in Publication Data
A catalogue record for this book is available from the British Library

Library of Congress Cataloging-in-Publication Data
Weiss, John, 1948–
The economics of industrial development / by John Weiss.
p. cm.
Includes bibliographical references and index.
(eb) 1. Industrialization–Developing countries. 2. Economic development–Developing countries. I. Title.
HC59.7.W4534 2010
338.9009172'4–dc22 2010003452

ISBN 13: 978-0-415-47371-2 (hbk)
ISBN 13: 978-0-415-47372-9 (pbk)
ISBN 13: 978-0-203-84680-3 (ebk)

Contents

Figures

Tables

Preface

This book is about industrialisation in what we used to call 'developing countries', although the heterogeneity of recent experiences confirms this to be a rather unhelpful blanket term. It follows from my earlier efforts published by Routledge, *Industry in Developing Countries* (1990), and *Industrialisation and Globalisation* (2002). Like these earlier books, this seeks to combine material of interest to both student and professional audiences and, as appropriate, draws on empirical work that I have been involved with over the years, as well as secondary material I have come across, particularly through my work in recent years with International Development Organisations. It tries to marry simple economic concepts with empirical evidence and applied work related to industrialisation. No single simple interpretation is pursued, but it aims to give readers a sense of the range of debate and approaches. Some of the more specialist material is presented in boxes and can be omitted by readers wishing to get a quick sense of the arguments. It is intended that the book will be useful to students studying courses on Development both at the undergraduate and masters levels, as well as to Development professionals wishing to revisit some of the arguments about and evidence on industrialisation.

All authors owe a debt of gratitude to their families for the distraction that writing creates and for the disruption to family life. My debt is particularly strong, and I want to acknowledge the wonderful support and patience of Francis and our sons Alfred and Antonio. Antonio was my technical advisor for word processing and formatting. Rob Langham of Routledge encouraged me to produce the book and commented on some of the earlier drafts. Masters students at Bradford University over the years will have come across some of the material on trade and development. Remaining errors are naturally the responsibility of the author.

John Weiss

1 Industry and development

This book is about the drive to industrialise in the lower-income economies of the world. Manufacturing is the capacity to produce goods with labour, materials and inputs produced by others. Simple forms of manufacturing have characterised all organised societies but the application of steam power to production in Britain in the late eighteenth and early nineteenth centuries significantly increased the capacity for production, and since this first *Industrial Revolution*, economic progress has in many people's minds been linked with the capacity to produce and trade in manufactured products. Some of today's lower-income economies (principally China and India) once took a far higher share of world economic activity than they do today, and their current rapid industrial growth is in part a return to this position. Elsewhere, new nations emerged from periods of colonial rule that distorted their economies and arguably held back economic progress. Forty or fifty years ago, politicians and their advisers were unanimous that progress required industry, and a range of policy measures were applied to encourage industrialisation. This book aims to explore the case for industrialisation, the experience with the application of policies to support this process and the links between national activity and the widespread international movement of capital, goods and ideas now termed 'globalisation'. This chapter sets the scene by introducing terminology and definitions and surveying recent experience. Later chapters pick up the key issues raised here in more detail.

Some terminology

At the outset of this book, it is necessary to clarify the sense in which particular terms will be used. Productive activity is conventionally classified using the United Nations International Standard Industrial Classification (ISIC) which divides all economic activity into three broad divisions – agriculture, industry and services. In principle, the general term industry can be used to reflect all types of economic activity (e.g. the *transport industry*). Its narrower meaning as used here refers to activity where inputs are transformed into a different form of product, so that value is created at different stages of the production process. This activity can be thought of as manufacturing and will include the processing of natural resource-based products from agriculture and mining. Hence, industry in this narrow sense refers to *manufacturing industry*. However, a common statistical definition of industry includes not just manufacturing, but also mining, construction and the utilities electricity, water and gas (see Box 1.1).

Industrialisation is, therefore, the process under which manufacturing comes to play a significant role in total activity of an economy. What is a significant threshold beyond which industrialisation can be said to be achieved is open to debate;

Box 1.1 Industrial classification

The ISIC classification revision 3 divides productive economic activity into three broad categories with further sub-divisions within these: Agriculture including forestry and fishing (divisions 1–5), Industry including mining, manufacturing, construction, electricity, water and gas (divisions 10–45) and Services including transport, retail and wholesale and financial services (divisions 50–99).

Manufacturing is sub-divided at the 2-, 3- and 4-digit levels. The 2-digit classification is given as follows.

15 Food products and beverages
16 Tobacco products
17 Textiles
18 Wearing apparel, dressing and dyeing of fur
19 Tanning, dressing and processing of leather, including footwear
20 Wood and wood products
21 Paper and paper products
22 Publishing, printing and recorded media
23 Refined petroleum products
24 Chemicals and chemical products
25 Rubber and plastic products
26 Other non-metallic mineral products
27 Basic metals
28 Fabricated metal products other than machinery
29 Machinery and equipment
30 Office, accounting and computing machinery
31 Electrical machinery
32 Radio, television and communication equipment
33 Medical, precision and optical equipment
34 Motor vehicles
35 Other transport equipment
36 Furniture and other manufactures
37 Recycling

Source: http:www.unstats.un.org.

for example, one can suggest a share of national income for manufacturing of 25 per cent and of total exports of about 75 per cent; however, the cut-off point is essentially arbitrary. Furthermore, progress in industrialisation is reversible as discussions of *de-industrialisation*, defined as either an absolute decline in manufacturing or a relative fall in its share in either output or employment, indicate.

Development is best seen as a process of income growth, improvements in social indicators and structural economic change. Growth can occur in the short term without the latter two effects, for example, due to an export boom, although the expectation is that without at least structural change, this type of growth will not be sustained. *Developing countries* is a term used to cover a group of countries undergoing the process of development, in contrast with economies that are already developed. The developing–developed dichotomy has a long history of usage, but it suggests homogeneity within each group, that whilst always a simplification, has become increasing misleading with rapid growth in some and stagnation in others. A term used to cover countries as diverse as Cambodia, China and Cote d' Ivoire is not very helpful. Here, whilst we do on occasion revert to the term 'developing countries', as far as possible we try to specify what type of economy we are referring to. *Newly industrialised economies* (NIEs) are those which have created a significant manufacturing sector. There are no unique criteria for membership of this group, but it is usually applied to China, the economies of East and Southeast Asia and the larger Latin American economies. The term *emerging economies* has also been applied to basically the same group of countries. It is usually reserved for relatively high-growth economies that have opened their financial sectors to allow capital and stock market participation by international investors. In practice, although the origin of the term is slightly different, the *emerging economies* are in effect the NIEs.

In an alternative classification, the United Nations designates a group of *least developed countries* (LDCs) as those with the lowest incomes (typically less than US$900 per head annually), weak human assets and vulnerability to economic shocks. However, even within this group, there will be differences in population and market size, economic structure and resource endowments, which mean they face different constraints to growth and development. On the basis of income alone, large countries like India and Pakistan should be part of the group, but they are excluded on the grounds of the relative sophistication of their human capital and production structure. The standard World Bank classification is a distinction between lower-income, lower-middle-income, higher-middle-income and high-income economies (Table 1.1). Insofar as increases in income are accompanied by change in production structure, this distinction is at least an improvement over the blanket category of developing countries. However, even at similar income levels, economies can face different problems; for example, Mexico and Macedonia have similar income levels of around US$7,000 at 2005 prices, but they are quite different types of economy.

Technology is knowledge of ways of producing commodities. *Technological capability* is the capacity to create or adapt technology. Technology can either

Table 1.1 Country classification by income level

Income group	*Average per capita income 2005 (US$)*	*Industry share in GDP 2007/8 (%)*	*Manufactures share in exports 2005 (%)*	*Annual growth of manufacturing 1990–2000 (%)*	*Annual growth of manufacturing 2000–05 (%)*
Low	580	29	51	5.9	6.9
Lower-middle	1,918	41	68	8.5	9.4
Upper-middle	5,625	33	61	4.4	3.1
High	35,131	26	81	na	1.1

Source: World Bank (2007).

be embodied and codified in physical equipment or exist only in the minds of researchers; it can also be protected by private patents that restrict its use or freely available as a public good. Most of the global research and development is undertaken in high-income economies, so that for technical change to improve efficiency or product quality, poorer economies must rely on imports of new technology or on adaptations of existing technology.

The different sub-divisions or branches of manufacturing have different levels of *technological sophistication* in terms of the expenditure on research and development (R and D) as a share of the value of final product (Table 1.2). Products with high levels of R and D are expected to undergo the greatest change in either cost or quality (otherwise, the R and D investment is ineffective) and hence are expected to be the most *dynamic products* in terms of the growth of demand both domestically and internationally. High-technological-sophistication products are principally those in the ISIC sub-divisions of electronics, office equipment and scientific and precision equipment (these are within ISIC 29–33 in Box 1.1).

Table 1.2 Country classification by region

Income group: low and middle income	*Average per capita income 2005*	*Industry share in 2005 (GDP %)*	*Manufactures share in exports 2004 (%)*	*Annual growth of manufacturing 1990–2000 (%)*	*Annual growth of manufacturing 2000–05 (%)*
East Asia and Pacific	1,627	45	80	10.8	9.8
Europe and Central Asia	4,113	32	57	na	na
Latin America and Caribbean	4,008	32	56	3.4	1.7
Middle East and North Africa	2,241	41	20	3.8	6.4
South Asia	684	27	76	6.6	7.0
Sub-Saharan Africa	745	32	31	1.9	2.6

Source: World Bank (2007).

Low-technological-sophistication products are either goods made from simple labour-intensive production techniques, principally in sub-divisions of clothing, footwear and food products, or basic intermediates like paper, wood, rubber, glass and metals, where whilst production may require relatively high levels of capital per worker the production technology in use changes relatively slowly. Other activities lie somewhere between these extremes on the spectrum of technological sophistication. As a broad generalisation, as economies get richer, the share of high-technology products in their manufacturing sectors and export baskets tends to rise.

Uneven development

Economic historians like to stress that early industrialisation followed different paths in different countries, varying with their initial circumstances and the wider external economic environment in which they started on the process. Large-scale industrialisation started in Europe but spread in the later nineteenth century to the United States and Japan. At this time, today's developing countries were predominantly agricultural and were often colonised by the more industrialised economies. They exported agricultural goods and raw materials to the latter in return for manufactured goods. Modest industrial development occurred in some of the larger developing countries in the later nineteenth century, particularly in the larger Latin American economies of Brazil and Argentina and to some degree in India and China. This *colonial division of labour* with a set of richer industrialised countries trading with a set of largely non-industrialised poorer ones, often colonies of their richer trading partners, only started to change in the post-1945 period. Initially, change was relatively slow as industrialisation in poorer countries took time to take off.

It was fashionable in the development literature of 40 or 50 years ago for discussions of obstacles to the economic progress of developing countries based on ideas of *dependency* or *development of under-development*. The central idea was that links with the higher-income, developed economies, whether through past colonial or imperial ties, or contemporary trade and investment relationships, provided an inherent obstacle to industrialisation and wider economic development. Poor countries remained poor, because rich countries remained rich. Such views are much less prevalent today. Although there remain active debates about how the benefits from the world trading and investment system (the process of *globalisation*) are distributed, it has become clear that contrary to earlier pessimistic predictions some countries once termed 'developing' have made major strides in terms of economic progress. When these strides were confined to a few relatively small countries in East Asia (the original Asian Tiger economies of Hong Kong, Singapore, Taiwan and Korea), it was possible to point to special features of their experience. However, once rapid growth was experienced in the large, initially very poor countries of China and India, once perceived as the epitome of underdevelopment, this special case explanation became untenable. Today, it is recognised that how a country performs economically and how rapidly it industrialises will be driven by many factors, including its geographical location and the resources within its borders, the education and skill level of its population, and its economic ties with the rest of the world. In addition, the policy choices made by governments and the broad institutional framework of an economy (e.g. the quality of its bureaucracy, its courts, and its financial sector) all matter greatly. It is for these reasons that industrialisation in low- and middle-income economies has progressed at different rates in different places.

Nonetheless, it is one of the key features of the last 50 years of global development that a significant part of world industry has relocated to countries defined as developing at the start of the period. This is primarily because developing countries as a group experienced a more rapid rate of manufacturing growth than higher-income, developed economies. For example, overall developing countries by the UN classification accounted for around 29 per cent of world manufacturing production in 2005, which is an increase of nearly 15 percentage points since 1990. The share of developing countries in world manufactured exports is even higher at around 32 per cent in 2005.[1] This has meant the migration of many industries away from the older industrial bases of the world. The decline of textiles, steel and shipbuilding in the United Kingdom in recent decades, for example, and the rapid growth of these industries in China and elsewhere is evidence of this.

Table 1.3 illustrates this trend by summarising the global spread of manufacturing activity by UN country groupings and geographical regions. It highlights

Table 1.3 Regional distribution and growth of manufacturing value-added

Country group/region	*World manufacturing share 2005 (%)*	*Annual growth manufacturing 1995–2000 (%)*	*Annual growth manufacturing 2000–05 (%)*
World	100	4.3	2.6
Industrialised countries	69.3	3.7	1.1
Economies in transition	1.7	1.6	7.2
Developing countries	29.0	6.5	7.0
Sub-Saharan Africa	0.7	3.0	3.1
Sub-Saharan Africa excluding South Africa	0.3	3.7	3.5
South Asia	1.8	5.5	7.9
South Asia excluding India	0.4	5.0	8.7
Middle East and North Africa	2.2	6.4	6.4
Middle East and North Africa excluding Turkey	1.7	7.2	6.8
Latin America and the Caribbean	6.4	3.5	1.9
Latin America and the Caribbean excluding Mexico	4.7	1.8	2.8
East Asia and the Pacific	17.5	8.6	9.8
East Asia and the Pacific excluding China	7.7	6.2	6.1
Least developed countries	0.3	6.1	7.3

Source: UNIDO (2009, Tables 9.1 and 9.2).

Table 1.4 Structural shifts in production: agriculture and manufacturing sector shares in GDP (%)

Region	*1950*		*1960*		*1980*		*2005*	
	AG	*MAN*	*AG*	*MAN*	*AG*	*MAN*	*AG*	*MAN*
Asia (12)	49	10	39	14	25	22	13	24
Latin America (7)	22	16	18	21	10	24	7	18
Africa (10)	41	9	37	10	25	14	26	12
Developing (29)	41	11	33	15	21	20	16	18
Developed (16)	15	31	10	30	4	24	2	17

Source: Szirmai (2009, Table 2).

Notes
AG is agriculture and MAN is manufacturing.
Number of countries in brackets.

the continued slow growth of manufacturing in what are termed the industrialised economies of North America, Europe and Japan and its rapid expansion in parts of the developing world, principally East Asia, South Asia and the Middle East and North Africa. Growth in Latin America and the Caribbean and sub-Saharan Africa has been much slower. The LDCs have had relatively rapid growth by their own historical standards in recent years, but from a very low base.

Whilst a low level of income is associated with a low level of manufacturing, there has been a marked differentiation within the developing country group. The expansion of developing country manufacturing has seen a major change in the structure of production in most economies over this period with a decline in the share of agriculture in national income. Table 1.4 shows how sector shares in total national income have changed over time for geographical groupings of countries over the long period since 1950. The degree to which manufacturing has increased its share has varied significantly with a large increase in parts of Asia, only a very modest increase in much of Africa and an initial increase followed by a decline in the last 30 years in Latin America.

As noted in the foregoing, a number of the higher income of these economies are often termed *newly industrialised economies* (NIEs) on the grounds of the relative importance and sophistication of their manufacturing sectors. In addition, a few economies that were classed as developing in the past have graduated to higher income levels and to the developed category. These are the high-growth economies of East Asia, Korea, Singapore and Taiwan. The overall figures for developing country share in world manufactured value-added and exports cited in the foregoing section are slightly misleading in that these economies are included as developing countries, on the grounds that despite their high incomes today, they were developing countries when the data series started. Together the three accounted for approximately 17 per cent of developing country manufacturing in 2005. These three plus the countries listed as NIEs in Table 1.5 accounted for all but 18 per cent of the value-added attributed to developing countries in 2005, so there are many countries within the developing group which contribute very little.[2]

Table 1.5 NIEs and comparators

NIEs	*MVA per capita 2005 (2000 prices, in US$)*	*Growth of MVA per capita 2000–05 (% pa)*	*MVA in GDP 2005 (%)*	*Manufactures in total exports 2005 (%)*	*Medium-high-technology manufactures in total manufactured exports 2005 (%)*
Argentina	1372	1.6	17	56	32
Malaysia	1430	2.2	32	86	72
Mexico	1000	−1.2	17	82	75
Chile	978	2.3	17	52	12
Thailand	882	5.4	36	87	62
Brazil	749	1.3	20	73	48
South Africa	576	2.0	16	70	47
China	496	10.1	34	95	58
Turkey	465	3.3	14	91	41
Indonesia	259	3.7	28	65	33
Philippines	249	2.4	22	96	81
India	83	5.0	14	87	23
Comparators					
Singapore	6708	2.4	26	95	72
United States	5528	0.4	15	89	72
Taiwan	4144	3.9	25	97	70
Korea	3826	6.0	29	98	75
United Kingdom	3707	−1.1	14	86	65

Source: UNIDO (2009, Annex 1, Table B).

Note
MVA is manufacturing value-added.

There is no uniform classification of NIEs, but Table 1.5 gives the main candidates, showing the size of their manufacturing activity relative to population, the recent growth of manufacturing, the share of manufacturing in exports and as measure of technological sophistication, the share of medium- and high-technology goods in total manufactured exports. The figures for several higher-income economies are given for comparison. The larger Latin American economies are classed as NIEs on the grounds of their history of manufacturing (hence their relatively high manufacturing value-added per head of population), although as yet they are much less well integrated into global production than are the economies of East Asia and manufacturing growth has been slow (and negative in Mexico in per capita terms in recent years). Malaysia and Thailand have made substantial progress in manufacturing over the last thirty years and it is now over 30 per cent of total economic activity. Indonesia is also included because of its recent high manufacturing growth, although relatively manufacturing remains less important there than that in the other two East Asian economies. Although the Philippines has been the slowest growing economy in East Asia, it is often included in lists of NIEs on the grounds of its relatively high levels of manufactured exports. South Africa is the only African economy represented, because of the size and history of its manufacturing sector. China and India are included because of their rapid growth and the absolute scale of their manufacturing, although relative to population, manufacturing in India remains small. Turkey is often included as an NIE because of its lengthy history of industrialisation and relatively high manufactured exports. Table 1.5 confirms the much slower, and in the UK negative, per capita growth in manufacturing in the old established manufacturing centres of the United States and United Kingdom, reflecting an important global shift in the geography of industrial development.

One measure of progress in manufacturing is the degree to which countries can move to the production of technologically sophisticated goods. As we have noted, high-technology goods are those with a relatively high ratio of R and D to sales value. Comparative data on their relative importance in trade show that high-technology exports are much more important in East Asia than in the other NIEs. As discussed further in the following section, this is accounted for by the far greater success of East Asian firms in integrating into *global production networks*. Global production networks are the links between a lead or key firm and its suppliers in different countries. East Asian firms have become both lead firms and suppliers for others.

At the other end of the spectrum, there are economies that have either failed to raise their manufacturing growth significantly or have undergone a process of deindustrialisation. The LDC group had an average manufacturing value-added per capita in 2005 less than 10 per cent of that of all developing economies (using the UN country classification for both groups), with a majority of their exports primary products rather than manufactures. The contrast between average manufactured exports per capita from the LDC group in 2005 and the developing country average is stark with the former less than 3 per cent of the latter (US$13 as compared with US$487).[3]

In addition to these very-low-income economies, with no history of industrialisation a significant number of countries have also experienced *de-industrialisation*. This term can be defined in various ways. In a relative sense, it is a decline in the share of manufacturing in either the total production or employment of an economy. In an absolute sense, it is an actual decline in manufacturing production or employment. The latter interpretation highlights a more obvious problem, but reasons why relative deindustrialisation at a relatively low-income level may also be a concern are reviewed in Chapter 2.

The countries suffering absolute declines in manufacturing are principally either failed states suffering from internal conflict and the loss of government authority or the *transition economies* of Eastern Europe adjusting to the post-Soviet era and the break-up of Yugoslavia, with a significant decline in their previously uncompetitive manufacturing sectors. Hong Kong is an exception in that, whilst it has de-industrialised rapidly, this is due to a shift of industry to Mainland China and its concentration on high-value services. Table 1.6 gives data for economies that suffered the largest declines 1990–2002. The declines in some of the transition economies are very dramatic, although relatively industry still remains important in part because a similar decline has occurred in other sectors.

Table 1.6 De-industrialising economies

Economies	*MVA per capita 2005 (US$2000 prices)*	*Growth of MVA 1990–2002 (% pa)*	*Growth of MVA per capita 2000–05*
Hong Kong	921	−3.2	−6.3
Croatia	na	−3.8	na
Slovakia	1106	−3.0	7.1
Russian Federation	470	−5.0	6.1
Bulgaria	382	−3.7	9.2
Romania	471	−3.5	5.5
Ukraine	na	−9.3	na
Colombia	323	−1.0	2.2
Turkmenistan	na	−2.3	na
Kazakhstan	na	−4.6	na
Algeria	133	−1.7	0.9
Zimbabwe	41	−0.9	−13.1
Tajikistan	na	−10.2	na
Georgia	140	−10.7	6.9
Haiti	na	−6.5	na
Burundi	na	−2.8	na

Source: For columns 1 and 3 UNIDO (2009) and column 2 UNIDO (2005).

In the de-industrialisers, high-technology production is generally very small relative to other internationally traded goods. Comparable data for more recent years are not available for all countries in the table, but it can be seen that there has been a significant recovery since 2000 in many of the transition economies and Russia, so that the de-industrialisation noted here seems transitory rather than permanent in all but countries suffering a collapse in government authority (of which Zimbabwe is the best known example) and Hong Kong (where other factors are at work).

Manufactured exports

Manufactures now dominate world trade and typically are around 80 per cent of world exports in any year with developing countries (in the sense of the UN definition) accounting for nearly one-third of this. In the bulk of developing countries, outside the LDCs and the oil rich states, manufactures account for a majority of export revenue. In terms of regional distribution, the bulk of developing country manufactured exports come from East Asia (70 per cent in 2005), with approximately 40 per cent of these from China. Similarly, South Asia's rapid growth of manufactured exports is due principally to India. As noted earlier, it is possible to classify goods by their R and D content to identify goods by technological level. Table 1.7 gives the share of different country groups and regions in total manufactured exports and Table 1.8 gives export share with exports classified by their technology level. In recent years, developing countries have been gaining world market share in all technology categories. In the 1980s and 1990s,

Table 1.7 Manufactured exports by region

Region	*Share in world manufactured exports 2005 (%)*	*Annual growth of manufactured exports 2000–05 (%)*
World	100	9.7
Industrialised countries	65.9	8.3
Economies in transition	2.5	18.5
Developing countries	31.6	12.4
Sub-Saharan Africa	0.7	12.6
Sub-Saharan Africa excluding South Africa	0.3	13.2
South Asia	1.4	16.1
South Asia excluding India	0.2	6.7
Middle East and North Africa	2.2	15.6
Middle East and North Africa excluding Turkey	1.4	12.4
Latin America and the Caribbean	4.5	7.5
Latin America and the Caribbean excluding Mexico	2.2	11.9
East Asia and the Pacific	22.3	13.4
East Asia and the Pacific excluding China	13.0	7.8
Least developed countries	0.1	−2.9

Source: UNIDO (2009, Table 10.4).

high-technology products were the most dynamic in terms of export growth, although Table 1.8 shows this pattern was not continued in the first few years of the new century.[4] What appears to have occurred more recently is a relative shift in world demand towards resource-based manufactures, such as iron and steel-related and petroleum products, in part reflecting growing demand in China and India and the related boom in commodity prices over this period. It is not yet clear what pattern will emerge after recovery from the current global downturn and whether high-technology products will resume their rising share of world trade in manufactures in the longer term.

Table 1.8 Manufactured export growth by technology category

Category	*Developing country share in world trade 2005 (%)*	*Annual growth of world exports 2000–05 (%)*	*Annual growth of developing country exports 2000–05 (%)*
All manufactures	31.6	9.7	12.4
Resource-based	31.8	12.1	14.2
Low technology	40.3	9.6	10.0
Medium technology	23.5	10.1	14.8
High technology	38.6	7.3	10.6

Source: Calculated from UNIDO (2009, Annex II, Table 3).

Note
For coverage of technology categories see UNIDO (2009) Annex II.

In a number of industries (most obviously electronics), production has become fragmented as parts and components produced in one location are assembled or further manufactured in another to take advantage of cost differences between locations. These transactions, which sometimes take place within one large international firm and sometimes between a lead firm and its suppliers often based in different countries, represent the spread of *global production networks*. The growth of manufactured exports from many low- and middle-income countries reflects this pattern.

Export data are also available by product category. Table 1.9 gives developing country and regional shares in manufactured exports by selected types of product. It shows developing countries as a group taking more than 50 per cent of world exports in the labour-intensive, simple-technology categories of textiles, footwear and leather goods and over 60 per cent in clothing and travel goods. They also remain major exporters of the higher-technology electronic products taking over 50 per cent of world exports of office machines and data processing (including here computers and their components) and telecommunications and sound apparatus. East and Southeast dominate the group of developing countries, largely because it includes China and the first-tier NIEs. This dominance is particularly marked in the high-technology electronics categories. Latin America with a relatively long history of industrialisation over the twentieth century is under-represented in world manufactured exports with its share of such exports at less than 4 per cent, well below its share in world manufacturing value-added. Sub-Saharan Africa has failed to make major inroads into export markets and if South Africa is excluded its share in the world total for manufactured exports falls from 0.6 to 0.2 per cent.

Paths to industrialisation

The uneven development noted earlier has in the past been associated with different strategies for developing the industrial sector. One of the key lessons from recent economic history is that countries have rarely followed precisely the same sequence in terms of the pattern and institutional form of their industrial development. In the nineteenth century, the industrialising European economies, which followed Britain chronologically relied more heavily on the role of banks, for example, to mobilise savings for productive investment, as compared with the British experience where reinvested profits of firms themselves were more significant. In the twentieth century, in Japan and later in Korea, large conglomerate national firms were the driving force of industrial development, whereas in Taiwan, the medium- and smaller-scale private sector and the government were relatively more important. In Southeast Asia and China, foreign investors have played a key role. In Latin America, large national conglomerates have been much slower to emerge than those in parts of East Asia have, and industrialisation has also been strongly linked with foreign direct investment.

Similarly, in terms of the details of policy, the degree to which countries have chosen to open their markets to foreign competition and looked to exports as a

Table 1.9 Developing country share in world manufactured exports 2003–2006 by selected product category and regional group (%)

Products	*All developing countries*	*Sub-Saharan Africa*	*East and Southeast Asia*	*South Asia*	*Latin America*
All manufactures	32.0	0.6	24.8	1.3	3.6
Leather goods	52.4	1.0	31.9	5.4	12.8
Rubber manufactures	24.6	0.5	17.3	1.5	3.6
Cork/wood manufactures	31.8	1.3	23.6	0.3	5.7
Paper and paper manufactures	14.7	0.5	9.7	0.3	3.0
Textile yarn	53.5	0.4	39.0	7.7	2.2
Non-metallic mineral manufactures	31.9	4.4	14.0	6.7	2.6
Iron and steel	29.0	2.1	16.2	2.0	5.6
Manufactures of metal	30.1	0.5	23.0	1.4	3.5
Machinery and transport equipment	32.3	0.3	26.9	0.3	4.0
Power generating machinery	15.3	0.3	8.8	0.4	5.0
Specialised machinery	15.6	0.3	12.1	0.5	2.0
Metal working machinery	17.0	0.1	14.9	0.5	0.8
Other industrial machinery	19.3	0.7	14.4	0.5	3.0
Office and data processing machines	55.3	0.1	51.9	0.1	3.1
Telecommunications and sound apparatus	51.6	0.1	44.5	0.1	5.6
Electrical machinery	46.5	0.1	41.7	0.3	3.7
Road vehicles	15.7	0.5	8.5	0.3	5.2
Other transport equipment	18.2	0.5	13.4	0.4	2.3
Miscellaneous manufactures	42.1	0.5	32.9	2.7	3.3
Furniture	33.6	0.7	25.2	0.4	6.1
Travel goods, handbags	60.4	0.1	55.3	2.5	0.8
Clothing and apparel	65.3	0.9	45.5	7.4	3.8
Footwear	55.0	0.3	47.1	2.0	3.7
Professional and scientific instruments	26.1	0.1	21.8	0.3	3.6
Photo apparatus, optical goods	29.9	0.1	27.7	0.2	1.5
Miscellaneous not elsewhere specified	35.4	0.5	29.3	1.9	2.4

Source: Calculated from UNCTAD (2008, Table 4).

source of demand has varied considerably. Most countries today are members of the World Trade Organisation (WTO) and subscribe to its rules on the liberalisation of foreign trade. However, the speed and timing of this liberalisation has varied considerably. It is well established that today's developed economies offered various support measures to their industries at their take-off stage, and in particular, it is plausible to argue that free trade has been a policy of the economically strong, adopted when their economies were competitive enough to benefit from opening to foreign competition. This generalisation applies, for example, to the United Kingdom and United States in the nineteenth century, and to Japan in the 1960s, Korea and Taiwan in the 1980s and more recently China in the 1990s. None of these economies were early trade liberalisers, in the sense of opening relatively new industries to external competition, although all have benefited greatly from liberalisation when it came.

Being a latecomer, industrialising economy offers the potential for rapid growth as drawing on technology developed elsewhere economies can catch-up with more established competitors. This *catch up growth* explains some of the successes of the NIEs in the twentieth century; however, the process is far from inevitable as the uneven spread of industrialisation within the group of developing countries over that period illustrates.

At the risk of over-simplification, the key differentiating features of alternative strategies over the last fifty years relate to:

- Openness to trade and foreign investment.
- Reliance on the market or planning.
- Technology choice.

Trade and foreign investment

International trade has been growing more rapidly than world income for most of the last 50 years, so that trade has become an increasing share of economic activity in most economies. Trade in manufactures has been at the forefront of this process, and as discussed earlier, the group of developing economies (including all the NIEs) has increased significantly its share in world manufactured exports to over 30 per cent. This is in contrast with the early image of these economies, most of whom around 1960 were heavily reliant on primary exports (foodstuffs and raw materials) to pay for imports of manufactures they themselves could not produce. Fifty years ago, many saw this as an undesirable specialisation that would hold back the growth of these economies. A central aspect of the case for industrialisation was the argument that developing economies would face a decline in the prices of their primary exports relative to the prices they would have to pay for their manufactured imports. A decline in the *terms of trade* would mean more exports would need to be given up to purchase the same volume of imports, and thus real income would be lower compared with a situation where relative prices remained constant (see Box 1.2).

The initial declining terms of trade case for developing countries is associated most closely with the distinguished economist Raul Prebisch, who held senior position for the UN both in the Economic Commission for Latin America (ECLA) and in UNCTAD (United Nations Conference on Trade and Development). The Prebisch case is based on an empirical analysis of UK import and export statistics running from the nineteenth century to the mid-twentieth. Its theoretical basis rests on differences in market structure. Primary goods, it was argued, are largely homogenous products produced in competitive markets, where prices move in line with changes in demand and supply. Hence, for example, if a frost

Box 1.2 Terms of trade

The simplest version of the terms of trade is the *commodity terms of trade*, which compares an index number of export prices with an index number of import prices, so

$$\text{TOT}c = \text{P}x/\text{P}m \tag{1.1}$$

where TOTc is the commodity terms of trade, Px is an index of export prices and Pm is an index of import prices.

An alternative version focuses on the change in the purchasing power of exports in the *income terms of trade*. This reflects change in the capacity to import as exports rise. Hence

$$\text{TOT}i = \text{Q}x.\text{P}x/\text{P}m \tag{1.2}$$

where TOTi is the income terms of trade, Qx is an index of export volume and Px and Pm are as before.

Calculation of the terms of trade is relatively straightforward where commodities are largely homogeneous or standardised (e.g. wheat and sugar), but complex where goods are differentiated and experience changes in quality over time, as with many manufactures. Strictly, what should be charted should be price movements for goods of a fixed quality, and it is difficult to allow for new product development and technical change in assessing movements in manufactured goods prices. Empirical updates of trends in the terms of trade often adopt the expedient of basing estimates on movements in average prices. Average unit values are calculated as export revenue divided by an export quantity measure (such as weight or numbers of similar goods) for different trade categories and aggregated in an overall index. These indices for average unit values are used to replace Px and Pm in Equations 1.1 and 1.2.

in Brazil wipes out much of the normal coffee crop, world supply will fall and world prices for different grades of coffee will rise. Similarly, a good harvest will increase supply and bring down prices.

On the other hand, the market for manufactures, it was argued, is characterised by differentiated products and relatively small numbers of producers. In this *oligopolistic* market, firms will set prices on the basis of a mark-up over production costs. In some sectors, control over new technology may allow firms a near monopoly position, which in turn will allow a higher mark-up than where there is more competition. The key point about these differences in market structure is what they imply for changes in price in response to productivity gains due to technical change. In primary product markets, the lower cost due to technical change will push down prices. On the other hand, in the less competitive markets for manufactures the expectation is that at least part of the cost saving will go to owners in higher profits and to workers in higher wages with only a proportion (and possibly none) of the reduction passed on in lower prices. Hence, the asymmetry in market response creates a long-run tendency for higher prices for manufactures relative to primary goods. This structural analysis can be combined with a focus on demand differentials based on higher household income elasticities for manufactures than for primary goods; in other words, as incomes rise beyond a certain level, there is a well-established empirical tendency for the proportion spent on manufactures to rise and for that spent on primary products, principally foodstuffs, to decline. For raw materials, it was argued that technical change worked in the direction of conserving their use, thus restricting demand growth.

The Prebisch case has been subject to extensive empirical tests and debates on data sources, although the overall consensus is that it held fairly convincingly during the twentieth century with most non-fuel primary goods suffering a long-run real decline in price over the period. However, by the end of the century, although primary exports remain of great importance in some of the poorer countries as in much of sub-Saharan Africa, developing countries as a group had ceased to be predominantly primary exporters, so the original argument had less direct relevance. More recent discussion on the terms of trade has focussed on the different question of whether the price of manufactured goods exported by developing countries has shown a long-run decline relative to the price of manufactured goods imported by these countries. The key reason put forward as to why this has occurred is based on product characteristics and their implications for market structure. Insofar as developed country exports have a higher technology and skill content, this creates a barrier to entry for rival exporters and allows a mark-up above costs. However, where simpler labour-intensive manufactured exports are sold by developing countries market entry will be easier and hence competition will be greater leading to downward pressure on prices. The emergence of China, in particular, as a major exporter with its relatively low labour costs and competitive exchange rate policy is seen as a key factor depressing prices of simple labour-intensive manufactures.[5]

Recent short-term price trends on the world market have seen a dramatic reversal of the Prebisch case with prices of primary commodities, oil, metals and minerals and some foodstuffs rising significantly in nominal terms and relative to the price of manufactures. This was due to a combination of rising world demand (in part from the expansion of the large markets in China and India) and lack of supply capacity. How these trends affect individual countries depends on their exact mix of exports and imports. Over the period from the mid-1990s to 2006, for example, sub-Saharan Africa saw a major improvement in its terms of trade due to its oil and mineral exports, as did Latin America. However, East and Southeast Asia, where exports are dominated by manufacturers, saw a decline in the commodity terms of trade. However, even the developing country net exporters of manufactures, whilst suffering a relative price fall, saw their income terms of trade rise as a result of rising export volumes, so that more goods could be imported despite the adverse trend in relative prices.[6]

The Prebisch terms of trade argument provided a rationale to diversify exports out of primary goods and into manufactures which implied making domestically what was previously imported, or what came to be known as *import substitution*. A widely used distinction in the literature of the 1960s and 1970s was between *import substitution* and *export promotion* as alternative trade strategies. The former focuses on the domestic market previously dominated by imported manufactures and aims to replace these imports with domestic goods. The latter focuses on the export market as the principal source of demand. This distinction was always something of an over-simplification and has become largely redundant in the current more open trading environment.

Import substitution can be seen as a natural stage in an economy's evolution, since as local production capacity is built up the advantage of proximity to local markets will enable some domestic producers to compete directly with foreign suppliers. As all economies have developed, this type of import replacement has occurred. However, the term *import substitution strategy* usually refers to policy-induced change, not this process of changing relative competitiveness or *comparative advantage*. From the early 1950s until the end of the 1980s, a majority of middle- and lower-income economies operated controls on trade whether through import tariffs, quota limits on what could be imported or rationing of access to the foreign currency needed to pay for imports. In some instances, these measures were used strategically to promote new industries, but in many cases their primary motive was to restrict demand for foreign goods, as there was an overall scarcity of foreign currency which did not allow all potential import demand to be financed (*a balance of payments constraint on growth*). The indirect, and in some cases unintended, effect of these restrictions on foreign trade was to create a protected domestic market for local firms who could charge prices well above those of imported goods, due to the barriers to importing which sheltered local firms from foreign competition. Countries going down this path normally commenced local manufacturing with technologically simple, often labour-intensive products, such as clothing, textiles, shoes, toys and processed agricultural products, like beer, tobacco and foods. This has been described as the first stage or *primary import substitution*. *The secondary import substitution* stage is where countries move to the replacement of imports of capital-intensive engineering goods and equipment.

The efficiency of the industry that grew up in this way behind relatively high protective barriers was the subject of a large number of detailed studies, most of which concluded that unless trade protection is accompanied by supportive measures to improve efficiency and is clearly defined as temporary, not permanent, it will simply allow the continuation of high-cost, internationally uncompetitive production. The literature largely concluded that the strategy of early opening-up to the world market through *export promotion* offered both efficiency gains through the stimulus of international competition and a much larger and more dynamic market than that available domestically, which is restricted by low incomes, small populations or both. Within export promotion, one can also draw distinctions. One version focuses on a shift in incentives and the removal of biases against exporting to encourage the export of goods destined originally for domestic sale (sometimes termed *export substitution*). Alternatively, the strategy can be based on the export of goods destined solely for the world market, for example, as supplies to an international lead firm (a strategy of *integration with global production networks*).

However, the lines between import substitution and export promotion become blurred once one looks beyond the extremes of both strategies. This is partly because many countries underwent policy shifts at different times veering between greater and lesser degrees of protection and export orientation (see Box 1.3). It is also partly because in several notable instances both strategies were pursued

Box 1.3 Openness and trade policy reversals: 1960 to early 1990s

Sachs and Warner (1995) produced a well-known index of trade openness based on a combination of subjective judgement and quantitative data. In their index, a country was classed as closed to trade if it had one or more of the following characteristics:

- A socialist economic system.
- A state monopoly of major exports.
- Non-tariff barriers covering more than 40 per cent of imports.
- Average import tariffs above 40 per cent.
- A black market exchange rate depreciated by more than 20 per cent relative to the official rate.

Taking the period from the early 1960s to early 1990s, countries are grouped into those fully open over the period, those where open policies were reversed, those that opened up in the late 1980s and those that were fully closed over the whole period. The countries in each group are given next. For the countries with policy reversals and where liberalisation came late in the period the years, they are classed as open are given in brackets.

Fully open economies:

Barbados, Botswana, Chile, Hong Kong, Indonesia, Jordan, Malaysia, Mauritius, Singapore, Taiwan, Thailand, Yemen, Korea.

Policy reversals:

Bolivia (1960–74, 1985–92), Costs Rica (1960–61, 1985–92), Ecuador (1960–82, 1989–92), El Salvador (1960–61, 1991–92), Guatemala (1961, 1989–92), Honduras (1960–61, 1991–92), Jamaica (1962–73, 1990–92),

Kenya (1963–67), Morocco (1960–64, 1984–92), Peru (1960–67, 1991–92), Sri Lanka (1977–83, 1991–92).

Late liberalisers:

Argentina (1991–92), Benin (1991–92), Brazil (1991–92), Colombia (1986–92), Gambia (1985–92), Guinea Bissau (1987–92), Guinea (1986–92), Guyana (1988–92), Mali (1988–92), Mauritania (1992), Mexico (1986–92), Nepal (1991–92), Nicaragua (1991–92), Paraguay (1988–92), Philippines (1988–92), South Africa (1991–92), Tunisia (1989–92), Turkey (1989–92), Uganda (1988–92), Uruguay (1990–92), Venezuela (1989–92).

Fully closed up to 1992:

Algeria, Bangladesh, Burkina Faso, Burundi, Cameroon, Central African Republic, Chad, China, Congo, Dominican Republic, Egypt, Ethiopia, Gabon, Haiti, India, Ivory Coast, North Korea, Madagascar, Malawi, Mozambique, Myanmar, Niger, Nigeria, Pakistan, Rwanda, Senegal, Sierra Leone, Somalia, Tanzania, Togo, Trinidad, Zambia, Zimbabwe.

There can be some dispute about these classifications in individual cases; however, in general, they do illustrate the policy shifts in many countries. The size of the late-liberaliser group gives an indication of the opening to foreign trade during the late 1980s. Most Latin American economies are in this category with some from sub-Saharan Africa. A majority of the fully open economies over the whole period are from East Asia, although whether this is an accurate classification all of these is open to question. Botswana and Mauritius are the only representatives from sub-Saharan Africa and Chile is the only Latin American country in the group (although it is only fully open post-1976). Countries with policy reversals are largely those where macro-economic problems created a need to conserve foreign exchange and reintroduce trade restrictions. As of the early 1990s, the largest group are those with one or more of the fully closed characteristics. Included here are most of sub-Saharan Africa, and the large economies of China, India, Pakistan, Bangladesh and Egypt. It is a measure of how far things have changed that today few if any of these economies (the main exception is North Korea) would be classified as fully closed by the Sachs-Warner criteria. For example, whilst South Asia remains the part of the world economy with the highest rates of import tariff, average rates are now well below 40 per cent, the figure used as an indicator of a closed economy in the original index. In 2006, average rates of import tariff were: India 19 per cent, Pakistan 14 per cent and Bangladesh 15 per cent.[7]

Source: Sachs and Warner (1995).

simultaneously sometimes differentiating between industries, sometimes between locations in the same country and sometimes between sales by the same firms. For example, in Korea in the 1960s and 1970s, government policy imposed export targets on the firms that were initially set up as import substitute activities and firms cross-subsidised their exports through the high profits generated by sales in the protected domestic market. Similarly, the spread of export processing zones in many countries from the 1980s onwards offered locations in which production for export was encouraged, whilst firms outside the zones continued to sell import substitute goods in the protected domestic market.

Until very recently, experience in China is the most dramatic example of the mixing of the two strategies. Until the mid-1990s, the domestic market was heavily protected, whilst Special Economic Zones were established in the eastern coastal provinces to encourage foreign firms to locate in China and produce the goods that subsequently have flooded the markets of the world. Within the zones, tariff and quota restrictions on imports were lifted so that foreign firms could import the parts and components they needed to produce for export. Today the trade reforms linked with membership of the WTO have opened up the markets of most economies and biases against exporting are now largely removed. Options to apply import substitution as a strategy are not completely ruled out by the WTO rules, but most countries are now very careful in how far it is applied to avoid retaliatory trade controls and anti-dumping charges by their trading partners.

The degree of reliance on foreign direct investment (FDI) has been another important source of comparison between countries, where FDI is defined as the purchase of assets by firms from another country where the foreign firm takes an active management role and holds more than a minimum proportion (typically 10 per cent) of the total share capital. This is in contrast with passive foreign investor involvement through the purchase of shares in *portfolio investment*. Most FDI takes place between higher-income economies but about one quarter of the stock of FDI assets both in total and in manufacturing alone is held currently in developing countries or economies in transition.[8] Recent trends have seen an absolute rise in FDI in manufacturing, but a relative shift towards FDI in services.

Some countries have historically have had a relatively low FDI presence outside of the extractive sector due to their low incomes, small markets and unattractive investment climate (e.g. much of sub-Saharan Africa). Others have until recently had relatively low levels of FDI due to what was perceived as an unwelcoming attitude on the part of governments (e.g. India and other parts of South Asia). East Asia (most recently China) and much of Latin America have been the principal recipients of FDI to developing countries.

Given the way in which data are recorded and the diversified nature of many of the international firms that undertake FDI, it is difficult to gauge precisely how important FDI is in manufacturing in particular economies. Table 1.10 brings together estimates from diverse sources which may not be directly comparable, but which give a broad indication of the role of FDI in selected economies in the 1970s and again in the 1990s. FDI plays a far greater role in employment in

Table 1.10 Share of foreign-owned firms in manufacturing employment

Countries	*1970s*	*Countries*	*1990s*
Argentina	12 (1970)	China	4 (1997)
Brazil	30 (1977)	Brazil	13 (1995)
Colombia	28 (1970)	Indonesia	5 (1996)
India	13 (1975)	Sri Lanka	54 (1996)
Korea	10 (1978)	Turkey	3 (1990)
Malaysia	34 (1978)	Malaysia	44 (1994)
Mexico	21 (1978)	Mexico	18 (1993)
Philippines	7 (1970)	Vietnam	15 (1995)
Singapore	72 (1980)	Singapore	52 (1996)
Taiwan	28 (1976)	Taiwan	21 (1995)
Hong Kong	10 (1980)	Hong Kong	16 (1994)

Source: For 1970s Weiss (1990, Table 2.5) and sources cited therein; for 1990s Weiss (2002, Table 2.7) and sources cited therein.

manufacturing in the smaller economies being particularly prominent in Singapore and Malaysia. Foreign-owned firms have been active in technologically sophisticated branches of manufacturing (like electronics, computers, precision equipment and pharmaceuticals); however, it is difficult to establish a clear link between technological complexity and FDI since they are also active in more traditional branches like tobacco and food products, as well as in medium-technology branches like automobiles.

Where FDI has assumed a key role in many economies is in the export of manufactures where it has linked economies with global production networks and international buyers. Again, accurate estimates of the extent to which this has occurred are difficult to obtain but in China, Southeast Asia, Mexico and parts of Central America foreign-owned firms are responsible for a very significant share of total manufactured exports. Current estimates put this at around 55 per cent for China, for example.[9] In terms of the two dimensions of openness – to foreign trade and to foreign investment – there is no obvious association in terms of country classification. For example, in the 1970s and 1980s, some of the major import substitution economies, like Brazil and Mexico, relied heavily on US FDI as a prime mover in their industrial sector, whilst others like India, Pakistan and most of sub-Saharan Africa did not. Similarly, of the original set of export promoting first-tier NIEs – the four Tiger economies of Hong Kong, Singapore, Korea and Taiwan – FDI has played and continues to play a major role in the first two, but a much smaller role in latter two economies.

Firms with their head office in the NIEs and a majority share ownership from these countries have also become active as foreign investors, although in 2005 there were only six such firms in the world's top 100 non-financial international firms (or *transnational corporations* as they are often termed). These are in petroleum exploration and refining (Petronas, Malaysia), cement and other non-metallic minerals (Cemex, Mexico), telecommunications (Singapore Telecommunications), electronics (Samsung and LG, Korea), and diversified holdings (Jardine Mattheson, Hong Kong).

If the largest 50 firms from NIEs are considered as foreign investors, there is a clear dominance of firms from East Asia, reflecting the high growth that has occurred there over the last 30 years. The composition of the top fifty international firms from the NIEs in terms of their share in foreign assets is shown for 1998 and 2005 in Table 1.11

Many of the firms represented in Table 1.11 are non-manufacturing, and cover petroleum refining and extraction (e.g. Petrobras of Brazil, Petroleos de Venezuela and the China National Petroleum Corporation) as well as various service activities and utilities like telecommunications (e.g. Telekom Malaysia). The major manufacturing firms are in electronics (Samsung and LG of Korea), computers and related activities (the Lenovo group of China and Acer of Taiwan), chemicals and plastics (Formosa Plastic group of Taiwan) and motor vehicles (Hyundai and Kia of Korea). Sub-Saharan Africa is represented only by South African firms in industrial chemicals, domestic appliances and metals and metal products.

Overseas investment by firms from East Asian NIEs has been for a variety of motives: to relocate production to lower wage cost locations in the same region

Table 1.11 Share of top fifty non-financial international firms from NIEs in total foreign assets of the NIEs (%)

		1998	*2005*
East Asia		64.9	79.0
Of which			
	Hong Kong	22.0	28.0
	Korea	16.7	13.1
	China	8.8	11.1
	Singapore	7.2	9.5
	Taiwan	2.4	8.8
	Malaysia	6.3	8.5
	Philippines	1.5	0
South Asia	India	0.8	1.4
Latin America		28.3	14.9
Of which			
	Mexico	5.9	8.2
	Brazil	7.6	4.5
	Venezuela	7.3	2.2
	Argentina	4.1	0
	Chile	3.4	0
Sub-Saharan Africa	South Africa	6.0	4.7

Source: 1998 UNCTAD (2000, Table 3.15) and 2006 UNCTAD (2007, Table A.1.14).

(e.g. Korean FDI in Thailand and Vietnam or Taiwanese FDI in China); to serve domestic markets in other countries through local production rather than exporting (e.g. Korean and Taiwanese FDI in China); and to obtain strategic assets like technology or brand names through the acquisition of firms from developed economies (e.g. Korean FDI in the United States). There has also been an expansion of FDI from Latin American NIEs, although these firms tend to be smaller than their East Asian counterparts and to have advantages based on management and finance more than their technological capacity. Hence, their focus tends to be in technologically more mature branches, like transport equipment, engineering, cement, steel and glass.

Planning or the market

A distinction has also been drawn between planned and market-driven industrialisation. The former aims to set physical targets for individual firms and sectors and allocates investment funds and raw materials in line with requirements determined by these targets. To generate growth priority is placed on capital and intermediate goods (commodities to make other commodities). The latter uses the price mechanism to identify demand and allows resources to flow between firms in response to consumer and producer demand. The Soviet planning system as developed in the 1930s and applied with modification well into the 1980s provides the model for detailed central planning. For some time it proved successful at generating high rates of overall investment (since the government could control total consumption) and a major expansion of physical production. It proved much less successful, however, in generating technical change and quality improvements and in matching physical output with what consumers required.

This central planning model was applied with local modifications in the satellite states of Eastern Europe and in the development context in the then socialist states of China, North Korea, Vietnam, Lao PDR in Asia and to some degree in Mozambique in Africa and Cuba and Nicaragua in Central America. Intellectually there is nothing contradictory about socialist regimes using the market as a means of resource allocation. The Stalinist command economy model of the 1930s provided the blueprint summarised in the foregoing, but other aspects of the socialist tradition, such as the New Economic Policy practised briefly in the Soviet Union in the 1920s or the academic literature on socialist economics in the 1930s setting out conditions for optimality under public ownership, allow for market relationships between firms, workers and consumers. Nonetheless, in practice socialist industrialisation was associated with a closed economy and barriers to foreign trade and FDI and with a focus on capital and intermediate goods production. Both political change in the old Soviet bloc and the limitations of central planning in what were very poor socialist developing economies subject to major external shocks, have combined to end this system. Even in economies that remain nominally socialist like China and Vietnam economic policy now allows far greater use of markets and controls over foreign trade and FDI have largely been removed.

These countries now participate fully in international trade with, for example, both China and Vietnam, full members of the WTO.

The planning systems that were applied elsewhere under the guise of national Five Year Plans were largely systems of controls rather than of detailed command plans of the Soviet variety. In the development context, they were applied either in mixed economies with a large public sector, where state-owned enterprises were set either physical or financial targets (e.g. in India, Algeria and Egypt) or in economies where the state, despite not owning a large number of productive enterprises, controlled access to resources like credit or foreign exchange, set maximum prices for sensitive goods and erected barriers to foreign trade and FDI (e.g. India again, and Brazil, Mexico and Argentina during their import substitution phases). To describe such systems as planning, as is sometimes done, is a confusion, since it is now well documented that such systems frequently had serious unexpected (i.e. unplanned) consequences. Public sector manufacturing enterprises frequently did not meet their financial targets creating a strain on public finances, as losses had to be covered through central government expenditure.

Controls over credit, foreign exchange, commodity prices and foreign trade created what have been termed *distortions* or deviations from prices that reflect the scarcity of the items concerned. Under a market-driven system where prices determine incentives, but controls intervene, there is a major risk that resources will flow in the wrong direction, in the sense that they do not go to the uses with the highest return. Technically, distortions are said to create *allocative inefficiencies* and work at the World Bank estimated degrees of distortion in various developing countries in the 1970s. Whilst the results and approach were subject to controversy, nonetheless, the broad conclusion that the most distorted economies were those that pursued import substitution trade policies combined with controls in various factor markets was plausible. The most distorted group in the 1970s included Ghana, Nigeria and Tanzania in sub-Saharan Africa, Bangladesh and Pakistan in South Asia, and Argentina, Peru and Chile (in its import substitution phase) in Latin America.[10]

Policy change in most economies in more recent years has seen a dismantling of controls, a freeing of trade, removal of barriers to exporting and privatisation of public sector enterprises in manufacturing and public utilities. This wave of reform commenced initially in Latin America in the 1980s and spread elsewhere, often but not always, as part of policy conditionality attached to Structural Adjustment Lending, whereby the donor community provided funding for international debt repayment on condition that governments allowed markets a greater role. This shift to a market-based economic policy has not gone unchallenged as far as debates on industrialisation and international competitiveness are concerned. In economic theory, markets only create an optimal solution under highly restrictive conditions (such as perfect knowledge and no advantages of size due to increasing returns to scale). It is not difficult to devise models in which markets fail to produce an optimal solution (or produce more than one optimum) and where well-designed interventions in how they work can improve welfare. This forms the intellectual basis for what is termed *industrial policy*, in which governments aim to override market outcomes, for example, by influencing which firms grow or how they allocate their output.

Part of the basis for this approach is a more subtle interpretation of theory than simple *market fundamentalism*, but in large part it stems from an interpretation of the success of the NIEs, particularly Korea and Taiwan, where arguably at critical stages policy interventions played a key role in their successful industrialisation. Chapter 7 discusses the application of industrial policy in East Asia. There, where it worked effectively, policy was operated flexibly, so that as the economies graduated to a higher development stage, policy instruments that proved helpful at an earlier stage were abandoned in favour of a more market-sensitive approach. This experience is in direct contrast with the experience associated with import substitution programmes elsewhere, where distortions were both allowed to develop and to persist. Precisely what role government intervention should play in fostering industrialisation and greater competitiveness, in the context of basically market-driven economies, remains unresolved, but the point to be stressed here is that even if planning has now largely been abandoned in favour of the market, this does not mean that governments have no role in support of industrialisation.

Technology

Technology, reflecting both processes of production and the knowledge necessary for their application and improvement, plays a key role in modern theories of economic growth. How technology is applied and developed has also been used as a means of distinguishing between alternative approaches to industrialisation. One view in line with international trade theory is to argue that countries that applied technologies that were in line with their resource endowments and thus their short-run comparative advantage did far better than those that used technologies more suited to a higher-income economic environment. This translates into a simple contrast between labour and capital intensive technologies and products. Low-income economies, it is argued, have a supply of labour that is abundant relative to their supply of capital and hence the price of labour relative to capital will be lower there than that in higher-income economies, where it is capital that is relatively abundant. If prices for the factors of production labour and capital are allowed to reflect the underlying relative scarcities, poor countries will have a cost advantage in labour-intensive goods and production processes.

Countries that specialised in labour intensive activities, it is argued, saw a rise in the export of technologically simple labour intensive manufactures (like clothing, footwear and toys) and a significant increase in employment in export industry. On the other hand, countries that kept the price of capital relatively cheap (e.g. through controls on interest rates and an overvalued exchange rate between national and foreign currency) biased technology choice in a capital-intensive direction and encouraged specialisation in capital intensive sectors (like chemicals and steel). Such countries, it is argued, grew more slowly with much less employment creation in industry on a growth path which has been described as an *anti-comparative advantage strategy*. This interpretation is part of the wider critique of past import substitution policies and of attempts to control markets resulting in distorted price signals.

From this perspective, the early success of the East Asian NIEs (particularly the first-tier group of Korea, Taiwan, Singapore and Hong Kong) in the 1960s and 1970s has been interpreted as a *comparative advantage based strategy* of export-led industrialisation. It has been contrasted with the more capital-intensive development paths over the same period used by many other countries, particularly the larger economies in Latin America of Brazil, Argentina and Mexico and in South Asia by India, Pakistan and Bangladesh. This is the strategy of *secondary import substitution*, noted earlier, with the domestic production of capital intensive goods that were previous imported. In China, policies pre- the opening-up in the early 1990s have also been classed in the anti-comparative advantage category with the opening to foreign trade and FDI shifting the economy on to a higher-growth path based on comparative advantage.[11]

Comparative advantage evolves over time as can be seen by the changing export structure of the NIEs, for example, as the original labour-intensive exports were replaced by both capital and technology intensive goods (like electronics, engineering equipment, computers and related products). From a dynamic perspective, how economies develop their own capability and mastery of technology becomes a key factor in explaining their performance in industrialisation. As noted before an advantage of poor economies that are latecomers in the development story lies in the ability to draw on already developed technology from richer countries which can be imported through licence or FDI, copied, adapted, modified and in some instances improved upon. This is seen as the key factor behind the emergence of the NIEs – defined as in Table 1.5 to cover more than the high-growth economies of East Asia. With support from governments, firms in these economies could draw on the *technological rents* (i.e. the extra profits) created by access to foreign technology.

Not all the NIEs behave in the same way and historical influences (so-called *path dependence*) as well as policy choice have created major differences amongst them. One distinction in relation to technology policy is between the group of NIEs where large national firms or national champions emerged (often with state support) to develop their own technology and those countries where they did not. These national firms, often part of a group or conglomerate, were large enough to challenge foreign firms and used their scale and financial backing to invest heavily in developing a national technological capability. This allowed such firms to develop their own process technology and brand names. Examples include the firms noted earlier in the context of foreign investment, such as Hyundai, Samsung and LG of Korea, Lenovo group of China and Acer and Formosa Plastic group of Taiwan. On the other hand, in other NIEs whilst national firms have developed, they are generally significantly smaller than their foreign-owned rivals, and have tended to invest less heavily in developing an indigenous technology relying more on technology imports. As a consequence, they are less likely to be world market leaders or to develop their own brands for selected market niches (see Box 1.4).

Box 1.4 Late industrialisation

Alice Amsden has offered stimulating generalisations on the catch-up experience in what she terms *the theory of late industrialisation*, which gives the interventionist or developmental state a key role. New knowledge and the technology in which it is embodied create extra profits (or *technological rents*) for the enterprises that possess it and reinvestment of these rents in new equipment drives the process of industrialisation. A late start for poor economies in the post-1945 period allowed them to draw on imported technology from Europe and North America. However, state support was essential for industrialisation since new national firms could not compete with established producers abroad who could draw on their specific knowledge and experience of production. The imbalance in knowledge-based assets was too great for national firms to become established without some advantage conferred on them by their governments. The mechanisms of support varied over time and place but included import tariff protection, forms of production subsidy, the channelling of funds through development banks, and some cases direct public ownership. These favours were often (but not always) granted in return for an understanding of reciprocity so that performance standards (such as levels of exports or jobs created) were set. In the exceptional case of Hong Kong, where local firms could compete, the state did not intervene, because it did not need to.

In her analysis, experience across different types of follower economies is reduced to two broad patterns. In the more successful economies, state support created large enterprises seen as national industrial champions, often conglomerates with a range of industrial products. With state support, these large firms invested heavily in developing a national technological capability to build the economy's own technology base. This is termed the *Asian model* – with Korea and earlier Japan fitting the stylised description most closely. It is not clear if Malaysia and Thailand yet fit into this model. In the second pattern, state support was more diffused between firms and less concentrated on national industrial champions. Transnational corporations tend to play a bigger role and national firms to invest less in building their own capability, continuing to rely heavily on technology imports. This is termed the Latin American model. Although it broadly corresponds to experience in Brazil, Mexico and Argentina, it is not a geographical description, since Turkey is included here. The opportunities created by globalisation are seen as leading to a parting of the ways of countries in the two groups in the late 1980s, with countries in the Asian group (Korea, Taiwan, and more recently China and India) developing along an 'independent' technological path based on national knowledge-based firms and countries in the Latin American group (such as Brazil and Mexico) moving further along an 'integrationist' technological path with heavy reliance on foreign investment and imported technology.

The key factors explaining which countries followed which path are taken to be their pre-1945 history and their degree of income inequality. Historical colonial experience in Asia encouraged large domestic firms, since in the early years of independence, foreign-owned firms were nationalised and replaced by either local private or public sector firms. In Latin America, de-colonisation occurred in the nineteenth century and pre-1945 manufacturing already had a substantial foreign firm presence, which was not nationalised post-1945. In relation to income distribution, it is argued that countries, where the state invested heavily to create national industrial champions, were characterised by low levels of inequality, since an egalitarian environment made it possible to mobilise resources for an industrialisation project in pursuit of the greater national good. Conversely, in more unequal societies (such as in Latin America) governments were more reluctant to be seen to be transferring resources to a small number of firms or industrial groups.

Source: Amsden (2001).

A simple measure of the technological depth of an economy is the share of medium and high-technology products (as defined by the R and D to sales ratio) in total manufacturing activity. The United Nations Industrial Development Organisation (UNIDO) has used a simple measure – the average of the share of medium- and high-technology products in manufacturing value-added and their share in total exports – to assess technological depth. Countries are ranked by this indicator. For 2002, the data reveal five of the East Asian NIEs in the top 10 countries, whilst the highest ranking of any of the Latin American NIEs is Mexico at 16th, with Brazil at 25th. Other country comparisons between Asia and Latin America by this indicator are less clear-cut, however. Significantly, China still only has a modest ranking at 27th, below both Mexico and Brazil (see Table 1.12).

Conclusions

Uneven development has characterised economic performance amongst the heterogeneous group of *developing countries*. In general, manufacturing has grown relatively rapidly, outside of sub-Saharan Africa and the transition economies of Europe and Central Asia (where de-industrialisation has been significant) and the developing country group has come to supply a major share of world manufactured exports. In terms of the three dimensions of policy towards industry identified here, we can draw the following broad conclusions.

Countries with fast-growing manufacturing sectors have tended to become increasingly open to foreign trade. Countries which retained strongly protectionist

Table 1.12 Country ranking by index of technological advance: NIEs 2002

Country	*Index value*	*Ranking*
Singapore	0.832	1
Malaysia	0.707	3
Korea	0.674	7
Taiwan	0.649	10
Mexico	0.599	16
Brazil	0.528	25
China	0.515	27
Thailand	0.514	28
South Africa	0.491	29
Hong Kong	0.477	30
Argentina	0.423	37
India	0.391	41
Turkey	0.365	44

Source: UNIDO (2005, Table 10.1).

inward-looking policies did not fare well. However, many successful larger economies only opened up to foreign trade gradually after an earlier period of protection when the domestic market provided the key source of demand; Japan, Korea, and more recently China and India fall into this category. Hence, for larger economies, recent historical experience does not suggest that early and widespread trade reform was critical in stimulating manufacturing growth. In smaller economies, however, links with the international market, most recently through international specialisation as part of global production networks, have been important.

FDI tends to flow either to economies with growing domestic markets and a favourable investment climate (in terms of political and economic stability and good-quality infrastructure) or to smaller economies with a relatively low-cost and skilled labour force where firms can be incorporated readily in international networks. Econometric analyses of the links between FDI and growth have tended to find a causal connection that may run in both directions, but where the dominant relation is from higher FDI to higher growth. However, equally, it has been found that this relation does not hold for all types of economy and in particular the policy environment (e.g. in relation to foreign trade) and the education level are important mediating factors. This implies that at a macro-economic level to benefit from FDI policies must be supportive of growth and a minimum education and skills level must be reached. This helps to explain why FDI has been relatively weak as a stimulus to manufacturing in much of sub-Saharan Africa.

The old planning versus the market debate has now largely been resolved in that virtually all economies (with the possible exception of North Korea) have abandoned centralised planning. The market mechanism has proved to be a powerful tool in conveying information and generating incentives for investment in different manufacturing activities. However, in the real world, we know that the theoretical conditions under which markets will always create a socially optimum outcome do not exist. These real world *market failures* mean that *a priori* one cannot rule out interventionist government policies creating a superior outcome. The track record of interventions is at best mixed, nonetheless, we do have examples of successful industrial policy, principally from the East Asian NIEs. This means that success in manufacturing cannot always be simply attributed to the liberalisation of foreign trade and domestic markets. However, equally, whilst in principle governments can play a positive supportive role, this needs to be thought through carefully with a clear rationale for any specific intervention and an analysis of its potential consequences.

Technology plays a key role in most interpretations of manufacturing growth. The most successful economies have imported, copied, adapted and improved foreign technologies. In some cases, FDI has been an important catalyst, but in others, it has been domestic firms that have led this process. The great strength of the East Asian NIEs and their most important distinguishing feature from Latin American NIEs, for example, has been the technological capability and mastery of their firms as compared with those from Latin America. This has allowed the East Asian NIEs to diversify their exports into higher-technology, more dynamic products and to give their firms a competitive edge in establishing their own global production networks. Experience suggests that success in developing a technological capability requires government investment in both education and in the related infrastructure and basic research facilities needed to support the R and D activities of firms.

Further reading

The best surveys of current manufacturing production and trade are found in the annual reports from UNIDO (Industrial Development Report) and UNCTAD (Trade and Development Report). These give both up to date statistics and useful overviews of key topics affecting manufacturing. The concept of deindustrialisation is discussed in Tregenna (2009) and the references therein. Weiss (2002) in Chapters 1 and 2 discusses many of the issues relating to choice of industrial strategy in more detail. The earlier dependency literature is surveyed in Blomstrom and Hettne (1984). The emergence of the East Asian NIEs is examined in World Bank (1993) and reappraised in Stiglitz and Yusuf (2001). The late Sanjaya Lall produced the seminal work on the classification of commodities by technology level and on alternative policies for developing technological capability; for example, Lall (2000) on trade classification, and Lall (2001) on technology policy and technological capability. Lall *et al.* (2004) illustrate the spread of global production networks.

2 Engine of growth

What explains the divergence in growth of national income across countries noted in Chapter 1 has long preoccupied economists and development practitioners. Theoretically simple economic models are available to explain that growth is determined by increases in either factor inputs (at the most aggregate level labour and capital) or in the efficiency with which they are used. These are the immediate or proximate causes of growth. However, whilst we may be able to explain an increase in growth by reference to an increase in capital inputs due to higher investment, for example, this simply pushes the explanation back to what causes the higher investment. Hence, there is a need to seek out the underlying or fundamental causes of growth. Here, there is more choice of explanation and there has been a vast literature identifying various *fundamentals*, such as openness to trade, geography and climatic factors, institutional quality and the general climate for private investment. In addition, there is also a tradition that argues that economic structure matters and that for many economies the ability to expand their manufacturing sectors will be critical to the growth process at an early stage of development; this is sometimes termed the *engine of growth* case for manufacturing. This chapter explores this argument in the context of development and links it with the experience of the NIEs highlighted in Chapter 1. It also introduces current global concerns relating to poverty reduction.

Formal growth models

The starting point for formal analysis of growth is usually the Solow growth model after Nobel laureate Robert Solow.[1] This views the economy as an aggregate production function with a production relationship between labour, capital and output, within a framework of perfect competition. There are constant returns to scale, but diminishing returns to an individual factor when the accompanying factor is fixed. This means that output Y can be written as

$$Y = K^{\alpha}. (A.L)^{1-\alpha} \qquad (2.1)$$

where K is the stock of capital, L is the labour force and A is an efficiency measure, reflecting technical knowledge. The parameter α represents the elasticity of output with respect to capital and with constant returns $(1 - \alpha)$ represents the elasticity with respect to labour, for a given level of A. Growth in this model is obtained by taking the logarithms of the variables and differentiating these with respect to time so that

$$dY/Y = +\alpha dK/K + (1 - \alpha)(dL/L + dA/A) \tag{2.2}$$

where *d* represents change.

Equation 2.2 states that growth is determined by a combination of changes in efficiency, capital and labour, with the respective contributions of capital and labour determined their respective productivity. Empirical studies have found that dA/A, broadly reflecting technical progress but sometimes termed the unexplained residual, has been an important element in past growth experience. The original analysis by Solow found the residual to account for about 75 per cent of actual growth.

A key contribution of the original Solow model was the focus on long-run stability in the growth process (unlike the instability found in earlier models). This means that there is an inbuilt tendency in the model for an economy to move to (or converge on) a *steady state path* where income growth is constant, and income and capital grow at the same rate. Shocks in terms of changes in either savings propensity or efficiency can alter the path, but once their effect has worked through there will be a move back towards a new steady state (although at a different constant output per capital ratio).

Since a condition of equilibrium is a constant capital-output ratio this means the change in capital stock matches that in income so

$$dK/K = dY/Y \tag{2.3}$$

Combining this with Equation 2.2 gives

$$dY/Y = \alpha dY/Y + (1 - \alpha)(dL/L + dA/A)$$

and rearranging

$$dY/Y(1 - \alpha) = (1 - \alpha)(dL/L + dA/A)$$

so

$$dY/Y = dL/L + dA/A \tag{2.4}$$

Equation 2.4 confirms that in the Solow model, growth of income in the steady state equals growth of the labour force (assumed to equal population growth *n*) and technical change. This is a somewhat uncomfortable result since both variables are exogenous to the model and must be explained in other ways. Since the population growth rate is likely to respond only slowly to actions by governments this means that to raise growth a key focus of policy must be to increase the rate of technical change and the subsequent improvement in efficiency.

A major consequence of this analysis is that (counter-intuitively) the savings rate (s) has no impact on the steady state rate of growth. This can be seen by combining Equations 2.3 and 2.4. In the model all savings are invested so

$$sY = I$$

where s is the marginal propensity to save and I is investment. Assuming zero depreciation, investment equals the change in capital so $I = dK$. This means that

$$dK/K = sY/K$$

and from Equations 2.3 and 2.4 we have

$$sY/K = dL/L + dA/A \tag{2.5}$$

If the growth of the labour supply is given exogenously by population growth n and if technical change is either zero or also exogenous, the right hand side of the equation cannot change in response to changes in savings behaviour. This means that in the steady state if a higher share of income is saved, so s rises, for growth to remain constant, this must be offset by a rise in the capital-output ratio, or in other words a fall in Y/K. However, the rise in the capital output ratio will, with a given growth of the labour force, lead to a rise in the capital labour ratio and a rise in output per worker, or in other words higher income per head. This follows since through manipulations of the basic equations it can be shown that both the capital-labour and output-labour ratios are positively related to s, holding all other factors constant. Hence, in equilibrium, a rise in savings affects the level of income, but not its growth.

Extensions of the simple model have focussed on explaining either labour force behaviour or technical change. Most recent theorising under the heading of *endogenous growth* focuses on this latter aspect, given the established importance of technical change in growth. Efficiency improvement via technical change can be built in by making capital stock have an external effect (in addition to its direct effect α) through, for example, knowledge spillovers that add to productivity. In this very simple reformulation, we can write

$$Y = K^{\alpha+\beta}. (A.L)^{1-\alpha} \tag{2.6}$$

where β represent the impact of capital on general productivity growth through the knowledge externality and other terms are as aforestated.

More sophisticated analyses introduce other variables within the model that can influence technical change and thus productivity growth. The main candidates are investment in education or research and development or alternatively a variable reflecting the policy environment, such as a measure of openness to trade or institutional quality. Insofar as a large manufacturing sector helps technical change, for example, through R and D expenditure by firms or other knowledge effects discussed in the following section, this will increase growth.

Using the notation of R to reflect any such additional variable, A will be a function of R rather than varying independently. Hence, we have A(R) and inserting this into Equation 2.1 gives

$$Y = K^{\alpha}. [A(R).L]^{1-\alpha} \tag{2.7}$$

where, as before, α and $1 - \alpha$ are the direct productivities of capital and labour, respectively, but change in A is now not exogenous, but is influenced by the variable R. Total output now depends on K, L and R, with R reflecting some of the more fundamental causes of growth. A version of this formulation has been applied in various empirical studies that attempt to explain cross-country growth experience. R can thus be reflected in variables that proxy factors like the quality of institutions, geography, openness to trade, technological level, and investment in a particular sector such as manufacturing.

Stylised facts on manufacturing industry

Formal growth models as discussed before largely abstract from the structure of an economy. However, there is substantial empirical evidence to suggest that there is an association between the structure of an economy in terms of the relative importance of key sectors – industry, agriculture and services – and economic growth. In particular, the scale and nature of manufacturing activity appears to matter for economic performance, particularly at relatively low levels of income. Alternative growth models along these lines are discussed later in this chapter and in Chapters 5 and 8 (see Boxes 5.1 and 8.1).

There are theoretical reasons why an expansion of manufacturing may be a causal factor in improved performance that are discussed in this chapter. Empirically we can point to four key generalisations or stylised facts that broadly hold up to a minimum threshold level of development (as approximated by income per capita).

1. *As countries grow the share of manufacturing in GDP and employment rises.* The generalisation of a rising share of manufacturing in national income as income per capita grows up to a certain point is well established from the early development literature. If one plots the relation, it is best represented as an S shaped curve with the share of manufacturing rising at relatively low income levels stabilising at some point and then declining beyond that point.[2] A recent analysis for developing countries in Asia, for example, finds that the share of manufacturing starts to decline only at an income of US$10,000 per capita (in 2000 prices).[3]
2. *Countries with large manufacturing sectors tend to grow more rapidly than those with smaller sectors.*
   The link between manufacturing and GDP growth can be seen from observation of recent experience highlighted in Chapter 1. The contrast between East Asia and Latin America is particularly relevant. In the former we have rapidly growing economies with a relatively high manufacturing share in GDP, which

is as much as 35 per cent in China. In the latter as noted earlier manufacturing has been falling as a share in total activity and overall economic growth has been much slower than in East Asia. Between countries in Asia there is also a clear positive relation between growth of GDP and growth of manufacturing.[4] Sub-Saharan Africa, still the slowest growing developing region, has a low manufacturing share in economic activity, and a particularly low share in total employment, at an estimated 5 per cent of the formal labour force in 2000.[5] Similar conclusions on the link between manufacturing and growth are reached by formal econometric tests which explain GDP growth across countries by the initial income level of each country, country characteristics (like population size) and the share of manufacturing in GDP at the start of the period.[6]

3 *Accelerations in GDP growth tend to be associated with a rise in the share of manufacturing in total income and employment.*

Recently, attention has been paid to relatively short periods during which countries may experience either an acceleration or deceleration of growth. A relevant question here is how the structure of production changes during those periods and whether a shift towards manufacturing either precedes or accompanies faster growth? Again, there has been formal analysis of this for developing Asia with the conclusion that most growth episodes see a relative decline in agriculture prior to or during the period. There is some evidence of a link between changing output share for manufacturing and periods of rapid growth (defined as more than three consecutive period where GDP growth averages at least 5 per cent), which is stronger than for services, in part because a rise in the service share can also be associated with a growth deceleration as workers displaced elsewhere are absorbed in services.[7]

4 *Economies that have high value manufactured exports tend to have higher growth of both exports and GDP.*

During the expansion of world trade that has occurred in the past twenty years, it has become clear that it has been manufactures with a relatively high technology content that grew most rapidly and that such manufactures maintained their price margins despite falling prices for technologically simpler labour-intensive products. These trends emerged clearly in the 1990s, although since 2000 it is less clear that high-technology manufactures have been the most dynamic manufactured goods (see Chapter 4). Most countries have succeeded in diversifying their exports and increasing their exports of manufactures. Some lower-middle- and middle-income countries have gone further and increased their exports of technologically more sophisticated goods, even if they are only producing the labour-intensive components of these goods. Recent work has attempted to quantify the diversification of the export basket of a country by constructing commodity indices of technological sophistication. When measures of the sophistication of exports are used in analysis of growth they are found to be significantly and positively associated with growth. In other words, exporting more sophisticated higher-value exports helps growth once other explanatory factors are controlled for. These higher-value exports are predominately manufactures (see Box 2.1).

Box 2.1 What you export matters

Recent work has attempted to quantify the diversification of the export basket by constructing commodity indices of technological sophistication. This can be done by using a weighted average of the incomes of the exporters of a good to the world market. Hence, for example, a textile product exported predominantly only by the United Kingdom and Italy is taken to have characteristics (including technology) that differ from a textile product exported predominantly by Bangladesh and Cambodia. Two alternative measures of product sophistication have been put forward, one by Hausmann *et al.* (2006) and the other by Lall *et al.* (2006). Both base the index for each product on a weighted average of the incomes per capita of the exporters of the good. The only difference in approach is in the weights used. Hausmann *et al.* weight on the basis of a country's specialisation using the revealed comparative advantage measure.[8] Thus, the more specialised a country is in a product, the higher will be the weight its income per capita receives in the product index. Lall *et al.* weight on the basis of a country's share in world exports of a product. Hence, the more a country exports, the higher will be the weight on its income per capita.

Hausmann *et al.* are interested primarily in the link between their product index and growth performance. To develop this, they convert their product index (which is at a very disaggregate 6-digit level) into a single export index for each country (which they term EXPY). This aggregate measure is a weighted average of all product indices for the goods the country exports, with weights given their share in the country's exports. EXPY then becomes one of the explanatory variables in a model to explain growth. The result is that overall there is a significant positive relation between EXPY at the start of a period and subsequent growth controlling for other influences. The authors experiment with many variants of the basic equation and for different types of economy. For OECD (Organization for Economic Cooperation and Development) economies EXPY is insignificant, and in general, it works best for middle-income economies. The simplest version of the model gives the following result for the whole sample to explain GDP per capita growth 1992–2003

$$g = -0.42 - 0.015y + 0.060\ \text{EXPY}$$

$$(4.32)^{**}\ (2.37)^{*}\ (3.96)^{**}$$

$$R^2 = 0.35$$

where g is GDP growth per capita, y is income per capita at the start of the period and EXPY is the average income level of a country's exports at the start of the period. The t ratios are in brackets; *denotes significant at 5 per cent level, **denotes significant at 1 per cent level.

The various specifications give different elasticities, but the foregoing result suggests that a 10 per cent increase in EXPY is on average associated with an increase in annual growth of 0.6 percentage points. The preferred specification allowing for individual country characteristics suggests a lower elasticity of around 0.02, but there is still a significant positive relationship (see Hausmann *et al.* 2006, Tables 8 and 9). This analysis is extended by Rodrik (2006b) to look specifically at the case of China whose EXPY score is well above that predicted for its income level and which appears to explain at least part of China's high growth rate.

Interpreting the stylised facts

The story behind the pattern implied by the stylised facts is that as low-income economies develop, there is a move out of agriculture into higher-productivity activities, of which manufacturing is the key. As growth takes place workers also move out of agriculture into services and the service share in GDP also increases. Two economic factors drive this process – one relating to trends in demand and the other to productivity. On the demand side, it is well established that the share of income spent on food declines as income rises, whilst the expenditure share on manufactures rises with income. However, as incomes pass a threshold level, the expenditure share of manufactures stabilises and then starts to decline. These are proportionate (not absolute) expenditure reductions reflecting changing income elasticity of demand, since total expenditure will keep growing with income. Once the threshold income level is reached, the economy starts to diversify further with agriculture's share continuing to decline, that of manufacturing stabilising and that of services rising. At some point due to shifts in demand the manufacturing share in GDP starts to decline with faster growth in services.

The second factor influencing the shift in importance of different sectors is differential productivity growth. Historically there has been strong evidence that growth of productivity in manufacturing is more rapid than in services or agriculture, although there is some evidence that now newer computer-based service activity is also seeing rapid increases in productivity.[9] Faster productivity growth means that the price of manufactures will decline relative to services boosting the initial demand shift towards manufactures due to rising income. Later, when the income elasticity of demand for manufactures starts to decline, this favourable substitution effect will act as a partial offset and delay the fall in manufacturing's share in income. How employment shares are affected by faster productivity growth in manufacturing will depend on whether the favourable substitution effect, as unit wage cost has fallen (encouraging employment in manufacturing), is offset by the labour-saving impact of rising labour productivity. Empirical trends in most countries suggest that at some point the latter comes to dominate

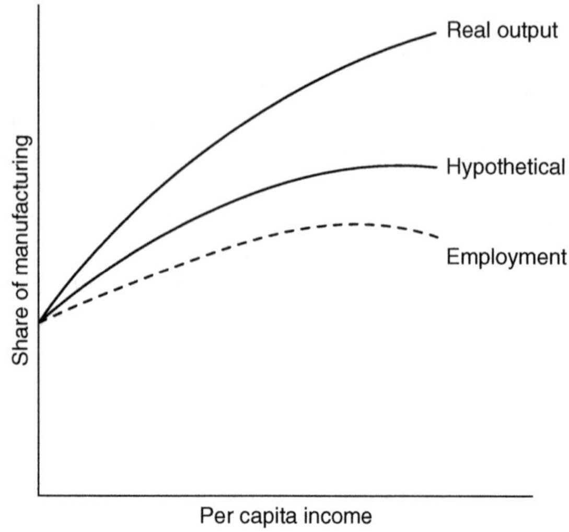

Figure 2.1 Manufacturing share and income level.

and manufacturing's share in total employment falls by more than its share in national income.

Figure 2.1 provides a schematic illustration of these trends. The horizontal axis plots income per capita and the vertical gives the share of manufacturing in both employment and output. For simplicity the units are chosen so that the manufacturing shares in output and employment are initially the same. All three curves reflect the S shaped relation noted before. The curve labelled *hypothetical* shows how these shares would evolve if productivity growth were the same across all sectors and so relative prices remain unchanged. Here, the employment and output shares of manufacturing remain the same and their evolution is determined solely by the income elasticity of demand. The curve rises initially reflecting a rising share of manufacturing as a result of an income elasticity of demand of above unity. However, over time, the curve turns down, reflecting a falling manufacturing share as the income elasticity falls below unity as incomes rise.

The hypothetical curve is an abstraction and by introducing productivity growth that is higher in manufacturing that elsewhere there will be a relative price effect that boosts the demand for manufactures causing its share in output to increase more rapidly than in the hypothetical case. This is shown in the upper curve denoted as *real output*. Here the curve also slopes upward but at a faster rate and turns down at a higher income level, because a combination of income and price effects is involved. However, the introduction of the productivity effect reduces the need for labour per unit of output. Thus, the employment share is reflected in a lower curve labelled employment which rises more slowly and turns down at a lower income level.

The speed and detail of this process has varied between economies, but it broadly represents historical change from as far back as the Industrial Revolution in nineteenth-century Britain and is being exemplified today in the major labour movement out of agriculture and into manufacturing in China. Where the manufacturing share in employment declines in the context of rising income and employment, this need not be a cause of concern, since it suggests that dynamic non-manufacturing activities are replacing manufacturing. It is a worry, however, where a falling manufacturing share occurs in the context of slow growth and job losses and where it is 'premature' in the sense of occurring at a relatively low level of income per capita and overall productivity. In most of Latin America, for example, the manufacturing share in income and employment is now very similar to that in Europe and North America whilst the income per capita level is much lower.[10] This reflects the much slower growth of manufacturing in the large Latin American economies as compared with the other NIEs in Table 1.5 and the declining share of manufacturing in GDP in the region shown in Table 1.4. This is sometimes described as *premature de-industrialisation*, and the risk is that with few new manufacturing jobs being created new entrants to the labour market will end up in low-productivity activities in services or informal parts of manufacturing.

Labour migration and the labour surplus

The labour migration out of rural and into urban areas noted earlier provides a theoretical starting point for understanding the dynamism of manufacturing. In low-income countries, the agriculture sector is typically based on relatively traditional low-productivity production techniques with a labour productivity well below that in manufacturing, construction and some services. This means that labour movement due to internal migration out of rural areas may give a significant boost to overall productivity if the migrants find work in higher-productivity occupations, such as in labour-intensive manufacturing. This in itself will be a once for all effect and will explain a move to a higher overall income level not a higher rate of growth. However, allowing for reinvestment out of the profits generated by the employment of migrants gives a dynamic dimension.

The key framework put forward to explain this process in the development context is the very well known Lewis model of a labour surplus economy, after the Caribbean economist Arthur Lewis (Lewis 1954). Despite its simplifications the basic insight of this model has been given contemporary relevance through its role in explaining recent Chinese experience. The thrust of the model is a contrast between a modern capitalist sector (which could be manufacturing, services or commercial agriculture) and a traditional agricultural sector. In the latter, a significant proportion of the workforce are in surplus supply, which means that either they contribute nothing to output (so their marginal product is zero) or that the small amount they do contribute could readily be covered by other household members should they migrate (so their marginal product is positive but low). To allow an adequate level of consumption per person in traditional agriculture it is assumed households share income equally so that each member receives the average product of the household. There is an incentive for workers in the traditional sector to migrate because of the higher productivity and wages in the modern sector.

They and their families will be better off provided they receive a wage which exceeds the average product of labour in the traditional sector plus an adjustment for the cost of migration and higher living cost in the modern sector (typically assumed to be in urban areas, although this is not essential). The key point is that at such a wage, because it is assumed there is a large labour surplus, employers in the modern sector can employ as many workers as they need without having to raise wages. In the short term therefore there is an unlimited supply of labour at the going wage or a *perfectly elastic labour supply curve*. If capitalists in the modern sector can employ workers at a constant real wage they can reinvest their profits to raise labour productivity and demand further, and because real wages are held down by the unlimited supply of migrants this surplus will continue to grow.

The process can be illustrated diagrammatically in Figure 2.2. The right hand portion shows average and marginal product curves in the traditional sector. Out of total labour supply of OLt the marginal product becomes zero at OLa, so that the labour surplus is (OLt – Ola). Strictly it can be larger than this where remaining family members compensate for any lost output due to migration by working harder. Output is maximised when OLa workers are engaged in traditional activity, and at this point, the average product is OWa. Migrants will be willing to move to the modern sector for a wage OWm (*the reservation wage*) that equals OWa plus a markup to compensate for the costs of migration (the original model took the markup to be 30 per cent of the average product). The left hand portion shows the demand for labour in the modern sector. This reflects the marginal product of labour for a given capital stock (so we have D1 for a capital level of K1 and a declining marginal product as employment expands for given level of capital). With workers employed at OWm and a labour demand of D1 the area ABWm will be the surplus accruing to capitalist employers which they can reinvest.

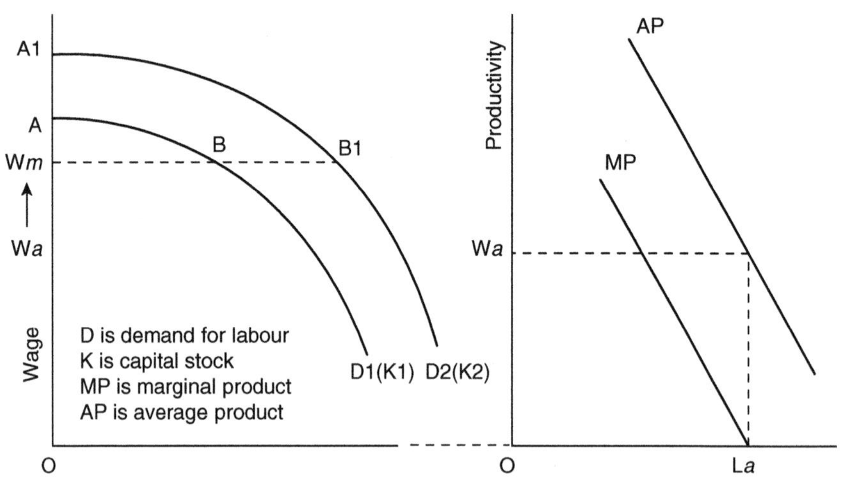

Figure 2.2 Lewis model of a labour surplus economy.

This reinvestment will create a new capital stock K2 and thus a new higher demand for labour D2 based on higher marginal productivity. The model implies that this process can continue with an expanding modern sector until the labour surplus is exhausted and real wages start to rise.

A large number of technical and factual qualifications have been raised in relation to this simple model. For example, it was pointed out that more than one migrant would leave the traditional sector for each new job created, as migrants would balance the expected value of higher incomes against the greater certainty of the average product in the traditional sector (although with weather-dependent traditional agriculture this average product would be far from certain in reality). The unemployment rate in the modern sector became the equilibrating device in this revised version of the model, so that rising modern (largely urban) sector unemployment accompanied migration. In addition, in the logic of the model it is not clear where demand for the expanded output of the modern sector would come from if real wages there did not grow. Exports will be needed to provide the demand outlet. Similarly if significant numbers leave the traditional sector with an unchanged total output, average product there will rise for those who remain behind. Since the wage necessary to attract migrants is a markup over the average product and this will raise the wage OWm that migrants need to justify leaving the traditional sector.

The model was a simplification and experience in a number of countries appeared largely at odds with its view of the world. For example, in much of Africa internal migration off the land was accompanied by rising urban unemployment and only modest increases in formal sector employment in manufacturing. In Latin America, as early as the 1960s, the rural areas had already lost large numbers of workers and the main body of labour surplus was in urban not rural areas. In parts of South Asia, internal migration faced cultural as well as economic barriers. However, the model has taken on a contemporary relevance, because it seems to be a reasonable explanation for recent Chinese growth. There productivity and average income remain very much higher in urban than in rural areas and most observers have identified a very large labour surplus (if not in the strict sense of a zero marginal product, then in the looser sense that workers' output contribution can be easily covered by family members working harder). Despite official obstacles to migration within the country, many people have moved location often to work in export oriented manufacturing in the coastal provinces, but also to do urban-based work in other parts of the country. Frequently they have left their families behind in their villages and have sent back remittances as a means of family support. The consequence of this internal migration has been both a contribution to poverty reduction in China and the dramatic expansion of a low-wage manufacturing sector. In turn, because of China's size and the export orientation of much of its manufacturing sector, from the mid-1990s, it can be argued that China became the marginal supplier of low-cost labour to the world economy. This has had important implications for the prices of manufactures on the world market and has had major impacts on consumers, producers and workers in the rest of the world.

If we take the Lewis model as a rough approximation of this process with demand for modern sector goods covered by exports, there will come a point at which real wages that the modern sector must pay will rise either because average product has risen in the traditional sector or because the cost of internal migration has increased. There is evidence that real wages are rising in parts of China and there is an ongoing debate as to how much of the labour surplus remains to be tapped. However, there seems little doubt that recent Chinese growth based on an export manufacturing sector that could draw on a vast reservoir of low-cost unskilled labour, broadly conforms to the labour surplus model.

Externalities

If it is established through historical experience and theory, that a shift from lower- to higher-productivity activities is part of the process of economic growth, this in itself does not establish a special case for manufacturing, since as the Lewis model makes clear what matters is having a dynamic sector organised on modern capitalist lines to absorb surplus labour. This could be sectors like commercial agriculture, tourism, mining or modern services, as well as manufacturing. In general, the case for a special role for manufacturing rests on two related general propositions.

> *The incidence of external benefits, defined as higher incomes for producers or consumers not directly associated with the initial investment is greater in manufacturing than elsewhere.*
>
> *The potential for productivity gains due to cumulative experience and experimentation is greater in manufacturing than elsewhere.*

In a broadly competitive economy with capital mobility and relatively little monopoly power one would expect the return on additional investment to be broadly similar across activities. If this is the case establishing that one form of activity is preferable to any other, requires a demonstration that there are external benefits not captured by the original investor, but which are real in that they accrue to someone in the economy. These externalities can of course be negative as well as positive and much recent discussion has stressed negative environmental effects. Externalities are important in a theoretical sense, because they demonstrate the inability of a competitive market system to reach a social optimum (termed *market failure*) and thus provide a major plank of the rationale for an interventionist policy to influence resource allocation. Technically two broad types are identified – *technological* and *pecuniary* externalities – reflecting the fact that externalities may be transmitted either directly (in which case they are technological) or through a market relationship (in which case they are pecuniary).

Strictly technological externalities arise where impacts on others have effects on their output that are not mediated through the market. Technically this means the output of one firm enters the production function of another. Hence:

$$Qi = f(Ki, Li, Qj) \quad (2.9)$$

where Qi is the output of firm i, Ki, and Li are the capital and labour inputs used by i, and Qj is the physical output of firm j.

However, since changes in output normally have monetary implications, many of the interesting effects are impacts on income and profits that can be thought of as pecuniary externalities. In this case, there is an externality where profits depend not just on a firms own inputs, but on the physical quantities of outputs of other producers. Hence, for firm i, there will be an externality if

$$Ri = f(Ki, Li, P, Qj) \quad (2.10)$$

where Ri is profit of firm i, Ki and Li are the capital and labour inputs used by i, P is a set of prices faced by i and Qj is the physical output of firm j.

Several examples of externalities are cited frequently in relation to manufacturing. A labour training externality arises, where producer j trains workers who subsequently leave taking their skills to firm i. The latter saves their training cost and gains the benefit from their higher productivity. Environmental externalities arise where a firm damages the environment, for example, through air or water pollution but is not charged for the damage it creates. Other firms and consumers will ultimately have to meet the cost of this damage either through their own mitigatory expenditure or through higher taxes.

More generally, there will be a series of inter-relationships based on the linkages between firms that can affect profitability. For example, expansion of firm j may increase profits of i if j's output is an input into i and is subject to increasing returns to scale so that unit cost and the price charged to i fall. Similarly, the reverse holds if i is a supplier to j so that the latter's expansion will raise demand for i; in this case i will benefit if it is subject to increasing returns and does not pass on lower unit costs in a lower price.

Negative effects on profits are equally possible where, for example, i and j are substitutes and expansion of j takes market share from i; similarly even if i and j are not direct competitors, expansion of j may push up the price of a factor used by both. These inter-relationships within manufacturing arise because of its interdependence. This is demonstrated in any input–output table where universally manufacturing shows more backward linkages (the purchase of productive inputs) and forward linkages (the sale of goods for further processing) than any other activity. This interdependence gives the scope for pecuniary externalities and given that manufacturing also involves more product variety than other forms of production, there is greater scope for imitation and modification of final goods.

Finally and possibly the most significant in this context is the potential for *knowledge spillover* externalities within manufacturing. This is where ideas developed by firm j are copied or modified by firm i possibly by simple imitation or by transfer of workers from j. Proximity of location between clusters of firms can play a key role here, with technical progress a continual process of trial, adaptation and modification. Imitation in developing new products is equally as important as in developing new production processes and the potential to stimulate entrepreneurship through the example and experience of successful first comers or innovators is a key aspect of knowledge spillovers.

Geographic proximity between producers as a means of maximising spillovers and other external effects, like labour availability, has received prominence in discussions relating to *agglomeration* effects and provides a rationale for the creation of Special Economic Zones and related measures to encourage the clustering of firms. The key potential advantages for a firm from proximity to other producers making similar things are:

- Access to a pool of skilled labour drawn to the area by the presence of similar firms.
- Spillovers though the sharing (or copying) of technological or marketing knowledge.
- A network of specialist suppliers drawn to the area by the presence of a sufficient number of user firms, where proximity to suppliers reduces transport costs and helps in ensuring timely delivery and reduces any co-ordination difficulties.

Box 2.2 summarises recent information on a survey of production clusters of firms across a range of regions that provides evidence of these positive agglomeration effects.

Box 2.2 Clusters of manufacturing firms

UNIDO (2009) reports on a study of ten clusters of firms in range of countries at different income levels. Each cluster consists of largely export-oriented firms in the same industry, plus their local suppliers and workers. Some (such as automotive firms in Buenos Aires, Argentina, garment firms in Phnom Penh, Cambodia and electronics firms in Penang, Malaysia) are largely integrated operations producing most of the parts and components that go into the final product, which is typically exported. Others (such as pulp and paper firms in Brazil, leather firms in Chennai, India and button producers in Qiaotou, China) produce goods that go elsewhere for further stages of manufacturing, either as direct exports or into goods that are exported subsequently. Some of the clusters (such as wood products in Lao, PDR and assembled cars in Jakarta Indonesia) produce principally for the domestic market, but these are the exceptions.

The electronics cluster in Penang provides the best example of technological dynamism and knowledge spillovers between foreign and local firms with evidence that some of the major international players in the industry (such as Intel and Motorola) conduct original design work in the cluster. Of the ten locations studied the most dramatic growth is found in the button cluster in Qiaotou, China which grew from virtually nothing to accounting for two-thirds of the world supply of buttons. Production started with the support of the provincial government when an Italian button firm contracted local suppliers to produce low-value buttons to its specifications. The cluster developed to encompass new design activity and the production of machinery for button manufacture.

Ten industrial clusters

Location	*Product*	*Annual export growth 2000–06 (%)*	*Number of firms surveyed*	*Principal drivers of exports*
Buenos Aires, Argentina	Automotives	15.3	50	Global integration of domestic subsidiaries into global value chains of international firms
South East Brazil (several sites)	Pulp and paper	13.4	13	Proximity to high-quality raw materials
Phnom Penh, Cambodia	Garments	24.1	87	Foreign firms utilising preferential access to rich country markets
Los Lagos, Chile	Salmon	18.6	50	Adaptation of best practice in salmon culture and processing
Qiaotou, China	Buttons	12.4	100	Connection with and upgrading in global production networks
Chennai, India	Leather	6.8	100	Institutional support for technological upgrading
Jakarta, Indonesia	Automotives	11.7	94	Specialisation within global production networks
Vientiane-Champasak, Lao, PDR	Wood products	5.6	100	Proximity to raw material and preferential market access for exports
Penang, Malaysia	Electrical goods and electronics	6.7	100	Foreign investment induced by high-quality infrastructure and financial incentives
Otigba, Nigeria	Computers and components	23.3	30	Local pool of educated entrepreneurs

Source: UNIDO (2009, Table 3.2).

The argument is not that externalities are absent elsewhere in the economy, but that their significance is far greater within manufacturing. This led in the past to industrial strategies based around types of goods judged likely to be important generators of externalities like a *basic industry* strategy (a focus on intermediate engineering goods, steel and metals) and a *capital goods* strategy (a focus on heavy machinery and equipment to make other machines). These are now largely disregarded on the grounds that they neglect the possibility of importing such goods more cheaply, but the externality case that lay behind them remains valid as a case for manufacturing in general; even if alone it is not enough to justify such specific strategies.

Increasing returns in manufacturing

The theoretical case for the special role for manufacturing involves not just greater externalities than in other sectors but a focus on dynamic increasing returns in the sense of declining unit costs as output grows over time. There is a long tradition in economics that contrasts increasing returns (i.e. productivity growth) in manufacturing with diminishing returns in agriculture with services treated as an appendage of manufacturing. This is distinct from an argument about increasing returns in a static sense, where unit costs fall as plant scale is expanded. Static economies of scale are found in many lines of activity; plantation agriculture may have lower cost per unit of crop output than that in small-holder agriculture and supermarkets are likely to have lower costs per product sold than that in small family shops. Furthermore, there will be a wide variation within manufacturing in the relation between higher output and decline in unit cost of production, with heavy capital-intensive activities showing the most scale effect. Table 2.1 summarises judgements on the degree of static economies of scale classifying sub-sectors of manufacturing into those with low-, medium- and high-scale economies on the basis of engineering and cost data (although this is now somewhat dated).

The key focus here is a dynamic rather than a static relationship, with dynamic increasing returns referring to the tendency in manufacturing for the growth of

Table 2.1 Static economies of scale within manufacturing

Low-scale economies	Wearing apparel, Footwear, Furniture, Textiles, Wood products, Leather products, Food products, Beverages, Tobacco, Other Manufactures, Plastics, Rubber products.
Medium-scale economies	Printing and publishing, Paper products, Metal products, Pottery, Glass, Non-metallic Mineral products, Iron and Steel, Professional Equipment, Electrical machinery, Non-electrical machinery.
High-scale economies	Petroleum and coal products, Nonferrous metals, Petroleum refining, Transport equipment, Other chemicals, Industrial chemicals.

Source: Cited in ADB (2007, Table 3.1.1).

output to be related systematically to the growth of productivity. Hence, it is not the level of output that drives the decline in unit cost but its cumulative growth over time. The mechanisms underlying this process in manufacturing are learning by doing, technological imitation, adaptation and modification and the gains from increased specialisation as manufacturing is increasingly sub-divided into more specialised forms. Unlike static economies of scale these dynamic gains should not be reversible if output subsequently declines, since they have created a higher skill and technological base for the sector.

The concept of dynamic increasing returns links with the discussion of externalities and linkages since they will be part of the process of productivity improvement. The complex set of linkages between firms found in manufacturing provides the mechanism for productivity gains in response to growing output. Historically, it is well documented that as the scale of the national market for manufactures grows, it allows the establishment of increasing specialisation and differentiation between firms (the *roundaboutness of production*), as newly specialised supplier firms are established through backward linkages from existing firms. Today, with the removal of many barriers to trade, this process has been heightened by the closer integration of most economies with the world market. The scale of the market is critical, since as it expands with growth, so will the opportunities for specialisation. Some of the resulting productivity gains will be internal to firms, but others will spillover as benefits to other firms, as discussed before.

The argument of the special role of manufacturing based on dynamic increasing returns originates principally from the Cambridge economist Nicholas Kaldor, who saw manufacturing as the only sector for which output growth and productivity growth were related. Productivity growth could occur in agriculture or in services, for example, but in his view, it was not related systematically to growth of output. For example, productivity growth in agriculture might be due to exogenous technical change in the form of new seed varieties or to the shift of workers off the land, not to the expansion of the sector itself and the increased specialisation and learning that this allows. This dynamic process may be at work in other sectors, particularly in the more modern branches of services based on information communication technology, but empirically the evidence suggests that it is in manufacturing that it remains most prominent.

Subsequent analysis for developing countries has shown that these results showing increasing returns hold for a range of sectors, not just for manufacturing.[11] However, the Kaldor argument goes further by asserting that manufacturing growth raises not just productivity in manufacturing, but through externality and spillover effects raises overall productivity in the economy as labour is transferred from lower-productivity activities into manufacturing and as manufacturing development stimulates improvements in the services that it uses. As Box 2.3 reports, there is evidence linking manufacturing with overall productivity growth; however, it appears that, unlike the earlier view of Kaldor which saw services as a largely passive element in the economy, the modern service sector is also emerging as an engine of growth and drawing workers into technologically dynamic activities with the potential for productivity growth.

Box 2.3 Kaldor's law and manufacturing

Kaldor's case was based on the relationship between output growth and productivity first established by the Dutch economist Jake Verdoorn and he put forward a simple empirical test (Kaldor 1966, 1967). He estimated two equations for a number of sectors from a sample of countries:

$$pi = a1 + b1.qi \tag{2.11}$$

$$ei = a2 + b2.qi \tag{2.12}$$

where p, q and e are labour productivity growth, output growth and employment growth, respectively, for sector i.

Equation 2.11 is the relation established by Verdoorn, which has been found to hold for many branches of activity. Since by definition, growth of output is the sum of growth of productivity and the growth of the number of workers ($qi = pi + ei$), it is possible for spurious correlations to be found between q and p, when changes in e are small. Hence, Kaldor's additional requirement to demonstrate the existence of dynamic increasing returns is that Equation 2.12 is also statistically significant with a coefficient $b2$ of less than unity. This implies that the growth of employment is less than the growth of output, so by definition, there will be a productivity gain.

Kaldor's original test was simplified in focusing only on labour productivity and can be modified by introducing a capital input and setting the analysis in a production function framework. This extended version of the test now requires that as output grows there will be increasing returns to scale so that combined factor productivity will be growing. This can be seen by using an aggregate production function for a sector i

$$\mathrm{Q}i = f(\mathrm{A.TFI}^{v}) \tag{2.13}$$

where Q is output, A is an exogenous factor for technology, TFI is a composite of capital and labour inputs (weighted by income shares for labour and capital) and v is the scale parameter, with v greater than 1.0 reflecting increasing returns.

If Equation 2.13 is differentiated with respect to time

$$q = a + v.tfi$$

where q, a and tfi are rates of change for output, technical change and total factor inputs, respectively. Rearranging gives

$$tfi = c + \alpha q \tag{2.14}$$

where $c = -a/v$ *and* $\alpha = 1/v$

Equation 2.14 provides the new test for dynamic increasing returns since it requires that $\alpha < 1$, so that total factor inputs grow by less than output. α will be below unity if $v > 1$, so we have increasing returns to scale. The tests using Equation 2.14 in the context of developed economies have found manufacturing to be the only sector where there is a consistent tendency for this effect (McCombie *et al.* 2002).

The impact of growth in manufacturing on the rest of the economy can be tested simply by regressing growth of manufacturing value-added on growth of GDP and comparing the results with similar analyses for services and agriculture. Dasgupta and Singh (2006) report this test for 50 developing countries for which data are available 1990–2000. The results are as follows

$$gGDP = 0.022 + 0.473.gManufVA \qquad R^2 = 0.98$$

$$(13.98)^* \ (67.53)^*$$

$$gGDP = 0.067 + 1.421.gAgVA \qquad R^2 = 0.69$$

$$(2.31)^* \ (10.44)^*$$

$$gGDP = 0.015 + 0.580.gServVA \qquad R^2 = 0.98$$

$$(8.53)^* \ (48.85)^*$$

t ratios are in brackets, *significant at 1 per cent level

where g stands for growth, Manuf, Ag and Serv refer to manufacturing, agriculture and services, respectively, and VA is value added.

The equations for manufacturing and services are robust statistically, but that for agriculture does not pass all the necessary diagnostic tests so less confidence can be placed on the link between agriculture growth and GDP growth. In these equations, the lower the coefficient on the sector growth variable the higher is the impact of the sector on GDP, since a lower rate of sector growth will be required to generate a given change in GDP. The coefficient for manufacturing (of 0.47) is below that for services (of 0.58). It should be noted, however, that the service sector is showing signs of dynamism (even at a lower rate) similar to that of manufacturing. Whilst some service activities in low- and middle-income countries, such as retail and wholesale trade and public bureaucracies, have low productivity, new dynamic elements of services are emerging, such as business and computer-based services, telecommunications and tourism. One interpretation of these results is that these latter dynamic elements are starting to dominate and that service sector as a whole is behaving in way similar to manufacturing and thus offering higher-productivity employment to that that available in agriculture. This argument is now particularly relevant in the context of India where service sector growth is seen as a key feature of recent development (see Chapter 8).

The same work also tests for another key assertion (see next) that overall productivity growth in the economy is explained positively by productivity growth in manufacturing and negatively by employment growth in agriculture. A relatively simple test for this is to use a regression model to explain overall labour productivity growth in an economy by the growth of manufacturing value-added and the growth of employment outside manufacturing. For the analysis across the same 50 countries 1990–2000 the results are

$$\text{g.Prod} = 0.003 + 0.408\ \text{g.ManufVA} - 0.286\text{g.AgEmp}$$

$$(0.526) \qquad (5.18)^* \qquad (8.96)^* \qquad R^2 = 0.76$$

$$\text{g.Prod} = -0.021 + 0.906\ \text{g.SerVA} - 0.276\text{g.AgEmp}$$

$$(3.09)^* \qquad (7.09)^* \qquad (10.04)^* \qquad R^2 = 0.83$$

where Prod is overall national labour productivity, AgEmp is employment in agriculture and other terms are as aforementioned.

The argument that manufacturing growth raises overall productivity growth and increased agricultural employment depresses it, is found to hold. However, the same positive effect on productivity elsewhere holds for services, which leads to the conclusion that the service sector is emerging as a dynamic factor in many countries, in the same way as manufacturing.

Manufacturing and other sectors

The engine of growth case for manufacturing based on increasing returns is sometimes misunderstood in the sense that it fully accepts that there is a key inter-relationship between manufacturing and agriculture particularly at a relatively early stage of development. A dynamic domestic manufacturing sector can provide inputs like fertiliser or farm equipment for agriculture, alternatively, through exports it can generate the foreign exchange to allow the importation of these inputs. On the demand side, by drawing workers out of agriculture it can also raise labour productivity for those remaining. On the other hand, a growing agricultural sector can provide wage goods for workers employed in manufacturing or raw materials for processing in agro-based industry. Critically, particularly where exports are still modest, growing agricultural incomes can be an important source of demand for manufactured goods. Thus, industrialisation can be held back by a stagnant agriculture sector, so that overemphasising manufacturing at the expense of agriculture can lead to a longer-term growth of manufacturing lower than would be possible with a more balanced strategy. Box 2.4 discusses a formal model in the spirit of Kaldor's original analysis to demonstrate this. What matters is that investment is allocated in line with expected returns (in a full economic sense and thus including external effects) and that bottlenecks are not allowed to develop in specific sectors.

Box 2.4 Industry–Agriculture terms of trade

A simple model can be used to explain the link between manufacturing and industry drawing on the work of Kaldor, who had stressed that although manufacturing may be the key sector for increasing returns, growth of manufacturing can be held back by a slow-growing agriculture due to a lack of demand for manufactures.[12] The analysis is based on a simple two sector (initially closed economy) model of industry and agriculture, with industry producing an investment good and agriculture producing a wage good (i.e. a good consumed by workers employed in manufacturing). Agriculture has surplus labour and is organised on a subsistence basis so that farmers sell their surplus to industry for consumption by workers. Wage determination is as in the Lewis model. Industry reinvests part of its output and sells the rest to agriculture. The relative price of the investment good (from industry) to the wage good (from agriculture) is the internal terms of trade (Pi/Pa), and this price ratio plays a key role in the analysis.

A series of equations set out the structure of the simplest version of the model. Savings in agriculture (Sa) are a proportion (sa) of agricultural output (Qa) so

$$Sa = sa.Qa \qquad (2.15)$$

Investment in agriculture (Ia) is the output set aside for saving divided by the relative price of industrial to agricultural goods p (i.e. the price of the investment good in terms of units of wage goods),

$$Ia = Sa/p \qquad (2.16)$$

Growth of agricultural output (dQa/Qa) will be the product of the investment ratio in agriculture (Ia/Qa) and the productivity of agricultural investment (σ) so

$$(Qa/Qa) = \sigma.\ (Ia)/Qa) \qquad (2.17)$$

where d is change in

Substituting for Ia from Equation 2.15 and Equation 2.16 gives $(dQa/Qa) = \sigma.\ (sa.Qa/p)*1/Qa$

which reduces to

$$gd = dQa/Qa = \sigma.\, sa/p \tag{2.19}$$

where *gd* is the growth of agriculture. It is written as *gd* to reflect the fact that growth of agriculture (with a constant savings rate) determines the growth of demand for industry. *gd* is positively related to savings (*sa*) and investment productivity in agriculture (σ) and negatively related to the internal terms of trade given as the price of the industrial good to the agricultural good (*p*). The relation with *p* can be drawn as a hyperbola with *p* on the vertical axis and *gd* on the horizontal. A rise in agricultural productivity will shift the curve outwards to the right, thus creating higher growth for a given internal terms of trade.

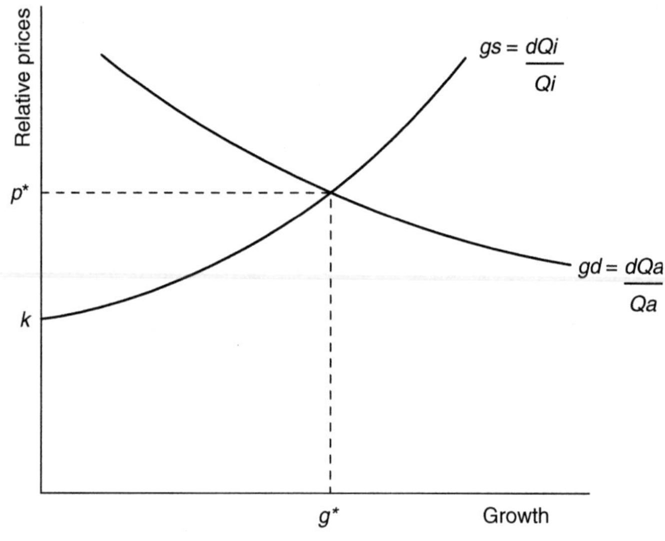

Figure 2.3 Internal terms of trade and growth.

A similar relation between growth and relative prices can be established for industry. Consumption of workers (*Ci*) is on agricultural wage goods (capitalist consumption is ignored) and will be a proportion k of industrial output (*Qi*), where *k* is the product of the labour input per unit of output (*l*) and the real wage (*w*) measured in terms of food ($k = w.l$).

Therefore

$$Ci = k.Qi \tag{2.20}$$

As with agriculture the growth of industry (*dQi/Qi*) will be the product of the investment ratio in industry (Ii/Qi) and the productivity of industrial investment (ψ) so

$$(dQi/Qi) = \psi\,(Ii)/Qi) \tag{2.21}$$

Investment in industry (Ii) is total industrial output (Qi) minus agricultural investment (Ia), so

$$Ii = Qi - Ia \tag{2.22}$$

However, from Equation 2.16 $Ia = Sa/p$

Agricultural savings (Sa) will be exchanged for industrial goods, as industrial workers wish to purchase (Ci) consumer goods, so that from Equation 2.20

$$Sa = Ci = k.Qi$$

Hence, substituting:

$$Ii = Qi - k.Qi/p = Qi\,(1 - k/p) \tag{2.23}$$

From Equation2.21 growth of industrial output (dQi/Qi) becomes

$$(dQi/Qi) = \psi\,(Qi\,(1 - k/p)\ {*}1/Qi$$

which reduces to

$$gs = (dQi/Qi) = \psi\,(1 - k/p) \tag{2.24}$$

Here, growth of industry is also written as gs reflecting growth of supply of industrial goods. It depends positively on investment productivity in industry (ψ) and the internal terms of trade (p) (i.e. the price of the industrial good relative to the wage good from agriculture) and negatively on the wage share in industrial output (k). The relation between gs on the horizontal and p on the vertical axis can also be plotted as a curve which cuts the vertical axis at k which gives the minimum relative price of the industrial good at which there will be zero growth (since there will be no reinvestment in industry). A rise in investment productivity (ψ) shifts the curve downwards to the right allowing a higher gs for a given p.

In the model, there will be an equilibrium terms of trade at which gd and gs cross (p^* in Figure 2.3). Setting $gs = gd$ we find

$$p^* = (\sigma.\ sa/\psi) + k \tag{2.25}$$

and

$$g^* = 1/(1/\psi + k/\sigma.\ sa) \tag{2.26}$$

From Equation 2.26 equilibrium growth g^* where demand for industry from agriculture (gd) equals industrial supply (gs) is related positively to investment productivity in both sectors (ψ and σ), and savings in agriculture (sa) and negatively to the wage cost ratio for industry (k). The equilibrium terms of trade shift in favour of industry (a rise in p^*), the higher are wage costs (k), savings in agriculture (sa) and the higher is productivity in agriculture (σ). Hence, from these last results technical change in agriculture (a change in σ) even if it may be lower than that in industry, nonetheless plays an important role in creating a favourable price effect and in stimulating industrial output.

This simple model has been used to highlight how a demand deficiency stemming from a slow growth of agriculture can hold back growth of industry. This can be seen from Figure 2.4. An attempt to force industrialisation by shifting the terms of trade against agriculture is reflected in the price ratio $p1$. At this relative price, industry has the capacity to grow at $g1$; however, this will not be attained, because demand from agriculture is only $g2$ at this price ratio. Industry can only grow beyond $g2$ if relative prices shift in favour of agriculture (with the maximum growth achieved for both sectors at the equilibrium price p^*) or if land-saving technical progress in agriculture shifts the gd curve upwards (so agricultural productivity σ rises). However, since technical progress in agriculture is exogenous to the model (and may be difficult to increase in the short-run in the real world), there is no reason why it should occur at a rate that allows industry to grow at its

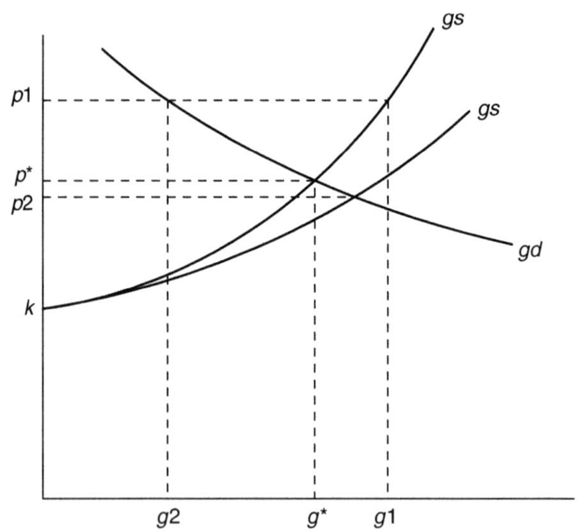

Figure 2.4 Changing the internal terms of trade.

maximum potential rate. Hence, a shift in relative prices will be required to maximise the growth rate for both sectors. Technical progress in industry on the other hand (a rise in ψ) will shift the *gs* curve downwards to the right and will create higher growth for both sectors and a lower internal terms of trade (e.g. at *p*2).

This analysis is for a closed economy and once exports are allowed they become an additional source of demand for industry. However, it is only in very small economies that one can expect exports to play a dominant role in demand from the outset. Historically, most industrialisation has seen agricultural demand playing a significant early role although as industry expands, exports become increasingly important, due to differing income elasticities of demand in domestic and world markets.

Source: Thirlwall (1986).

As we have noted, as incomes rise there is a clear tendency for resources to flow to manufacturing relatively more quickly than to agriculture and in some countries more quickly than to services. How far a rise in the relative scale of manufacturing is optimal will vary between economies, depending upon factors like their resource endowments, and the size of their population. Economies with major natural resource deposits (such as the oil exporters) will clearly rely relatively less on non-resource-based manufacturing and small countries without a large domestic market cannot be expected to support a relatively large manufacturing sector as easily as a much larger economy with a higher internal demand. However, natural-resource exporting economies are normally advised to diversify their export mix to reduce the risk of a market decline for their specialist products and to take advantage of potential gains from manufacturing. The natural-resource-rich economies of Australia and Canada, for example, have diversified in this way. Much smaller oil-rich economies in the Middle East are currently diversifying into services and oil-related processing activities. Similarly, some small economies (of which Singapore and Ireland are the most obvious examples) have supported a relatively large manufacturing sector through success in exporting. We know, however, that beyond a certain income level, demand patterns are such that the proportion (but not the absolute size) of domestic demand going on manufactures will decline. Exporting can delay this effect, but in all cases beyond a certain level of national income the share of manufacturing turns down.

Asian newly industrialised economies: a proof of the case?

Perhaps the strongest support for the engine of growth case for manufacturing comes from the growth experience of a group of Asian economies, which over the last 50 years or so have seen a dramatic increase in income driven in large part by their manufacturing sectors. The countries concerned are fewer than the list of NIEs in Table 1.5 and cover Korea, Taiwan, Singapore, Hong Kong (the original four Tigers), Thailand and Malaysia (as second-tier Tigers) and more recently China and to a lesser degree India. The earlier re-emergence of Japan after 1945 can also be seen in the same light. Their experience provides strong support for the view that there is considerable potential for poor countries to raise their productivity and grow rapidly due to the process of technological catch-up (or *late-comer industrialisation*). Poor countries will be operating well behind the international best-practice technology frontier, and this allows the opportunity for growth based on importing, adapting and applying technology of the more developed (or leader) economies. This process implies income and productivity convergence for successful follower economies relative to the established leaders, which is what we have observed for the Asian NIEs relative to Europe and North America.

The catch-up hypothesis must be interpreted to mean that follower economies have the *potential* to converge on the income levels of the leaders rather than that all followers will inevitably do so. Whether successful catch-up growth takes place is a function of the domestic institutional, educational and economic base of followers, which allows them to respond effectively to the opportunities created by the availability of international best-practice technology developed elsewhere. This realisation has led to a vast literature attempting to explain why some Asian economies have been highly successful in industrialisation over the last fifty years, whilst followers in other parts of the developing world have been much less so. One part of this explanation has been a focus on the role of the state, so that in most of these NIEs (Hong Kong is the obvious exception) in certain periods an active developmental state supported and encouraged industrialisation to help domestic follower firms to compete internationally. State industrial policy in these economies went through many changes over time and is currently much less interventionist than in earlier decades. Its impact remains controversial and key aspects are examined in more detail in Chapter 7.

Manufacturing and poverty reduction

One of the key contributions industrialisation can make to development is the creation of jobs for poor people. Again, it is clearly not the only sector that can do this, but historically in all countries which have industrialised this job creation has been an essential element in reducing poverty. Poverty is normally defined in the development context as having a level of consumption expenditure below the minimum necessary living standard to meet basic needs for food, shelter and others aspects of family life. This latter minimum standard is termed a *poverty line* and the proportion of the population below this line gives the most common measure of poverty (the *headcount* indicator). A vast amount of empirical work has studied poverty trends in recent years, with the basic finding that there are two major determinants of change in poverty – the overall growth rate of an economy and the initial level of inequality. In general, there is a strong negative relationship between growth and poverty with a stronger relationship typically reported at low income levels. On the other hand, high initial inequality will weaken the impact of a given growth rate on poverty reduction as the poor receive proportionately less of the benefits of growth.

Most governments have their own national poverty lines, which are typically higher in higher-income countries (e.g. that for Thailand is nearly twice that for Bangladesh).[13] However, for comparisons of international trends in poverty, a single international line is needed that can be applied across all countries. The World Bank initiated this work in 1990 by taking an average of the national poverty lines in a number of poor countries and converting them into a constant price value in US dollars. This requires estimates of national poverty lines in domestic prices adjusted to a single base year and then converted into US dollars at a purchasing power parity exchange rate. This latter adjustment is to ensure that a given domestic expenditure in different countries is equivalent to the same command over goods. The original international line derived in this way was set at US$1 per day (the *dollar-a-day* poverty line) and international poverty estimates were derived using this line.

Recently, the methodology for estimating international poverty has been revised by taking a new set of poverty lines in the poorest countries and using updated and improved purchasing power parity exchange rates. The new line for extreme poverty is set at US$1.25 per day in 2005 prices and is broadly comparable with the original US$1 per day at an earlier set of prices. This line reflects the national poverty lines in a set of very poor countries, most of which are from sub-Saharan Africa. As this line reflects very poor living conditions, analyses are also conducted using alternative lines. A higher line of US$2 per day, which is the median in all countries in the sample, is used to measure moderate poverty.

The estimates from this analysis for extreme poverty by region are given in Table 2.2. A key point to note is that overall global poverty is higher than was previously thought (approximately 1.4 billion persons as compared with 0.93 billion) although the rate of decline over time was similar to that estimated earlier.[14] The incidence of poverty as reflected in the headcount ratio varies greatly by region but in 1981, East Asia and the Pacific was the poorest region both in terms of numbers of the poor (because of the inclusion of China) and the share of the population deemed poor. As Table 2.2 reveals, a very large number of very poor persons were pulled out of extreme poverty in the period up to 2005, although many of these still remained in moderate poverty; 39 per cent of the population of the region were below the US$2 per day line, for example, in 2005.

Hence, one of the most striking features of the development experience of the last 30 years has been the very significant fall in poverty in the economies that experienced rapid economic growth driven by industrialisation – principally the East Asian NIEs. Poverty in East Asia has been reduced very substantially not just in Korea, Taiwan, Hong Kong and Singapore – the original Tiger economies – but also in their followers Thailand, Malaysia and more recently China. Extreme poverty as defined in Table 2.2 is all but eradicated in Thailand and Malaysia, for example, and in both countries the percentage of the population subject to

Table 2.2 Extreme poverty (US$1.25 per day at 2005 prices) by region: absolute numbers and headcount

Number of poor (millions)				
Region	*1981*	*1990*	*1999*	*2005*
East Asia and Pacific	1071.5	873.3	635.1	316.2
Of which China	835.1	683.2	446.7	207.7
Eastern Europe and Central Asia	7.1	9.1	24.3	17.3
Latin America and the Caribbean	42.0	42.9	54.8	46.1
Middle East and North Africa	13.7	9.7	11.5	11.0
South Asia	548.3	579.2	588.9	595.6
Of which India	420.5	435.5	447.2	455.8
Sub-Saharan Africa	213.7	299.1	381.6	390.6
Headcount (%)				
Region	*1981*	*1990*	*1999*	*2005*
East Asia and Pacific	77.7	54.7	35.5	16.8
Of which China	84.0	60.2	35.6	15.9
Eastern Europe and Central Asia	1.7	2.0	5.1	3.7
Latin America and the Caribbean	11.5	9.8	10.8	8.2
Middle East and North Africa	7.9	4.3	4.2	3.6
South Asia	59.4	51.7	44.1	40.3
Of which India	59.8	51.3	44.8	41.6
Sub-Saharan Africa	53.7	57.9	58.2	50.9

Source: Chen and Ravallion (2008, Tables 6 and 7).

moderate poverty is now modest at 12 and 8 per cent, respectively, in 2005. Even poorer countries in the region have seen large fall in poverty; in Indonesia it fell from 72 per cent of the population in 1981 to 21 per cent in 2005, whilst the comparable figures for Vietnam are a fall from 90 to 23 per cent.[15] This is in direct contrast with the much less successful experience in South Asia and sub-Saharan Africa, where although the headcount poverty index fell over the period (in the African case only modestly) the absolute numbers of the extreme poor rose with population growth.

Demonstrating precisely how far industrialisation alone contributed to poverty reduction in East Asia is difficult. If growth and income distribution are the key driving factors for poverty reduction, there will be complex interactions since the development of modern industry in previously agrarian-based economies will create new jobs, raise productivity and shift the distribution of income – all of which will impact on poverty and not all effects will work in the same direction. However, insofar as manufacturing was the key engine of growth in East Asia including China, as certainly seems to be the case, it will inevitably have served to bring down poverty. This is despite the fact that empirical work has demonstrated that in low-income countries, other things being equal, a given change in income generated in the agricultural sector or in rural-based activities tends to have a greater poverty reduction impact than the same income change in manufacturing or industry more generally. The weak direct poverty impact is due to the fact that in most poor countries the bulk of the poor is concentrated in rural areas and is affected most directly by agricultural and rural-based activity, although some of the latter could be agricultural processing or simple manufacturing. However, if manufacturing grows considerably more rapidly than agriculture (as typically happens at low income levels) the fact that a given unit change has a greater poverty impact in the latter will not be a major concern; see Box 2.5 for a comparison between China and India along these lines.

Box 2.5 Poverty reduction in China and India: tests for the impact of economic structure.

The impact of structure on poverty can be estimated in a pair of simple equations that separately make poverty a function of overall GDP per capita growth and the growth of sector incomes weighted by sector shares in GDP. Thus, where H is the poverty headcount

$$H = f(g) \tag{2.27}$$

$$\mathrm{H} = f(a_1.p,\ a_2.s,\ a_3.t) \tag{2.28}$$

where g is GDP per capita growth, p, s and t are the growth of the primary, secondary and tertiary sectors, respectively, and a_1, a_2 and a_3 are their shares in GDP (so $a_1 + a_2 + a_3 = 1.0$).

Estimating 2.27 in logarithmic form gives a poverty elasticity determined by the regression coefficient on g. Equation 2.28 allows a test for whether economic structure matters for poverty reduction, since if it does not the coefficients on p, s and t will be equal.

The results for an analysis of time series data for China and India are shown below. The secondary sector broadly corresponds to industry, the primary to agriculture and the tertiary to services.

Economic growth in general has a much bigger poverty reducing effect in China than in India, which is consistent with the data in Table 2.2 showing the relatively slow decline in poverty in India. The elasticities of the poverty headcount to a given change in growth are −2.6 and −0.99, respectively, meaning that a 10 per cent growth rate creates a 26 per cent reduction in the headcount measure of poverty in China, but only a 10 per cent reduction in India. The structure of sectoral growth appears to matter for poverty reduction in both countries, but in China it is the primary sector that matters, with the secondary and tertiary sectors having both lower and

Dependent variable H	*China (1)*	*China (2)*	*China (3)*	*India (4)*	*India (5)*
Independent variables: growth of GDP per capita	−2.60 (2.16)			−0.99 (3.38)	
Primary sector		−8.07 (3.97)	−7.85 (4.09)		−1.16 (2.96)
Secondary sector		−1.75 (1.21)			3.41 (1.84)
Tertiary sector		−3.08 (1.24)			−3.42 (2.74)
Secondary and tertiary sectors			−2.25 (2.20)		
R^2	0.21	0.43	0.42	na	0.75

Source: Chaudhuri and Ravallion (2007, Table 6.1).

Notes
na is not available from the source.
t ratios are in brackets without negative or positive signs.

insignificant coefficients. In India, the impact of the primary sector is much weaker than in China (probably due to greater inequality in land ownership) and the secondary and tertiary sectors appear to cancel each other out (as their coefficients are equal with the opposite sign).

However, this evidence does not rule out industrial or manufacturing activities playing a major role in poverty reduction. The authors point out that arithmetically if China had maintained the same overall growth but with each of the three sectors growing at the same rate (so if primary sector growth had been much higher than it actually was) the speed of poverty reduction over the 1990s would have been even higher (by more than 60 per cent annually) than was actually achieved. However, this counterfactual begs the key question of whether without the high rate of industrial growth the overall growth of the economy of over 9 per cent annually for nearly 30 years could have been achieved. Given the constraints on agricultural land in much of China and the limited demand elasticities for food this seems implausible.

Source: Chaudhuri and Ravallion (2007).

Expansion of the manufacturing sector offers low-income economies the prospects for employment creation and through it poverty reduction. For all but a few very large countries this will inevitably have to be based largely on export market sales, where competition is strong and where exclusion from global networks and the buying chains and market access they allow will be a serious constraint.

Another current worry is that with rising capital intensity in new technologies, employment growth in manufacturing may weaken. The degree to which manufacturing continues to offer an outlet for underemployed workers is now subject to debate since a phenomenon of recent years in some countries has been rapid manufacturing growth which has generated relatively few new jobs (*jobless growth*). Manufacturing employment statistics are particularly unreliable and in some instances what may be happening is that formal sector employment has grown slowly, whilst informal and less-well-recorded employment has increased more strongly. There is evidence that this is the case in India, for example, from where much of the jobless growth debate started.[16]

Table 2.3 gives estimated employment elasticities (proportionate response of sector employment to the growth of sector output) for different sectors for Asian countries. It can be seen that whilst these vary greatly across countries and between sectors, in no case does manufacturing have the highest employment elasticity and in some of the higher-income countries (Singapore, Korea and Taiwan) the elasticity is very low, at less than 0.15 (i.e. a 10 per cent output growth leads to an employment increase of less than 1.5 per cent). Where such elasticities reflect rising capital intensity and high labour productivity as part of the development of economies, they need not be a problem, since a strongly growing and competitive manufacturing sector can create a large absolute rise in employment, even if the investment per job is high. Where low elasticities are not associated with a competitive and dynamic sector there is a significant problem since low numbers of higher productivity jobs will be created. This is the concern over *premature deindustrialisation* noted earlier. The strong level of employment elasticities in services suggests that in some cases it is this sector which is attracting a significant share of migrant workers from agriculture.

Table 2.3 Employment elasticities in Asia by sector (1970–2004)

Country	*Manufacturing*	*Agriculture*	*Services*
Cambodia	1.2	1.15	1.42
China	na	na	0.75
Hong Kong	1.17	1.26	0.60
Indonesia	0.47	0.31	0.48
Malaysia	0.55	na	0.58
Pakistan	0.20	0.68	0.70
Philippines	0.81	0.50	1.05
Singapore	0.12	0.96	0.48
South Korea	0.14	na	0.68
Sri Lanka	0.28	0.76	0.68
Thailand	0.53	na	0.67
Vietnam	na	0.60	0.68
Taiwan	0.14	0.82	0.41

Source: Felipe *et al.* (2007).

Note
na is not available.

The implication is that whilst the development path to poverty reduction set out in the Lewis model, linking labour-intensive manufacturing with the removal of rural surplus labour, is in no sense inevitable, but at the early stage in a country's industrialisation it can prove to be a powerful mechanism for growth.

Conclusions

Manufacturing has a strong potential for dynamic growth through a process of technical change, linkages and learning that in theory should be greater than in other sectors. Under favourable domestic and international conditions, it holds great potential for rapid growth and historically, in all but natural-resource-rich economies, at early stages of development manufacturing has played a key role. This is not an argument for neglecting other sectors, since a stagnant agriculture can hold back manufacturing. The experience of the NIEs in recent decades shows that manufacturing holds the potential to alter very significantly the income prospects of poor economies. However, not all economies have been able to realise this potential. In a number of cases, the new manufacturing industry that has been created has been high-cost and uncompetitive, and has not created the basis for a dynamic transformation. Furthermore, how far countries can and should go in terms of shifting resources into manufacturing will vary with specific circumstances, both in terms of their domestic resource endowments and the international prospects they face. We take up the foreign trade aspect in the following chapter.

Further reading

Weiss (1990) Chapter 2 surveyed the Kaldor arguments and they have been examined empirically Dasgupta and Singh (2006) and McCombie *et al.* (2002). ADB (2007) provides a recent empirical analysis for Asian countries examining the patterns of structural change in these economies. The key role of manufacturing has been tested in a number of papers by Rodrik, including Rodrik (2006), and Hausmann *et al.* (2007).

The concept of late-comer industrialisation is set out in Amsden (2001). UNCTAD (1996), Stiglitz and Yusuf (2001) and Weiss (2005) examine the case of the first- and second-tier East Asian NIEs.

3 Trade and efficiency

There is a different way of assessing the role of industrialisation to that of the engine of growth case of Chapter 2. There is a longstanding view that international trade has been a facilitator and creator of growth in the past and currently offers poor countries a way to raise incomes and create employment. The issue this and the following chapter address is how manufacturing industry fits into this story.

Countries exchange many different goods though trade. At one extreme quite different types of product may be exchanged (*inter-industry trade*). Kenya may export coffee to Germany and import cars in return. Alternatively, only slightly differentiated products may be traded (*intra-industry trade*). China may export simple unbranded shirts to Italy and import high-fashion shirts in return. Both sets of exchanges in principle expand the market for each other's products and allow the participating countries to specialise in either broad product categories in the inter-industry case or niche markets within a given category in the case of intra-industry trade. International trade is rarely completely free in the sense of a total lack of interventions by governments or regulatory bodies. Most governments intervene in some way and nowadays the World Trade Organization (WTO) provides a set of rules governing trade. Government policies have an impact on how markets function and even under WTO rules biases can be created for or against particular countries or activities. In addition there are barriers to international trade that have nothing to do with policy interventions, but arise from the cost of moving goods between countries (*trade costs*).

The basis for the potential gains from international trade is specialisation in the production of goods which a country can produce relatively cheaply, that is specialisation along the lines of *comparative advantage*. Since the comparison is between costs of goods within one country, there must always be something in which that country has a comparative advantage, in that a good is cheap relative to everything else that the country can produce. A majority of the goods that are sold on world markets are a form of manufactured product; hence, how far countries can take advantage of the potential gains from trade will have a large impact on their manufacturing sectors.

Gains from trade

Drawing on international trade theory, many have argued that unlike the arguments in Chapter 2, it is not meaningful to distinguish between broad sectors, like manufacturing or agriculture. In this view, it is far more important to differentiate between activities that produce goods that can be bought and sold on the world market (*tradable sectors*) and those that focus exclusively on the domestic market (*non-tradable sectors*).[1] In addition, within tradables, given the vast range of possible products, there will be only a limited number in which an economy has a comparative advantage.

This reasoning is associated with *Neoclassical* or market-based views of development that stress the importance of specialising on the basis of an economy's comparative advantage. Hence, it is not manufacturing per se that is important, but within manufacturing the goods that a country can produce relatively efficiently and thus export successfully to the rest of the world. There are different explanations for comparative advantage differences between countries corresponding to different theories of trade. Cost differences can arise though differential access to technology (*Ricardian* models), different resource endowments (*Heckscher-Ohlin* models) or increasing returns to scale (*New Trade Theory* models). However, regardless of the origin of cost differences, the idea that specialisation should be where comparative costs are lowest has had a key influence on policy across most countries in recent decades. The case has both static and dynamic dimensions.

In static terms, assuming a perfectly competitive two commodity framework, with full employment and diminishing returns to scale, it can be shown that trade without restriction (*free trade*) leads the economy to a higher level of welfare than does no trade (*autarky*). With diminishing returns the maximum output of each commodity (*a* and *b*) with a given level of resources is shown as a bowed out curve QQ1 in Figure 3.1 (*the production possibility frontier*). At any point the slope of QQ1 shows the amount of one commodity sacrificed for additional production of the other (the *opportunity cost*). Thus, the opportunity cost of a unit of *a* is the loss of *b* as a result of the diversion of resources to the production of *a*. Extending beyond a simple two commodity framework a country can be said to have a comparative advantage in goods in which its opportunity cost is lower than that in its trading partners.

In Figure 3.1, without trade, efficiency in terms of maximising production and meeting consumer preferences, will be at point x where the line reflecting the relative domestic prices for *a* and *b* is at a tangent to QQ1. At this point, there will be equality between the slope of QQ1 and the slope of the price line (PP1). The slope of QQ1 gives the relative cost of production (i.e. the opportunity cost of *a* divided by the opportunity cost of *b*) so at this point of tangency, the relative cost equals the relative value of the goods as reflected in their relative prices (the domestic price of *a* divided by the domestic price of *b*). The no-trade scenario means there are barriers to trade, either policy-induced or natural barriers posed by geography and high transport costs, and these barriers will impact on domestic

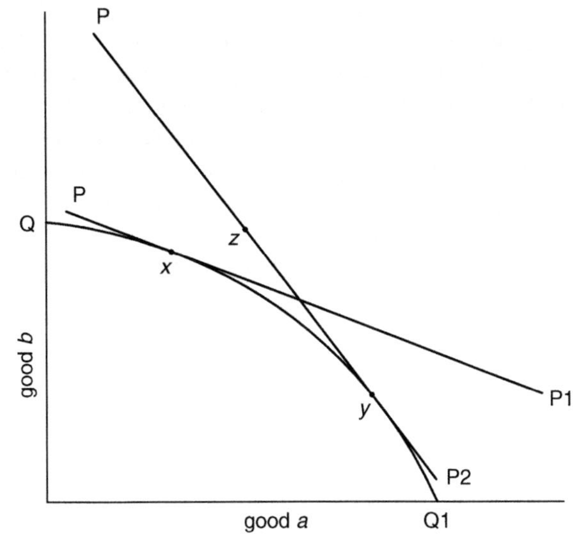

Figure 3.1 Allocative efficiency with international trade.

prices, so that relative domestic and world prices differ. This is shown by price line in Figure 3.1 of PP2 reflecting relative world prices (the world price of *a* divided by the world price of *b*). With trade, efficiency requires production at point *y* where the ratio of opportunity costs now equals the world price ratio. This will be a superior outcome to production at *x* for any set of consumer preferences since with the possibility of trade an economy can move along the world price line PP2 exporting *a* (e.g. manufactures) in return for *b* (say food). If such exports take place, it is possible to consume more of both goods (e.g. at point *z*) than in the no-trade scenario, so that the outcome is unambiguously positive.

This analysis is highly abstract and based on critical assumptions regarding flexibility (so that in any reallocation of production between *a* and *b* full employment is maintained) and on the lack of impact of a country's actions on the relative world prices it faces (*the small country* case). However, it provides the rationale for specialisation on goods for which a country has a comparative advantage, defined as a low opportunity cost. As set out here, specialisation is partial in that with trade a country increases the production of one good, whilst reducing that of the other and continuing to produce both. In this model, full specialisation does not occur due the assumption of diminishing returns to scale.[2]

A more dynamic version of the gains from trade case focuses on the link between openness to trade and economic growth. Versions of the aggregate growth model discussed in Chapter 2 are applied including a measure intended to reflect the degree of openness of trade policy with the expectation that there will be a positive relation between openness and growth. This remains an area of controversy due to the difficulty in finding an adequate proxy for the stance of trade policy. A widely used indicator – change in the share of exports plus imports in GDP – has been shown to be closely correlated with economic growth. However, trade share in GDP is an outcome (or endogenous) variable and does not reflect policy per se; for example, it may rise or fall due to commodity price fluctuations that are independent of any change in policy. Results obtained using this variable are suspect, whilst other proxies for trade policy (such as average tariff rates) also have their limitations. Hence, whilst there is widespread agreement that fast-growing countries tend to trade more with the rest of the world, establishing the direction of causation has proved more controversial.[3]

Identifying comparative advantage

It is possible to identifying comparative advantage simply by examining an economy's trade structure and identifying the goods in which it has already specialised. This *ex post* approach involves calculating the *revealed comparative advantage* (RCA) ratio. This measure of specialisation compares the share of a given product in a country's exports with the same product's share in world trade. Hence, for product i and country j the RCA is

$$\mathrm{RCA}i = (\mathrm{X}ij/\mathrm{X}jt)/(\mathrm{X}i/\mathrm{X}wt) \qquad (3.1)$$

where $\mathrm{X}ij$ is exports of i by country j,

$\mathrm{X}jt$ is total exports of country j,

$\mathrm{X}i$ is total world exports of i and

$\mathrm{X}wt$ is total world exports.

Hence, if RCA is greater than 1.0, the country is more specialised in a good than would be expected given the good's size in world trade, and the higher is RCA, the greater is this relative specialisation. Although widely used, due to the fact that it can be calculated readily, the RCA ratio is a very crude means of identifying comparative advantage, since current or past specialisation need not reflect the efficiency (i.e. the opportunity cost) involved in producing particular goods. *Ex post* specialisation, for example, may be due to historical links between countries and the trade preferences on offer or to policy support through export subsidies. The RCA ratio also says nothing about the dynamic potential of different patterns of specialisation. Recent work has extended this simple RCA ratio by looking at dynamic potential of products and the ease or difficulty of moving between different patterns of specialisation. It builds on the simple RCA measure by incorporating a measure of the value of a product based on the weighted average income level of its exporters on the world market (see Box 2. 2). The idea is that goods produced by high-income countries have intrinsically higher worth (due to their technology content and market prospects) than goods produced by poor countries. Goods that have similar characteristics to these high-income products are thus deemed to have greater potential for structural transformation and thus should be the targets for industrial policy. If individual products can be given a unique numerical score representing their contribution to structural transformation, then totalling this score across all products in a sub-sector or branch will give a numerical measure per branch that can then be compared with stated government priorities. Thus, for example, if clothing is a designated priority but the total score for all clothing products is low relative to the manufacturing or national sub-sector average this information casts doubt on the reliability of a priority on clothing, at least in terms of its contribution to structural change. Box 3.1 illustrates the approach.

Box 3.1 Mapping individual products

As part of their contribution to the analysis of industrial policy, Hausmann and Klinger (2006a, 2006b) put forward a highly novel approach to product scoring working with over 1,000 products. The value of a product is defined by the index discussed in Box 2.1 and based on the weighted average income per capita of the exporters of the product on the world market with weights determined by their revealed comparative advantage (RCA) in that product. Goods with high values are thus those in which rich countries are specialised and those with low values are those in which poor countries are specialised. Thus, for example, in the simplest case of a good exported by only two countries, India and the United States with the following data

India: income per capita US$1,000 and RCA 1.2
United States: income per capita US$40,000 and RCA 0.8

the *value* placed on the good (which the authors term PRODY) will be

US$1,000*0.6 + US$40,000*0.4 = US$16,600

where the India weight is 1.2/2.0= 0.6 and the US weight is 0.8/2.0 = 0.4.

There is evidence that countries that move into high value (i.e. rich country type) goods do not do so randomly, but because these products are already close to the products they already export in terms of the capabilities and skills required. Hence, the concept of distance between products becomes important, since it will be easier to produce something if the skill set needed is close to that required for a good that is already produced. Thus, the second measure derived is one of distance between products, what the authors' term *proximity*.

Proximity is calculated for pairs of individual products (*i* and *j*) based on the probability that countries in the world have a specialisation (RCA above unity) in both. Goods, thus, are similar where there is a high probability that if a country is specialised in *i* it will also be specialised in *j*. Proximity *d* between *i* and *j* is estimated as the smaller of the two probabilities that if a country has a specialisation in *i* it also has specialisation in *j* and vice versa. Where goods are very similar this probability and therefore *d* will be high. Data on PRODY and *d* can be estimated at the individual product level.

In addition to a measure of value and of distance, a third product dimension is introduced. This is a measure of potential structural transformation, what the authors' term *strategic value*. This refers to the potential value that can be created by goods in which a country does not yet have a specialisation. Products have a high strategic value if they are similar to goods with a high value (as given by PRODY), so that it is relatively easier to move from these goods to high-value products than from goods for which distance (as measured by *d*) is greater. Estimation of strategic value for an individual product requires calculating the total strategic value for the export bundle of a country (what the authors' term *open forest*) and then estimating the additional contribution to this total of achieving a RCA of above unity for any individual product in which the economy is not yet specialised. Total strategic value (TSV) for a country is calculated as the distance-weighted value of products that it could potentially produce, but for which it does not have a current comparative advantage. Simplifying the original formulation for country *c*

$$\text{TSV}c = \Sigma_k[(d_j/\Sigma_k d)*\text{PRODY}_j] \qquad (3.2)$$

where there are *k* products in total and a country has a specialisation in *i* goods but not in *j* goods (where $k = i + j$). TSV is therefore a weighted average of value (PRODY) for all *j*. Countries for which TSV is high are seen as at an advantage compared with those where it is low, since it is hypothesised that closeness (a high *d*) makes it easier to obtain a comparative advantage and a high TSV means that the goods in which the country might be competitive in future have a high value.

The three measures of PRODY, proximity and strategic value provide a product level score which is meant to reflect their potential for structural transformation. Their units are standardised in relation to their mean and standard deviation, so that the three measures can be combined into an overall product index. This can be done using different weighting systems of which the simplest is to give each dimension equal weight. If product scores are aggregated by sub-sector categories this gives a ranking that can inform decisions on sectoral priorities.

This highly disaggregate approach is novel, but it is complex since changes to the weights used may affect rankings. Furthermore, structural transformation may not be the only objective of industrial policy. The authors apply this approach in the context of South Africa and note that employment creation is also a key objective. To incorporate this added dimension, they use the share of unskilled labour in value added as an indicator and standardise this in the same way as the other indicators. They focus on products with a RCA below unity and combine all four indicators PRODY, proximity, strategic value and unskilled labour share. They aggregate product scores by the sub-sectoral priority categories of the industrial plan to see how the different sub-sectors compare. The score when the aggregation uses equal weights for each dimension is

Sub-sector	*Average score*
Machinery	0.24
Agriculture	0.19
Basic chemicals	0.11
Plastics	0.02
Coke and refined products	0.02
Metal fabrication	–0.04
Textiles	–0.07
Clothing	–0.20
Aerospace	–0.29

Source: Hausmann and Klinger (2006b, Table 2A).

As a means of highlighting individual products even focusing on over 1,000 products may be too aggregate. However, the sub-sector groupings reveal that two priority sectors – clothing and aerospace – score consistently poorly and appear as outliers. Only by giving a very high weight to employment does the clothing sector score well and aerospace never does so. Hence, the approach provides a check on how meaningful *a priori* selections of priority activities in industrial strategies are.

Measuring domestic resource costs

A considerably more rigorous approach as compared with the simple RCA involves the calculation of an efficiency measure the *Domestic Resource Cost* (DRC) ratio. This estimates the domestic resources required to generate a unit of foreign currency (*foreign exchange*) through various different activities. An economy has a comparative advantage in the goods for which the DRC ratio is below the economic value of foreign exchange (often termed *the equilibrium exchange rate*).

Formally the DRC ratio for good *j* can be expressed as

$$\text{DRC}j = (\Sigma anj.\text{P}n + \Sigma alj.\text{P}l)/\ (\text{P}j - atj.\text{P}t) \tag{3.3}$$

where *n* refers to non-traded inputs used to produce *j*, *l* to labour inputs and *t* to traded inputs; *anj* is the physical inputs of non-traded input *n* per unit of *j*, *alj* is the physical inputs of labour *l* per unit of *j* and *atj* is the physical inputs of traded input *t* per unit of *j*; Σ refers to the summation for all *n*, *l* and *t*; P*n* and P*l* are the opportunity cost values of *n* and *l*, and P*j* and P*t* are the world price values of output *j* and traded input *t*.

Comparative advantage in *j* requires

$$\text{DRC}j < \text{EER}$$

where EER is the equilibrium exchange rate.

A simple way to express the DRC ratio is convert the both sides of the ratio into a common currency. When this is done efficiency requires that DRC/EER < 1.

The denominator of Equation 3.3 gives the net foreign exchange earning from product *j* allowing for the necessary traded inputs into *j* that use foreign exchange. The numerator of Equation 3.3 gives the opportunity cost of the domestic resources (non-traded inputs and labour) that go into the production of *j*. If the numerator is in domestic currency and the denominator in foreign exchange then Equation 3.3 becomes equivalent to an exchange rate for product *j*, in terms of the domestic resources required to create a net foreign exchange effect. Hence, for example, if its costs 12 Pesos in domestic resources to earn or save US$1 of foreign currency (or its equivalent in other currency) and the long-run real value of a US dollar is estimated at 15 Pesos, then the cost of generating the foreign currency is below its long-run value and a country can be said to have comparative advantage in the good concerned. Hence, within manufacturing, we have a means of distinguishing between activities (e.g. cotton shirts) in which an economy has a comparative advantage and those where it does not (e.g. automobiles).

The DRC ratio can be calculated at different levels. It may be done ex ante for planning purposes with revenues and costs projected for the life of a project. In this case, strictly both sides of Equation 3.3 should be discounted present values. Alternatively, it can be calculated ex post for a single year. Where this is done an annual capital charge at the specified discount rate is required to capture the opportunity cost of the capital committed to the activity. Strictly, due to the existence of scale and terms of trade effects and it may be misleading to rank activities by the size of the DRC ratio, with those with the lowest DRC taken as the most competitive. However, as a broad generalisation, such ranking is unlikely to be very inaccurate and was the way in which the indicator was often used in practice.

The DRC ratio can be used to answer basic questions such as what part of the production process can be carried out relatively efficiently in a particular country. The analysis of automobile production is a good illustration. Many countries established assembly activities whereby imported parts and components would be assembled into a car or truck behind tariff protection. The activity was commercially profitable only because a high tariff on imported cars or trucks raised their price to often more than double what it would cost to import the vehicle itself. However, once the cost of importing the parts and components was allowed for, the net foreign exchange saved was low relative to the cost of assembly creating a high DRC ratio, well above any realistic estimate of the value of foreign exchange. However, this did not mean that no automobile activity was efficient since some local production of parts might still have a relatively low DRC. In Mexico, in the early 1980s, for example, approximate estimates based on input–output data suggested that on average final production of automobiles was highly inefficient (with a DRC of around 2) whilst some body parts and components could be produced efficiently (a DRC of below 1).[4] Since that time the automobile sector in Mexico has undergone considerable restructuring with the closure of a number of plants and the concentration of the sector around the major international firms. After the high-cost production of the early 1980s, large exports emerged principally to the United States as part of the North American Free Trade Agreement. Significantly, the main firms now active in the sector in Mexico are Japanese (Honda and Toyota) and European (Volkswagen and Mercedes) with the US producers Ford and General Motors, which once dominated the sector having lost a considerable share of the market.

Changing comparative advantage

A key feature of comparative advantage is that for most economies it will change over time. Countries that have a specialisation in one line of activity need not continue specialising in that line indefinitely. Natural resource exporters may find such resources (such as oil reserves) depleted, with additional supplies only available at steeply increasing marginal cost. Exporters specialising in low-cost manufactures (like clothing and toys) may find that rising wages make them uncompetitive. At the higher technology end of the spectrum technological breakthroughs in one country may undermine the competitive position of producers in another. These illustrations broadly correspond to alternative explanations as to why trade takes place. Probably the clearest example of this process at work is the dramatic shift in the composition of Korean exports during its high-growth phase 1960–90. At the start of this period Korea's largest export item was iron ore (about 13 per cent of exports), by 1980 the largest item was textiles and garments (around 30 per cent of the total) and by the end of the period it was electronics (also around 30 per cent).[5]

This shift in specialisation across countries has been rationalised in the theory of *the stages of comparative advantage*. Based on a resource endowment explanation of trade, this argues that, at low income levels, countries will specialise in either primary and natural resource products or where they are lacking in such resources in simple low-cost manufactures utilising their low-wage labour supply. As economies develop, the primary exporters will diversify into low-wage manufacturing in response to rising internal demand and perhaps also rising

Table 3.1 Stages of comparative advantage

Stage	*Factor endowments*	*Exports*
One	Natural resources	Primary products
	Labour surplus	Labour-intensive manufactures
Two	Rising wages and higher savings	Resource-based and capital-intensive manufactures
Three	Skilled and educated labour	Human capital-intensive manufactures

costs in the primary sector due to the physical limits on land and resource stocks. Furthermore, as wages rise in response to economic growth, low-wage manufacturers will gradually shift into more capital-intensive activities in response to the change in relative factor prices. At a final stage, when greater technological mastery is attained due to an improvement in the human resource base of an economy specialisation will shift towards more human capital-intensive, higher-technology products. In summary, resource endowments and relative factor costs will change as economies evolve and even in the absence of direct government intervention this will create the incentives for resources to flow into different lines of specialisation (see Table 3.1).

This sequence is a simplification of real world trends, but broadly speaking it is a helpful starting point for considering the evolution of trade. Other explanations of trade flows, such as differential access to technology (e.g. through FDI) or increasing returns to scale that allow producers that get into a line of production early on to build up expertise and specialisation (*first-mover advantage*) can also be added to complement the shifting resource endowment explanation. The stages approach also broadly matches the *flying geese* theory popular in Japan to explain the migration of industries from Japan to other parts of East Asia (initially principally to Thailand, Malaysia and Indonesia and more recently to China and Vietnam) after 1980, in response to rising wage costs in Japan. As wages in turn rose in the second-tier NIEs, China and then Vietnam became relatively more important destinations for Japanese FDI. Hence, industries migrated within the region like flying geese. US investment in Mexico and the smaller countries of Central America can be explained in the same manner. This FDI generated trade between the origin country (e.g. Japan) and the host (e.g. Thailand) as goods made with the foreign investment were exported back to the origin country (and also to third countries).

Can policy change comparative advantage?

Whilst comparative advantage should be seen in dynamic terms, there is considerable disagreement as to whether governments have a role in assisting or steering this process. The engine of growth argument discussed in Chapter 2 implies that special support for manufacturing will boost economic growth, although in principle it is neutral as to how this support should be offered and whether it should be for import substitute or export production. Both import replacement and exporting can occur though decisions based on market incentives (a so-called natural process) or they can be stimulated by intervention (e.g. through import tariffs and quota restrictions on imports or through export subsidies). In the past, many governments attempted to force the pace of industrialisation through such measures, particularly as part of import substitution strategies. A large empirical literature in the 1970s and 1980s provided evidence that this was often a very high cost strategy, creating serious economic inefficiency.

Part of the evidence used the DRC indicator discussed earlier to identify the costs involved. Many protected activities saved relatively little foreign exchange due to the need to import raw materials and capital equipment (so the denominator of Equation 3.3 was small) whilst at the same time using large amounts of domestic resources (so the numerator was high). Table 3.2 summarises a number of studies from this period showing the relatively small proportion of manufacturing branches deemed efficient (i.e. where the economy concerned was found to have a comparative advantage at the estimated equilibrium exchange rate applied). In some extreme cases, a negative DRC was found, implying that the denominator of Equation 3.3 was negative so that the activity used more foreign exchange in imported items than it actually saved. This is an example of gross inefficiency and is only possible where producers are highly protected, so they can sell their output at prices well above world levels. Although less evidence is available,

Table 3.2 Domestic resource costs (DRC) under import substitution: selected countries

Country	*Year*	*Range DRCs*[a]	*Number of branches studied*	*Number of branches with negative DRC*[b]	*Number of efficient branches*[c]
India	1963–65	Rs 2.7/US$– Rs 1049/US$	75	6	na[b]
	1968–69	Rs 5.9/US$– Rs 259/US$	75	4	17
Chile	1961	0.28–12.6%	21	0	6
Turkey	1965–69	TL 10.2/US$– TL 93.9/US$[e]	16	na[d]	10
	1981	0.5–10.2	14	1	4
Ghana	1967–68	0.19–20.4	39	8	9
Tanzania	Early 1970s	TSh 2.9/US$– TSh 12.2/US$[e]	24	0	17

Source: Compiled from Weiss (2002, Table 3.3), which gives details of original sources.

Notes

a DRCs are given as exchange rates or ratios; where the latter are used they are the ratio of domestic resources required per dollar saved where the dollar is converted at the equilibrium exchange rate.

b Negative DRC implies loss of foreign exchange.

c Efficient activity is where the DRC is below the equilibrium exchange rate or where the ratio is below 1.0.

d na is not identifiable from the original source.

e TL is Turkish Lira and TSh is Tanzanian Shillings.

there were also cases in which exporters operated inefficiently in the sense of DRC ratios above the equilibrium exchange rate, since export subsidies allowed high costs of production to be covered.

Interventions of this type also had profound implications for the incentive structure both within manufacturing and between manufacturing and other sectors. Highly protected activities saw a large rise in their relative profitability thus creating a strong incentive for resources to shift into those sectors. Insofar as protection was linked with high-cost production, this distorted resource allocation and moved it in a direction that was contrary to short-term comparative advantage. The formal means of quantifying this incentive effect involved the calculation of the effective rate of protection (ERP) indicator for different sectors and activities within these; the higher the ERP the greater the incentive relative to a non-intervention scenario.

Effective rate of protection

A widely used technical measure of the incentive impact of policy intervention is the effective rate of protection (ERP). This compares value added in a line of production at actual domestic prices – that is including the effects of trade policy interventions like import tariffs, import quotas and export subsidies – with what value added is estimated to be in the hypothetical situation that there are no barriers to trade and all internationally traded goods are sold at world prices. Hence, in its simplest form for activity *j* this is

$$\text{ERP}j = (\text{VADP}j - \text{VAWP}j)/\text{VAWP}j\ \% \tag{3.4}$$

or rearranging

$$\text{ERP}j = [(\text{VADP}j/\text{VAWP}j) - 1]\ \%$$

where VA is value added and DP and WP refer to domestic and world prices, respectively.

Thus, an ERP of 20 per cent means that due to protection, value added is raised by 20 per cent compared with what it would be in the free trade or non-intervention case.

Since value added is the difference between output value and the value of the sum of all purchased inputs, ERP will be determined by the extent to which protection affects the relative prices of output (in this case *j*) and purchased inputs (all *i*). All trade policy interventions will cause a divergence between domestic and world prices, with import tariffs and quotas and export subsidies raising domestic prices above world levels, and with input subsidies lowering them. If we use t to depict the proportionate price change created by trade intervention, Equation 3.4 can be re-written to show the relative effect on output and input prices. Now we have

$$\text{ERP}j = (tj - \Sigma aij.ti)/(1 - \Sigma aij) \tag{3.5}$$

where *ti* and *tj* are the proportionate price effects for output *i* and input *j* and *aij* is the value of input *i* per unit of output *j* at world prices; summation is for all inputs. Equation 3.5 makes it clear that ERP will be higher the greater is the price effect on output relative to the price effect on inputs and the smaller is the share of value added in output. Hence, it is possible for activities that sell in highly protected domestic markets, but which buy inputs that are subject to low tariffs and no quotas, and have a low value added, to show very high ERP. Conversely, for activities (most notably exports) which sell in competitive world markets without any subsidy, but which face tariffs or quotas restricting their purchase of imported inputs, ERP will be negative, implying that value added is reduced as a result of the protective system.

This discussion has glossed over some of the theoretical complications, particularly related to the treatment of non-traded goods which do not enter into international trade. In the simplest version of Equations 3.4 and 3.5, they are included as part of value added. It is possible therefore for the ERP indicator and the DRC measure discussed before to be very similar. The key issue here is what is included in value added and what domestic prices are used to value non-traded inputs and labour. If actual domestic prices (as opposed to estimates of opportunity cost for labour and the non-traded inputs involved) are used in the DRC ratio then the DRC can be thought of as equivalent to VADP/VAWP and from Equation 3.5

$$\text{DRC} = \text{VADP}/\text{VAWP} = \text{ERP} + 1 \tag{3.6}$$

Although, as we discuss further in the following section, theoretically there is no reason why all activities should have the same ERP, in practice it is argued that wide variations in the impact of protection will create serious resource misallocation effects. For example, a government may wish to discourage the import of luxury saloon cars and impose a very high import tariff (of say 200 per cent), whilst other imported goods enter at an average rate of about 20 per cent. This restriction on such cars will push up their price in the domestic market, and because it has become so expensive to import these cars it will become highly profitable to assembly them locally, provided parts and components can be imported at the average rate of 20 per cent. The value added component in such assembly will be low (say 20 per cent), and assuming domestic prices are raised by the full extent of import tariffs then putting these figures into Equation 3.5 gives an ERP of

$$\text{ERP} = (2 - 0.8*0.2)/0.2 = 9.2$$

or 920 per cent.

In other words, value added is increased by more than nine times relative to the zero tariff case.

Similarly, an export activity will typically have negative protection provided it faces tariff or quota restrictions on the inputs it uses and receives no export subsidy.

For example, such an exporter facing the 20 per cent tax on its imported inputs and with a value added content of 60 per cent will have a negative ERP. Here, from Equation 3.5 we have

$$\text{ERP} = (0 - 0.4*0.2)/0.6 = -0.133$$

or −13.3 per cent.

In other words, value added is decreased by about 13 per cent relative to the zero tariff case.

When such calculations were carried out for economies pursuing import substitution strategies, they generally produced results showing a wide range of ERP values for different sectors and different activities within sectors, normally with little economic rationale and in some cases creating incentives that were in direct contradiction to stated government priorities. For example, in the 1960s and 1970s in several countries domestic production of capital goods was seen as a key element in import substitution since without domestic capital goods investment could be held back by a scarcity of foreign exchange. However, often capital goods production had much lower effective protection that did the production of consumer goods which were treated as lower priority

As an illustration, in Mexico in the early 1980s, the industrial plan of the Ministry of Industry set as a key priority the domestic production of the capital goods of engineering and equipment. This was on the grounds that the latter were an essential component of investment and if the investment rate was to be raised to generate faster growth, demand for these goods in turn would increase. If domestic capacity were not available, the goods would have to be imported increasing expenditure on imports and putting a strain on the balance of payments. Expansion of their local production was thus seen as a means of reducing what was perceived as a balance of payment constraint on growth. However, this objective was in contradiction to the incentives created by the system of tariff protection. Import tariffs at that time were high for imported consumer goods (such as cars, electrical products and clothing) but low for equipment. High tariffs on consumer goods raised their price and would either reduce consumer demand or shift it to locally made goods. However, this was judged preferable to having high tariffs on imported equipment since this would raise their price and reduce investment. Lower investment was perceived as much more of a problem than lower consumption because of the subsequent impact on growth. Whilst understandable, this reasoning overlooks the incentive effect of tariffs, since the tariff structure created much higher effective protection (taken in higher profits and wages) in the production of the highly protected consumer goods sectors and much lower effective protection in capital goods and equipment. The bias in the protective structure was only addressed in later years as the country moved to a much less differentiated system of import tariffs.[6]

This incentive effect of protection can also be viewed the other way around from the perspective of exporters. It has been common complaint from developing country exporters that they faced higher tariffs in the markets of richer countries if they wished to export processed agricultural products, like coffee or cocoa, than if they wished to export them in an unprocessed form. This meant relatively high effective protection for developed country processing firms at the expense of poor exporting countries wishing to raise the value-added content of their exports.

Different rates of protection

A common use of the ERP indicator is to compare across sectors, within sectors and between domestic and export sales. In general, in most economies pursuing import substitution, protection for manufacturing was much higher than for agriculture, which was often negative. Negative protection for agriculture arose in some cases, because it was an unsubsidised export activity with farmers facing import tariffs and restrictions on imported inputs like fertiliser and in other cases even if the latter restrictions were not imposed, farmers received a price for their produce from Marketing Boards that was below the equivalent world price (after deductions for transport and marketing). In other cases, where agricultural produce was for domestic sale, output prices may have been controlled below world levels in an effort to subsidise urban consumers. Table 3.3 summarises a set of

Table 3.3 Effective protection manufacturing and agriculture: selected economies

Country	*Manufacturing*		*Agriculture*	
	Year	*%*	*Year*	*%*
Kenya	1967	92	1974–75	–19
Tanzania	1966	116	1979	–45
Ghana	1972	105	1979	–90
Ivory Coast	1970–72	62	1970–72	–28
Senegal	1972	70	ns	–32
Korea	1978	32	1978	57
Malaysia	1971	38	1973	30
Philippines	1978	44	1974	18
Thailand	1978	70	1973–74	–7
Taiwan	1969	14	1969	–4
Pakistan	1970–71	181	1975–76	–30
Sri Lanka	1979	38	1979–80	–10
Egypt	1966–67	42	1976	11
Argentina	1977	38	1969	–13
Bolivia	1980	24	1980	14
Chile	1967	217	1967	–5
Colombia	1980	37	1979	29
Mexico	1979	11	1979	–2
Peru	1980	52	1980	46

Source: Weiss (2002, Table 3.1); most estimates were compiled originally by Agarwala (1983).

ERP estimates for manufacturing and agriculture across a range of countries for the 1960s and 1970s at the height of the import substitution period. It can be seen that in many countries at this time, particularly in Africa, agriculture was penalised severely with overall negative ERPs. In only one case, Korea, did manufacturing have lower ERP than agriculture and even in cases where agricultural ERP was positive overall (as in the Philippines and Malaysia, for example) it was still below that of manufacturing. Today under the WTO rules, this situation has been reversed with most countries protecting farmers living standards by imposing higher protective barriers to agricultural trade than for manufacturing (see Table 3.5).

Furthermore, within manufacturing, there were also wide variations in protection granted to different activities. As an illustration, Table 3.4 reports data on one country in sub-Saharan Africa, Malawi, showing a wide range from the strongly negative protection for tea exporters to the highly protected textile, leather and beverage producers. Such wide variations were not uncommon in cases where tariff rates were high and widely dispersed and value-added content was relatively low.

Until relatively recently, a common pattern of import tariff was for tariffs to escalate, being low or zero on raw materials and capital goods, but much higher on consumer goods. As stated earlier, this led to high ERP for consumer products (as ti was low relative to tj). Most countries have moved to a small number of tariff rates and a relatively low overall average. Theoretically to avoid the creation of uneven incentives and to create 'a level playing field' requires a policy of uniform tariffs; in other words the imposition of single rate of import tariff. Only under this system will ERP (as measured by equation 3.5) be the same for all activities, since if $ti = tj$ from Equation 3.5 the ERP will be ti %. In this instance, the actual tariff rate on output (or *nominal rate of protection*) equals the effective rate. Even in this case theoretically getting an exactly equal ERP for all activities will be impossible due to the fact that there will be a different

Table 3.4 Effective protection within manufacturing: Malawi 1991

Sub-sector	%
Food products	–1.4
Tea manufactures	–30.5
Beverages	109.6
Tobacco products	7.4
Textiles	101.0
Leather/footwear	125.3
Wood/paper	52.2
Chemical products	71.1
Plastic products	28.6
Metal products	19.1
All manufacturing	48.9

Source: Mulaga and Weiss (1996).

non-traded content in the value added of each activity and the price effect of protection on non-traded goods will vary with their traded good content. However, in practice, setting a uniform tariff goes as far as is practicable in this equalisation of incentives.

The policy implication drawn from this analysis is that trade policy should aim to equalise incentives between sectors and activities, lower overall barriers to trade and remove any bias against exporting. This move towards equalisation of incentives, whilst wholly in line with the trade theory discussed here, contradicts the policy implications of the engine of growth argument examined in Chapter 2, which suggests that there is a case for special support for manufacturing. We return to this contradiction next.

WTO rules

Most countries have undertaken a version of trade reform either under the auspices of the General Agreement on Tariffs and Trade or more recently as members of the World Trade Organisation (WTO). In addition, bilateral and regional trade agreements that remove all barriers to trade between members have also become common. The general aim is to lower trade barriers, with WTO membership offering new members the attraction of the same access to markets as that enjoyed by all existing members (the *Most Favoured Nation* tariff). Thus, in most countries, import tariffs have both been lowered and been made more uniform and import quotas have been prohibited unless under emergency circumstances.

Countries joining the WTO must negotiate with their trading partners and agree to remove quota barriers to imports and set maximum rates for their import tariffs (*bound tariffs*). Differential rates of import tariff are allowed with relatively higher rates (*tariff peaks*) allowed for 'sensitive' items where domestic producers feel threatened by import competition. In principle, all measures that distort foreign trade, such as export subsidies, dumping (defined as the sale of goods for export at a price below either the cost of production or the price in the domestic market), and non-tariff measures that discriminate against imports, are banned. However, countries can impose temporary restrictions on imports in the face of strong growth that threatens to disrupt the domestic market (an *import surge*) or due to short-run balance of payments difficulties. There are clearly defined rules as to how long these temporary measures should remain in force and how restrictive they can be and in practice there is flexibility and 'temporary' can last as long as eight years.

As noted in the foregoing section, subsidies that distort trade either by promoting exports or import substitutes, are ruled out, with some temporary exemptions for least developed economies (LDCs), since WTO rules recognise the special position of such economies and allow a phased introduction of a number of measures for newly joining LDCs. However, subsidies are allowable for certain categories of expenditure – R and D, regional development and environmental protection – provided they do not discriminate in favour of domestic activity. The provision of differential support for R and D as between firms is 'actionable' in that it can be challenged and prohibited if damage to trading partners can be proved. However, even where WTO rules on subsidies are flaunted by an individual country (so their activity is formally actionable) action under WTO rules is only taken if there is proof of serious injury to trading partners. Where the country concerned is a small player in world trade for the commodity concerned, this will be unlikely. Export performance, which has been used in the past as an indicator of how far individual firms or sectors are meeting national development objectives and hence as a criterion for the allocation of public funding, can no longer be used in this way if a country is a WTO member.

Two potentially important aspects of the WTO rules are that countries must agree to restrictions on industrial policy measures that may distort trade (the *Trade Related Industry Measures* or TRIMs) and to the protection of intellectual property in the form of patents and blueprints (the *Trade Related Intellectual Property* agreement or TRIPs). The former prohibits the use of industrial policy measures that impact on trade; for example, the requirements that foreign investors:

- Export a certain proportion of their output (*export targeting*).
- Export a value sufficient to cover their import needs (*import balancing*).
- Source a certain proportion of their inputs from domestic producers rather than imports (*local content targeting*).

These measures were used in the past by governments in their dealings with foreign investors, particularly in the automobile sector.[7] The TRIPs agreement is intended to prohibit copying of innovations and to impose patent protection equivalent to that operating in the United States.

Most newly joined members negotiate maximum bound tariff rates that are above their actual rates to allow some freedom of manoeuvre. They also choose to keep rates that are significantly higher than average for certain sensitive items, whilst at the same time lowering the number of possible tariff rates. For example, when Cambodia joined the WTO in 2003 the number of rates (or tariff bands) was reduced from 12 to 4, in the range of zero to 35 per cent. For sensitive goods, the highest maximum rate agreed was 50 per cent. The average bound rate was set at 20 per cent, whilst the average actual rate in 2003 was 16.5 per cent. As an LDC, Cambodia could phase in its WTO commitments. For a ten-year period, it retained the right to offer tariff-free access for imports used in exports (but not in domestic sales), although this was a trade-distorting measure. However, although allowable, it declined to exercise its right temporarily to apply agricultural export subsidies, on the grounds that these were unaffordable for the government. It was also given an extension of four years before implementing the legislation on patent protection (TRIPs). The industrial policy agreement TRIMs was judged to be irrelevant as Cambodia had no such industrial policy measures for foreign investors and hence had no plans for targets for exports or minimum local content.[8]

Table 3.5 summarises the average of bound (i.e. maximum) tariffs and the average of applied (i.e. actual) tariffs for a number of middle- and lower-income countries.

Table 3.5 WTO Average tariffs: bound and applied (%)

	Total	*Agriculture*	*Non-Agriculture*
India			
Average Bound[a]	49.2	114.2	34.9
Average Applied (2005)[b]	19.2	37.6	16.4
Trade-weighted Applied (2004)	14.7	60.6	12.3
Brazil			
Average Bound	31.4	35.5	30.8
Average Applied (2006)	12.3	10.2	12.6
Trade-weighted Applied (2004)	8.2	10.3	8.1
Mexico			
Average Bound	36.1	43.7	34.9
Average Applied (2006)	14.0	18.2	13.3
Trade-weighted Applied (2005)	11.9	21.3	11.2
China			
Average Bound	10.0	15.8	9.1
Average Applied (2006)	9.9	15.7	9.0
Trade-weighted Applied (2005)	4.7	15.4	4.2
Mozambique			
Average Bound	97.4	100.0	6.6
Average Applied (2006)	12.1	16.4	11.4
Trade-weighted Applied (2005)	9.1	9.5	9.0
Tanzania			
Average Bound	120.0	120.0	120.0
Average Applied (2006)	12.7	19.0	11.7
Trade-weighted Applied (2005)	9.7	23.6	8.3

Source: WTO website www.wto.org.

Notes
a Simple average of final bound tariffs.
b Simple average of most favoured nation (MFN) tariffs.

It is clear that most countries are much less protectionist than the agreed bound rates suggest. This is particularly the case for the lower-income economies from Africa. It is also clear that Agriculture, not Industry, is now the most protected sector (particularly for India). Finally, the data reveal a discrepancy between protection levels in China and in the other three NIEs – Brazil, India and Mexico – with China's trade-weighted average tariff less than half that in the others, which can be interpreted as an indication of China's commitment to the global trading system.

Export policy

There will be a bias against exports whenever the ERP for domestic sales is above the ERP for exports, and one formal definition of an *export promotion policy* is one in which these two ERPs are equal. However, this will only be the case either:

- Where there is total free trade, so all *ti* and *tj* in Equation 3.5 are zero for all outputs and inputs.
- Alternatively, where protection is employed and impact of import tariffs for domestic sales is exactly offset by export subsidies that raise the value of export sales.

During periods of the import substitution, a common accusation was that trade policy operated with a strong anti-export bias due to the much greater profitability of selling in the protected domestic market. In many countries, in reaction against import substitution, exports were sometimes given special treatment, on the grounds that exporting confers special benefits not associated with domestic sales. Principally these special benefits are taken to include:

- Access to a much larger market than that available domestically (hence allowing economies of scale to be achieved).
- The exposure of domestic firms to international competition (hence encouraging greater efficiency and cost reductions).
- Access to best practice international technology (where domestic firms establish links with international firms in global supply chains).

Special measures to support exports included various forms of export subsidy such as lower profits tax rates for profits from export sales or preferential access to low-cost credit for export production. These subsidies have the equivalent effect of raising *tj* for exporters in Equation 3.5 and thus raise ERP for export sales. Export subsidies are contrary to WTO rules and although they continue to be practiced in various guises (particularly in relation to agriculture) they are prohibited for all but the poorest countries.

A subtler and less obvious form of export subsidy arises where an economy manages its exchange rate at a deliberately undervalued level to encourage exports. Formally, an undervalued rate can be thought of as an actual rate that is below the long-run equilibrium rate (where the latter is in today's prices and allows for realistic levels of long-run capital movements in and out of an economy). If the long-run rate is Pesos 8/US$ and the current actual rate is Pesos 10/US$ this implies that for every dollar earned exports are receiving 25 per cent more in Pesos than is warranted by the underlying conditions (the *fundamentals*) of the economy. As exporters are the only group that earn foreign exchange directly through their production, they will be the key beneficiaries of this policy. These various forms of export support have a clear relevance to contemporary difficulties in the WTO with developed country producers (the European Union and the United States) continuing to subsidise their agricultural exports and China still accused of deliberately holding down the value of its currency to boost its exports (despite some upward adjustment in recent times).

In most countries in recent years export policy under WTO rules has aimed reducing the bias against exporting by lowering protection on domestic sales whilst removing the negative ERP that arises whenever import tariffs (or higher prices due to quota restrictions) raise the cost of imported or locally produced traded inputs; from Equation 3.5, this arises when $tj = 0$, whilst ti is positive. Removal of these import tariffs gives exporters access to inputs at world prices, normally seen as key pre-condition for competitive export production. Different mechanisms can be used to achieve this. First, import tariffs on such inputs may be abolished for all importers not just exporters. Second, and alternatively, this abolition may be only for exporters though a refund or drawback scheme; here the tariffs are paid but are claimed back once export sale has taken place. Third, exporters may face a different customs regime to other producers, for example, due to their location in an *export processing zone*, specialising in sales to the export market and where the normal tax regime of the country does not apply.

The concept of special zone relates to any arrangement that gives special encouragement to firms to locate in a specific location. Export processing zones (EPZs) are a particular form of such zones that offer investors a free trade environment in which they can produce goods for the export market using imported inputs that they can purchase free of the prevailing national rates of import tariff. Special zones may also offer a package of other incentives such as profits tax holidays, free or subsidised factory space and subsidised access to utilities like power and water.

EPZs were initially seen as a means of gradually introducing trade reform into unreformed economies, creating 'islands of free trade'. This explains the large numbers of such zones which have proliferated since the 1970s. Estimates from the International Labour Organisation suggest that 130 countries operate these zones and that they employ as many as 66 million workers worldwide (two-thirds of these in China).[9] China has used special zones (essentially EPZs) very effectively and whilst initially focused on the coastal areas they have spread all around the country.

EPZs offer several potential benefits for countries:

- Employment for the workers who obtain jobs in the zones.
- Learning effects if local firms located in the zones learn through spillovers from the activities of foreign firms located there.
- Tax payments from foreign firms in the zones (although these are reduced by tax holidays).

However, they also create costs in terms of infrastructure investment in the zones, and where services and utilities are provided at a subsidised price that does not cover the costs involved. Whilst some zones have seen a strong interest amongst from firms and a dramatic expansion in employment, others have seen factory space and infrastructure facilities underutilised, so that the record of such zones is very mixed.[10]

Performance after trade reform

Trade reform, in terms of lowering or removing barriers to trade, is expected to stimulate a shift of resources in line with an economy's comparative advantage and hence create an improvement in economic performance. Figure 3.2 gives the standard illustration of this utilising the framework employed in Figure 3.1. In static terms, trade reform is deemed to have two effects that both stimulate improvements in productivity.

Now unlike Figure 3.1 it is assumed that in the absence of trade there is inefficiency so that the economy is operating at point *u* well within the production frontier. Production at *u* means that more of both commodities can be obtained from the available resources if these are used more productively. Hence, in the no-trade protected scenario, two types of inefficiencies will be present. The first refers to the gap between points *u* and *x* where the latter is on the production possibilities frontier. This gap reflects the fact that producers are not maximising output at the set of domestic prices PP1 because of their sheltered position protected from foreign competition (*technical inefficiency*).

A second inefficiency arises from the fact that producers are missing the opportunity to trade along the price line PP2 and reach a higher level of consumption, for example, as at *z*. This *allocative inefficiency* is reflected in the difference between points *x* and *y*. The overall cost of inefficiency can be measures in terms of consumption by the difference between consumption at *u* (with no trade and technical inefficiency) and consumption at *z* (with free trade and no technical inefficiency).

In this model, trade reform (i.e. a move to free trade) is deemed to remove both types of inefficiency. First, by opening up the domestic market it will provide a competitive stimulus to previously protected domestic firms. In response, firms will shift to the production frontier (provided managerial incentives operate as required). Second, by changing the set of relative prices facing firms, resources will shift from less efficient to more efficient firms and there will be a partial specialisation along the lines of comparative advantage. In Figure 3.2 after reform production of *a* expands and that of *b* contracts. These effects are relatively short term and will create a once-for-all increase in income.

For trade reform to create an increase in growth, as its proponents argue, some other mechanism must be at work. Several are possible depending on the growth model that underlies the argument. The most plausible is that an open trade policy gives greater access to foreign technology, either embodied in imported plant and equipment or disembodied in ideas, designs or patents made available through exposure to foreign trade. This will allow growth to accelerate through a *catch-up* process as follower economies adapt and apply new technology superior to that available domestically. Growth effects in Figure 3.2 are shown as an outward shift in the production frontier to QQ2.

Explanations of trade based on resource endowments suggests that the sectors (and the activities within these) which will expand after reform will be those that use intensively an economy's abundant factor, which in the case of lower-income

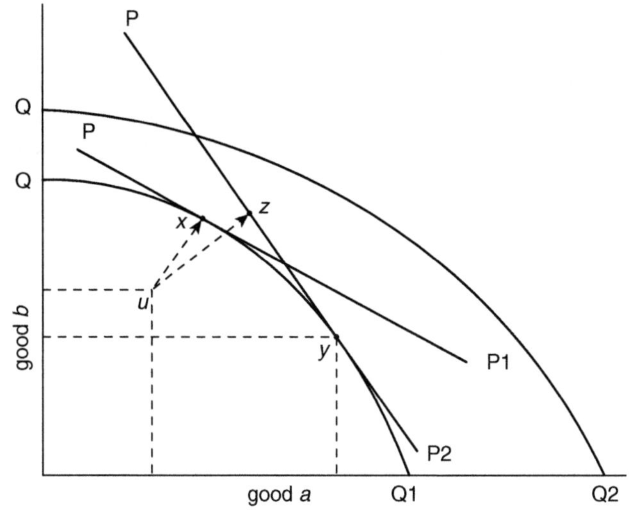

Figure 3.2 Opening to trade and resource reallocation.

economies will be unskilled labour. Similarly, the relative price of these goods will be expected to rise, thus creating a shift in income in favour of unskilled workers (see Chapter 4).

Trade reform and manufacturing efficiency

Trade reform has had negative impacts on manufacturing where it has led to the contraction of previously protected import-competing activities and where the displaced workers have not been absorbed elsewhere either in export manufacturing or other sectors. This cannot happen in the simple framework underlying Figures 3.1 and 3.2 as full employment is assumed. However, in real world situations, such unemployment has occurred both on a short-term and on a long-term basis, and given the lack of unemployment benefits in most low-income countries which allowed periods of job search this can result in a permanent movement of workers into informal sector activity. The decline in formal sector manufacturing employment post-reform was most marked in Latin America and although new jobs were created in export industries, in countries like Brazil and Mexico there was a net decline in manufacturing employment over the 1990s.

However, positive outcomes are also possible depending on how firms respond to the new set of price incentives and the competitive pressure following a lowering of barriers to import. With import protection sheltering domestic producers, a working hypothesis is that lower protection will stimulate cost reductions and that the higher the previous protection, the greater will be the cost reduction and efficiency improvement. A number of studies have tested this proposition and although earlier work found no real link, more recent analyses from countries as diverse as

Brazil, Chile, Korea Mexico and Malawi, have found a relationship, even if it is sometimes statistically weak (see Box 3.2).

The precise mechanism at work remains unclear, but from detailed firm level studies it does not appear that trade opening is associated with significantly longer production runs at plant level. Possible explanations for the link between the lowering of protection and higher productivity are greater competitive stimulus to remove the managerial slack underlying technical inefficiency, and stronger incentives to invest in and greater access to new foreign technology. In addition, there is evidence that during trade reform the mark-up of price above operating costs (*price–cost margin*), which is an approximate measure of monopoly pricing, falls and that this fall is related to the degree of tariff reduction faced by firms. A fall in such margins will imply lower profits and may also reflect higher

Box 3.2 Manufacturing efficiency and trade reform

The most satisfactory means of testing for a relationship between trade opening and subsequent efficiency improvement is to use case studies of individual economies over time. A relatively simple approach is to use manufacturing survey data across different manufacturing branches to test for a relationship between a productivity variable and either the initial level of or in change in a measure of protection across branches. For example, total factor productivity (TFP) growth (the proportion of change not explained by higher capital and labour inputs) can be explained by factors like output, technology and an indicator of protection like the effective rate (ERP) discussed earlier.

Hence,

$$\text{TFP} = \text{gVA} - (a_1.\text{gK} + a_2.\text{gL}) \quad (3.7)$$

where *g* indicates growth, VA is value added, K and L are capital and labour inputs, respectively.

TFP can be expressed as a function of output (Q), a measure of technology (T) and protection (ERP)

$$\text{So TFP} = \text{f (Q, T, ERP)}$$

and can be estimated empirically in a regression as

$$\text{TFP} = a + b_1.\text{Q} + b_2.\text{T} + b_3.\text{ERP} + e \quad (3.8)$$

where a is a constant and e is the error term.

Equation 3.8 can be estimated in levels or in rates of change. If trade reform is to stimulate efficiency the level of ERP will be negatively associated with TFP, and the decline in ERP will be positively associated with the change in TFP.

Mexico underwent a major trade reform in the mid-1980s and its impact on manufacturing has been studied extensively. Using variants of Equation 3.8 two studies found a significant negative association between lowering of trade barriers (as captured by a fall in the ERP) and productivity growth, so the greater the reduction in protection the stronger the productivity stimulus. However, another study based on individual plant level data finds no relation. Here, the only relation is between initial openness to trade (as approximated by the share of imports in production) and subsequent productivity growth, so it is the more open branches pre-reform that show the greatest efficiency gains.[11]

Cross-sectional regression models of the type implied by Equation 3.8 suffer from the problem of not being able to control adequately for influences that vary over time. Ideally, this requires panel data analysis across individual firms over a number of years. This allows the estimation of an equation that explains productivity by branch level protection, combined with firm specific characteristics (these can be measured by individual variables like firm age or output scale or more simply through individual firm dummy variables), and cyclical macro-developments (through annual dummy variables). Hence, in the simplest form, TFP for firm j can be estimated from the regression relation:

$$TFP_{jt} = a + b1.ERP + b2D_j + b3D_t + e_j \qquad (3.9)$$

where j is for firm j, t is for year t, and D is a dummy variable of unity for j and t.

Brazil is an economy that underwent trade reform in the late 1980s with a subsequent productivity increase. A more sophisticated version of Equation 3.9 is estimated for a large sample of firms in Brazil with the result that there is a significant negative coefficient on the protection indicator in analysis for the level of TFP. Furthermore, of the 50 per cent growth in TFP over the period 1990–94, the majority is put down to trade reform, with cyclical effects playing only a minor role.[12]

productivity which is passed on to consumers. As part of trade reform, lower margins have been found in a number of diverse countries (e.g. Brazil, Mexico and Morocco) with the interpretation that trade reform has 'disciplined' domestic producers and weakened their monopoly power. However, whilst these results imply trade reform creates positive improvements in performance, it will be only one of a number of factors at work. The precise impact of changes in import tariffs and quotas will vary with factors like the macro-economic environment, market structure within which firms operate and speed and the manner in which reform is implemented. Given these qualifications, it is not surprising that some studies find no support for the trade reform–productivity link.

If trade reform stimulates greater exports and if exporters have a higher productivity level or rate of growth than domestically oriented firms, this shift in production structure away from the domestic market will itself bring an improvement in performance. Most empirical studies, both cross-country and involving detailed firm-level data, concur that export-oriented firms have a superior productivity performance to non-exporters. There is dispute over causation, however, since exporting may create better productivity performance (e.g. due to competitive pressure in international markets or access to foreign technology supplied by foreign buyers) or the more productive firms may choose to export (so *self-selection* is at work). The latter was the conclusion of a well-known study of firms in Columbia, Mexico and Morocco, where experience of exporting (*learning by exporting*) was found to be unrelated to productivity, when other factors are allowed for. Hence, whilst we can be confident that exporting and strong performance go together at the firm level, this does not prove that exporting actually causes this performance.[13]

There can be broad agreement that a competitive environment for firms can stimulate efficiency improvements and that as part of a wider programme, trade reform can help improve productivity. Whilst it has been difficult to find dramatic examples of productivity spurts after trade liberalisation, nonetheless the widespread collapse of previously protected manufacturing where it has occurred has largely been due to macro- and institutional factors rather than trade opening per se, so that the negative effects predicted by opponents of liberalisation have also been difficult to demonstrate.

What is left of the special case for support of manufacturing?

Given this theoretical analysis and empirical evidence, what is left of the special case for manufacturing based on its potential for externalities, technical change and productivity growth, examined in Chapter 2? Can the discussion here be reconciled with the earlier analysis? The key point to note is that international trade theory has long recognised that interventions to support particular sectors or activities, which may not be competitive in the short run, can be justified on long-run grounds. The starting point is the *infant industry argument* which states that new firms require time to learn how to produce efficiently and that, in the short term, they may not be in a position to compete with longer established producers. However, competitiveness can be achieved over time, through *learning-by-doing*.

This firm-level case can in turn be extended to whole sectors in newly industrialising economies. The normal diagrammatic representation is as in Figure 3.3 which shows a unit cost curve (AC) of an infant firm related to time on the horizontal axis. Unit costs are compared with price from an established overseas producer OP shown as constant and quality differences are assumed away. Both unit costs and the competitor price are in constant prices, so inflation is not

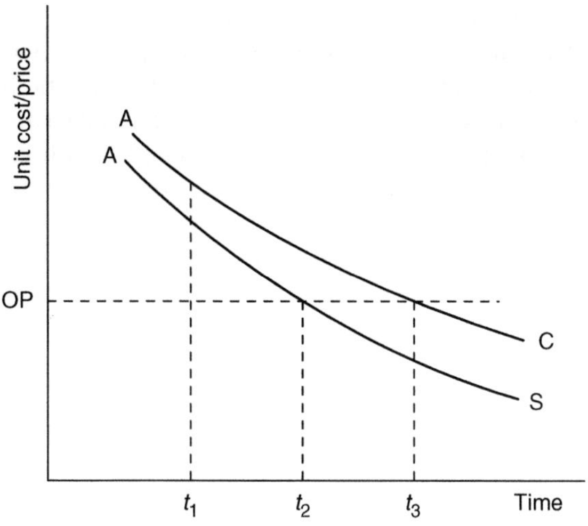

Figure 3.3 Infant industry case for protection.

considered. At time t_1 the firm is new and uncompetitive, whilst it reaches competitiveness at time t_3, after which it should be able to export. Insofar as positive external effects are created by the firm this can be represented as a new cost line where the positive external benefit per unit *e* is subtracted from the firm's own unit cost to give a net social cost AS (so AS = AC – *e*). The significance of this is that with positive externalities in broader social terms, competitiveness is attained earlier at t_2.

In the short term, however, for an infant producer to survive will require either:

- A barrier (either a tariff or a quota) blocking imports at the cheaper price (so the tariff inclusive price rises to equal or exceed domestic cost) or,
- A subsidy from government to allow the producer to cover the difference between its cost and the cheaper import price or,
- Cross-subsidisation by another part of the firm itself.

In the first case, the short-run costs are borne by consumers, in the second case by tax payers and in the third by the firm's owners. However, there will also be benefits from longer-term competitiveness to set against the short-term higher cost of local production as compared with imports, so that infant industry protection is a form of social investment, with its costs accruing to different parties depending upon how the subsidy is financed.

In Figure 3.3, the mechanism through which the infant industry matures is simply learning. A slightly more sophisticated version of this argument introduces the idea of technical change and a minimum efficient scale of production as necessary to apply new technology. In Figure 3.4, DD represents domestic demand, P*m* is the cost of imports in the domestic market (before any import tariff), and P*e* is the export price (the difference between P*m* and P*e* is accounted for by transport and distribution costs). At low output levels, such as OQ, unit costs in the infant producer are high and the supply line is horizontal at P*d*S, where P*d* is the price that covers average unit cost. Domestic production will require an import tariff of *t* (where *t* = P*d* – P*m*). If an infant firm can be sheltered in its domestic market, with growing demand, it will become feasible to invest in a new technology subject to economies of scale. In Figure 3.4, once demand grows beyond OQ*, it will be profitable to invest in a new technology with a supply line SS subject to falling cost. With the expansion of domestic production, unit costs will fall and the protective tariff *t* can be reduced. At output OQ1, the firm will become competitive with imports and at OQ2 it can export competitively.

Qualifications to the infant industry argument

Protection by import tariff thus either allows the firm to learn through production (as in Figure 3.3) or to invest in new capacity embodying best practice technology (as in Figure 3.4). Where there are positive externalities and capacity for further productivity growth, supporting infants can in principle bring strong long-run gains, for reasons discussed in Chapter 2. If the capacity for infants to grow is stronger in manufacturing that elsewhere and if external benefits are more prevalent there, the engine of growth case can be supported. How does this analysis link with the trade theory discussion? Several points must be noted.

First, the infant industry argument is not necessarily one in support of import tariff protection. It makes a case for supporting new or infant activities so they

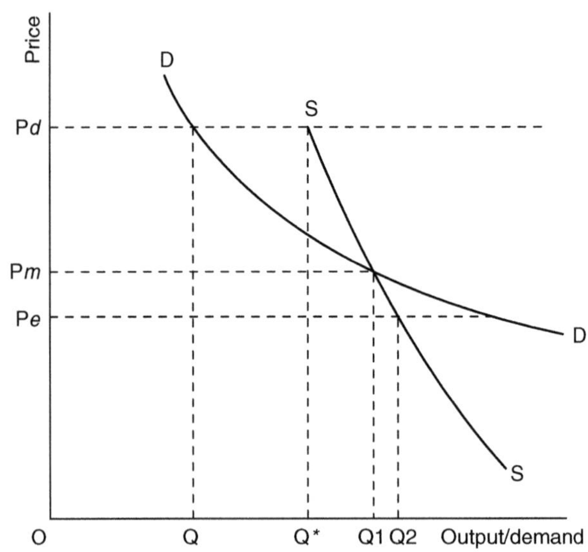

Figure 3.4 Economies of scale and infant protection.

can grow to become competitive. Support can come in different ways, for example, in tax incentives, subsidised credit, subsidised inputs like power or factory space or cash transfers. Import protection is simply one mechanism, but it is one that hits consumers of the good concerned directly. Subsidies of various types are paid for by general taxpayers and with taxes spread over a large number of products the distortionary impact of supporting production of a specific good out of taxation is likely to be less than that created by a single import tariff on the item itself. On the other hand, support through import tariffs requires no extra taxation, as it is self financing through the charge on consumers of the protected product. It is therefore easier to implement, explaining its past attraction for governments.

Second, as noted, a successful infant industry can be seen as a form of investment with initial cost (where domestic unit costs are above competitor prices) and later benefits (where domestic unit costs are below competitor prices and with possible positive externalities). As with any other form of investment, assessment of desirability requires a comparison of the future stream of costs against the future stream of benefits (with both streams discounted to the present to give *present values*). Only if the latter exceeds the former will the investment in protection be justified. However, where benefits exceed costs, the question then becomes why can firms not anticipate this and set up the activity alone without public support. To explain private sector inactivity requires reference to various market imperfections:

- The firms may lack information (but if so why should we expect the government be better informed?).
- They may have difficulty borrowing from banks to fund this investment.
- Or they may prefer not to take the risk involved.

Reforming credit markets to better supply long-term finance to potential private investors in new activities has been a strategy adopted in recent years in many countries. However, whilst desirable in itself, it is at best an indirect means of industry support on infant grounds. Where investment does not take place because benefits are external and do not accrue to the original investors the theoretically preferable solution is to subsidise directly the activity that generates the external benefit. For example, if the source of the externality is knowledge creation, R and D should be subsidised; if it is training, there should be support to meet the training costs of firms; if it is product innovation that can be imitated support can be linked with patenting and enterprise start-up. Trade protection is a feasible, but undoubtedly *second best*, means of providing support, since it raises cost to consumers and alters relative prices faced by both producers and consumers. However, it is relatively easy to implement and raises revenue for governments.

Third, studies of protected firms have revealed that learning by doing as implied in the move down the cost curve over time in Figure 3.3 is only the simplest type of learning and is far from automatic. Successful learners also actively invest in training and knowledge acquisition. A key issue is how far firms will have an incentive to do this if they are sheltered from competition behind protective import tariff or quota barriers. In theory, different assumptions can be made about the response of firms. For example, higher sales in a protected market due to barriers to imports may give an incentive to spend more on design or product adaptation as the cost can be spread over a larger number of units of output (this matches the shift to the new technology at point OQ* in Figure 3.4). On the other hand, with a protected market firms and their managers may lack the competitive pressure to minimise costs or improve quality. This is the technical inefficiency illustrated in Figure 3.2 and captured by the high DRC estimates reported for protected firms in many different countries from the import substitution era (see Table 3.2).

Fourth, where economies of scale are important, the infant industry case has to explain why the higher output necessary for the introduction of new technology cannot be achieved by reversing incentives and encouraging exports rather than import substitutes. In fact, logically the argument can equally be applied to 'early' export promotion with initially high-cost exports subsidised to allow unit costs to fall to achieve subsequently competitive cost levels at some future date. These subsidies could either be publicly funded by governments or from the individual firm themselves. However, today, as we have seen for non-least-developed countries, imposition of export subsidies is against WTO rules and could be subject to retaliatory measures or anti-dumping charges.

Conclusions

Theoretically, where one sector, such as manufacturing, is subject to more positive externalities than another, the case for special support remains valid. Theory implies the need for selectivity within manufacturing, limiting special support to the activities with the greatest potential for productivity growth and external benefits. Furthermore, most observers now agree that to avoid the inefficiency found in the past, any such special support should be relatively modest in terms of its impact on value added and be on offer only for a limited period to build up a sense of competitive pressure amongst producers. Hence, the case for selective limited trade protection of parts of manufacturing cannot be disregarded totally, particularly if it leads to subsequent exports of competitive products. However, past experience suggests that the well-established international brand names from the developing world such as Tata (for trucks and buses from India), Acer (for computers from Taiwan), Brasilia (for aircraft from Brazil) and Corona (beer from Mexico), where success was built initially on domestic sales, are the exceptions rather than the rule. Many more national brands produced for protected domestic markets failed to make significant breakthroughs into exports and either remained small and domestic or were taken over by international firms. This does not mean that competitive manufacturing cannot be established in the group of developing countries, but rather that the environment in which it is most likely to thrive is one that is basically open to foreign trade with only selective and modest protection for limited periods.

Further reading

The classic analyses of the cost of import substitution policy as a means of promoting manufacturing are in Little *et al.* (1970), Balassa (1982) and Krueger (1978). Weiss (2002, Chapters 3 and 4) surveyed these arguments in detail. Surveys of the impact of trade reform on growth and productivity improvements are in Rodrik (1992), Tybout (1992) and Winters (2004). Weiss (1999) looks at results specifically for Mexico in the 1980s and 1990s.

4 Globalisation and industrialisation

One of the key features of recent developments in the world economy has been the reduction in costs of transport and communications. It has become considerably cheaper in real terms to move goods across national borders due to a reduction in transport cost (e.g. due to the use of large container sea vessels) and to communicate between buyers and sellers and between head offices and affiliated firms (e.g. through the Internet, videoconferencing and cheaper air travel). These reductions in the cost of doing business internationally (what is termed *trade cost*) have had important implications for decisions relating to choice of supplier and of production location and for trade in manufactured goods. The concern of this chapter is how these trends have affected industrialisation in the NIEs and middle- and lower-income economies. It discusses the impact of trade costs, the rise of global production networks, the particular problems of low-income regions like sub-Saharan Africa that have had difficulty in integrating into the world market and emerging competition from China and India. Finally, it looks at the implications of dealing with climate change for the location of industry globally.

Trade costs

A key feature of globalisation is the decline in the cost of moving goods and generally doing business across international frontiers (*trade costs*). These refer to all the costs other than the production cost in getting a good to the final user. Declines in such costs have been a major stimulus to global trade and investment. Different categories of trade costs include transport (port, rail and road links), customs delays, time of goods in transit, management and communication cost between countries, cost of holding stocks and cost of changing currencies, as well as import tariff and non-tariff barriers to trade. With trade liberalisations of recent years under the auspices of the WTO, the latter two aspects have become relatively less important. Empirical work has shown that trade flows can be sensitive to reductions in transport costs, including time cost of delay.[1]

Trade costs form a potentially important barrier to trade that improvements in infrastructure can reduce. They provide a form of protection that allows domestic produces to capture a higher level of value added, whilst still remaining price competitive with foreign suppliers. Non-tariff trade costs should in principle be incorporated in estimates of effective protection, since they act as a barrier to trade in the same way as tariffs and lower the return to exportables and raise it for import substitutes (see Box 4.1).

Box 4.1 Trade cost and protection

The Effective Rate of Protection (ERP) concept discussed in Chapter 3 can be extended by incorporating the additional protection created by transport and other trade costs. Hence, ERP becomes:

$$\text{ERP}i = (ti - \Sigma aji.tj)/(1 - \Sigma aji) + (ri - \Sigma aji.rj)/(1 - \Sigma aji) + (ni - \Sigma aji.nj)/(1 - \Sigma aji) \quad (4.1)$$

where *i* is the final product, *j* is an internationally traded production input and *aji* is the coefficient for units of *j* per unit of *i* with no policy barriers to trade and no international trade cost; *ti* and *tj* are the rate of tariff or tariff equivalent of policy-induced trade barriers on *i* and *j*, respectively, *ri* and *rj* are the transport costs per unit of *i* and *j*, respectively, and *ni* and *nj* are the non-transport trade costs per unit of *i* and *j*.[2]

The first term gives the potential proportionate increase in value added due to policy-induced protection, the second term gives the proportionate increase due to transport costs and the third the proportionate increase due to other international trade costs. In other words, the sum of these gives the increase in potential income to domestic factors in comparison with a situation where there are zero tariffs, no quotas and no trade costs. Trade costs, thus, potentially increase natural (as opposed to policy-created) protection and since they can vary significantly between products, they can impact on relative prices.

Before one can incorporate trade costs in a calculation of effective protection one needs an estimate of their magnitude (i.e. the coefficients *ri* and *ni* in Equation 4.1 above). Quantification of trade costs can be done by case studies that survey product prices at different stages of the supply chain. This is arguably the most desirable way of quantification in empirical work, although alternative simpler approaches have also been tried, mostly focussing on the transport component.

One approach is to take the difference between the *cif* (cost–insurance–freight) and *fob* (free-on-board) prices of a commodity as a measure of international transport and insurance costs. Hence, for trade between countries *j* and *k*

$$ri = (ci - fi)/fi \quad (4.2)$$

where *ri* is transport and insurance costs per unit of *i*, *ci* is the *cif* import price in *k* and *fi* is the *fob* export price in *j*.

If an aggregate trade cost measure r is required, Equation 4.2 will have to be weighted by the share of i in the total value of trade between j and k (wi), so

$$r = \Sigma_i((ci - fi)/fi)^*wi \qquad (4.3)$$

The difficulty with this approach is the lack of consistency in price data at the *cif* and *fob* levels, which may be aggregated across different products. This can lead to wide variations in ri between products that appear unlikely to reflect the actual situation.[3]

Another approach uses international freight rate data as a direct measure of transport cost. Here, individual commodity data will rarely be used and r (excluding insurance) will be estimated as a weighted average across commodities so

$$r = \Sigma_i si.qi \qquad (4.4)$$

where si is the shipping cost for commodity i per physical unit shipped from country j to k and qi is the share of i in the volume of trade between j and k.

Although use of shipping rates has the advantage of obtaining direct data on transport costs like the use of the *cif-fob* margin, it omits other elements of trade cost. Hence, as a third approach, an index of infrastructure quality (e.g. based on an aggregation of road density, paved road network, rail network and telephone lines per person) is often combined with one or other of the transport costs estimates in an econometric model. Here infrastructure quality is used as a proxy for the non-transport components of trade costs. The econometric model applied is normally a variation of the gravity equation, so that

$$Yjk = f(d, Z, T, I, \varepsilon) \qquad (4.5)$$

where Yjk reflects trade between two partners, d is distance between them, Z is vector of country characteristics, such as income per capita, T is a measure of transport cost between the countries, I covers a separate index of infrastructure for both countries and ε is an error term. The responsiveness of trade to T and I gives an indication of the importance of trade costs. Such analysis will not give a direct per unit estimate for the impact of non-transport costs. However, if the volume effect of I on trade is combined with an assumed price elasticity, this will allow the estimation of an implicit price effect (or tariff equivalent).

Source: See Weiss (2007a) and Dee *et al.* (2007).

Whilst arguments about the importance of trade costs are widely recognised, there is a lack of empirical evidence on their size. It is now widely asserted that after various rounds of tariff reductions trade costs are more important than policy barriers to trade. Representative international trade costs for industrialised countries based on a combination of transport and non-transport costs are said to be as high as 74 per cent, compared with average tariffs of less than 5 per cent. Of these international trade costs, roughly one-third are transport related. If international trade costs for inputs are below those for outputs the representative effective protection rate created by trade cost (terms two and three in Box 4.1) will be higher still.[4]

Globalisation and trade

One way of interpreting globalisation is as a process through which trade costs are reduced. This is the perspective in the *new economic geography* literature, which differs from the standard trade theory examined in Chapter 3 in its key assumption of increasing returns to scale (so unit costs fall as output expands). Increasing returns can be either internal to a firm or external due to the presence of external benefits created by the activity of other firms. In new economic geography models where firms choose to locate is determined by the interaction between factor endowments (which determine wage costs), market size (which impacts on scale effects internal to a firm), external benefits (the scale of which will be determined by the linkages between firms) and trade costs. The key prediction is that at very high levels of trade cost, there will be a tendency for firms to locate close to the market for their goods, whilst at low levels of trade cost, differences in wage costs between countries are likely to be the key determinant of location. At intermediate values of trade cost, it is likely that the influence of external benefits relative to other factors will be greatest, leading to a tendency for firms to cluster close to each other in a few countries and locations within countries (in a process of *agglomeration*). Once an industrial concentration becomes established, it will take a major reduction in trade costs to create a counter-tendency towards *dispersion* to new countries.

The implication is that the impact of globalisation will lead to a modest dispersion of industrial location with only a few new industrial centres, where external effects are important, emerging at least in the short term. This is consistent with the empirical observation of the emergence of only a small number of newly industrialised economies (NIEs). Once production becomes established in an industry, there are advantages through increasing returns that can be built on in a cumulative fashion. International dispersal of activities like manufacturing (but the arguments apply to any increasing returns sector) requires either large cost increases in established production centres (e.g. due to rising wages or congestion costs) or major falls in trade costs. From this perspective, the rise of the first- and second-tier NIEs, in part the result of FDI flows from the older established producer Japan, represents one of stage of industrial dispersal, with rapid growth in China, also strongly influenced by FDI flows in part from the NIEs themselves, a more recent dispersal stage. Hence, economies that lack the flexibility to move quickly into increasing return activities may find that once producers in rival economies become established, the process of catch-up may be lengthy and difficult.

The advantage gained by a country that establishes an industry early (*first mover advantage*) in the presence of positive externalities can be illustrated for two countries. In total there are n firms divided between countries 1 and 2 (so $n_1 + n_2 = n$) (see Figures 4.1 and 4.2). In both figures, the horizontal axis gives the number of firms in each country measured by the distance between a given point and the right and left hand axes. The vertical axis gives firm profitability (p). In Figure 4.1, the line from the left hand axis shows profitability in country 1 as declining as the number of firms increases, on the assumption that as the number of firms increases the price of the scarce factor in 1 is bid up for each firm. The same applies to country 2, and there is equilibrium at E with equal profit rates and both countries producing the good concerned. At E with perfect information, there is no tendency for a firm to move from 1 to 2 or vice versa, as this will lower not increase its profit, so the equilibrium is stable.

Figure 4.2 introduces positive externalities (e.g. due to knowledge spillovers) which are large enough to offset the impact of firm numbers on factor price, so that profit rates in each country now increase with the number of firms. The profit lines in each country are therefore upward sloping. The new equilibrium at U is unstable because there will be an incentive for a firm to leave one country and move to other, since the extra firm will increase the profit rate in the recipient country and reduce it in the country from which it has left. This gives other firms an incentive to follow in a cumulative process. The stable equilibrium, where there is no incentive for firms to move, are either E_1 or E_2 where all firms locate

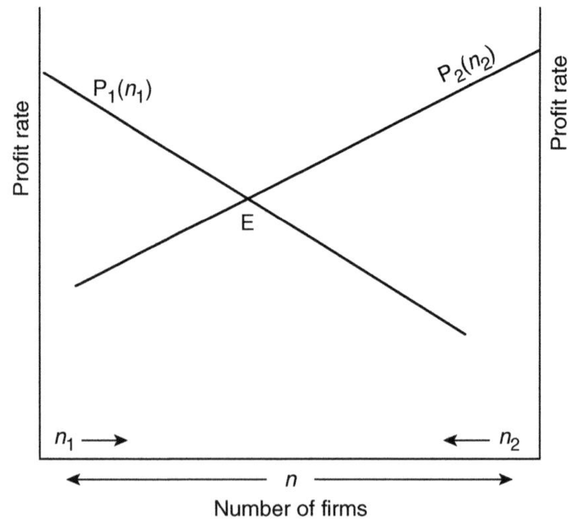

Figure 4.1 Stable equilibrium under globalisation.

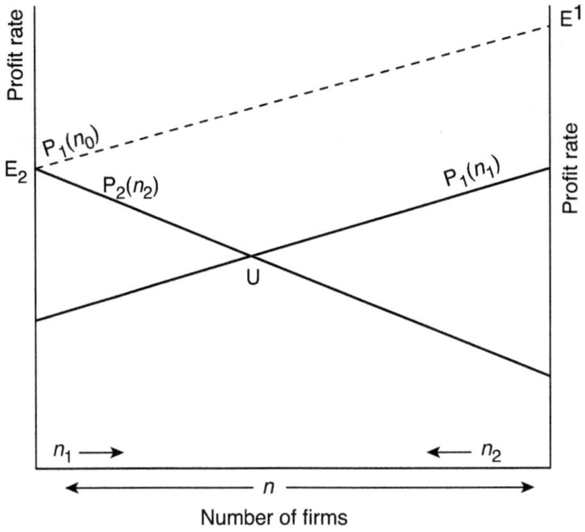

Figure 4.2 Unstable equilibrium under globalisation.

in either country 1 or country 2, respectively. These are multiple (i.e. non-unique) equilibrium and theory cannot predict which will be the outcome. Once established in a country, an industry can build on the first mover advantage in a cumulative fashion.

Falling trade cost can be introduced in the model as an upward shift in the profit line. If the impact of trade cost is only on country 1, due for example to its improved air or sea links with a third country market, this will be reflected in a rise in its profit line, so the rate of profit in 1 rises for a given number of firms located there. However, if originally firms concentrate in 2 (with an equilibrium at E_2), it will require a very large fall in trade costs (*a catastrophic change*) to create a new equilibrium where firms concentrate in 1 (at E^1). This will only occur if the profit line in 1 rises to the dotted line (since only with this line is the starting rate of profit with no firms in 1 equal to the rate of profit with all firms in 2 (so $P_1(n_0)=P_2(n_2)$). Hence, with external economies and increasing returns, in these models, it will take large changes in trade costs to offset the tendency towards concentration.[5]

Global production networks

A major result of falling trade cost has been the fragmentation of production globally through the emergence of *global production networks*, whereby the production, distribution and sale of commodities are divided between different locations in the world economy. Much of the growth of manufactured exports from the developing country group and in particular from East and Southeast Asia has been due to the spread of global production networks driven by foreign (or *transnational* in the sense that they operate globally) firms. All manufacturing activity can be decomposed into a range of different activities which are as follows:

- Research into product design and technology.
- Logistics when the necessary inputs and raw materials are purchased.
- Production when the inputs and raw materials are converted into a product.
- Sub-division of production with components of a good produced in different locations.
- Distribution of the finished product to wholesalers.
- Marketing of the good to the final user or consumer.

At each stage of this process, value is created and hence the use of the term *value chain* to refer to these various links in the chain or network.[6] Manufacturing has always been characterised in this way, but in the last three decades the dramatic fall in transport and communication costs globally has made it attractive to firms to break up these stages and locate those that require relatively more labour in countries where wage costs are low, keeping some skill and knowledge-intensive stages in high-income countries. Thus, international firms might retain R and D and marketing at their headquarters (e.g. in the United States or European Union), but locate all or parts of their production in a low-wage country (e.g. in Vietnam or China).

The technology of some activities makes it relatively easy to sub-divide the production process itself. For example, parts and components for automobiles can be produced in different locations and shipped to another for assembly (see Box 4.2). In clothing, cloth may be spun or woven in one location and cut and made up in another. Such sub-division has resulted in a dramatic growth in international trade in parts and components for manufactures. This trade has typically been organised by large lead firms from rich countries that either establish their own subsidiaries in lower wage economies or sub-contract to independent supplier firms from these countries. In some countries and sectors, this has been encouraged by preferential tariff arrangements. Thus, for example, there are tariff exemptions in the United States for articles originating in the United States but assembled or made-up elsewhere and exemptions for goods from parts of Africa under the African Growth and Opportunities Act (AGOA) scheme. Similarly, regional trading agreements, like the Association of South East Asian Nations (ASEAN) and the Southern Region Trade Agreement (MERCOSUR) that allow for zero tariffs on trade between members, also encourage this process of trade in parts and components.

Across manufacturing activities, the intensity of fragmentation or subdivision within these networks is largely driven by four factors. These are:

- *The technical divisibility of the production process*. The contrast here is between a continuous process production, as found in chemicals for example, which is technically difficult to subdivide and production, as in automobiles or electronics, which can be subdivided into discrete stages and undertaken at different sites.

Box 4.2 Toyota automobile production network

Toyota like other Japanese car producers has established production facilities in China both to serve the Chinese market and for export. Toyota selects different production sites for its different car models with key research and design work conducted at its research centre in Nagoya, Japan. The new energy efficient Prius model was designed at Nagoya and assembly of the Prius takes place at Toyota's plant in Nagoya. However, the assembly is based on engines, parts and components that have been produced not just in Nagoya, but also in Toyota's plants in two locations in China, Shanghai and Guangzhou. These Chinese plants in turn obtain components from local Chinese supplier firms, who are thus part of the overall production network. The cars assembled in Shanghai and Guangzhou are then sold in Japan and also exported back to China. In the case of the Camry model, research and design work again takes place at the Nagoya centre but assembly is now in China at the Guangzhou plant. Engines, parts and components are made both in Guangzhou and also in Shanghai and Nagoya for shipment to Guangzhou for final assembly. Again, some local Chinese supplier firms are involved in making components for the three plants. Camry models are sold in China as well as being exported to Japan and third country markets.

Source: Kuchiki (2008).

- *The factor intensity of production*. Labour is still largely an immobile factor internationally and firms seek out low-wage locations. However, for fragmentation to be viable, the wage cost saving from locating a stage in the chain in low-wage economies must be sufficient to justify the extra trade costs (particularly in transport and management) involved. This will primarily be the case for labour-intensive forms of production.
- *The technological complexity of production*. Not all labour-intensive stages can be shifted to low-wage locations if skill levels and mastery of technology are weak. Hence, the design stage of production, which is skilled-labour intensive, is often retained in the home base of a transnational company with only the technologically simpler stages relocated.
- *The value–weight ratio for the product*. It will be financially viable to ship low-weight-high-value items long distances as part of such networks or chains. However, where the weight-to-value ratio is high, transport costs may make such an arrangement unattractive (cement is the classic example of this).

Electronics is the sector where all four conditions for fragmentation are found most strongly. It has many separable production processes, some of which are highly labour intensive and require relatively low skill levels. The value-to-weight ratio can also be very high. In contrast in automobiles, although there are separable production processes, most require significant mastery of technology to operate effectively and many components are relatively heavy making transport over long distances unviable. Although fragmentation to lower wage economies has increased in automobile production (as illustrated in Box 4.2) for these reasons, it remains far less extensive than in electronics.

A standard distinction is between global production networks (or value chains) where the lead firm is a producer (*producer-driven chains*) and where the lead firm is a retailer or buyer (*buyer-driven chains*). Producer-driven chains are where the lead firm purchases its inputs from suppliers elsewhere in the chain, often in different countries. As part of this process, it will provide designs and necessary production technology to its suppliers and sell the finished products to retailers. Producer-driven chains are based on the market power of firms in capital or technology-intensive sectors like automobiles, heavy machinery, aircraft and computers, with market power based on barriers to entry created by either investment requirements or knowledge of production technology. Profits are determined by volume of production or by technological breakthroughs that lower costs.

In buyer-driven chains, the organisational dynamic stems from the buying firms that set up a series of links with suppliers, often in low-wage economies. Buyers can be either large retailers that design their own products (like the Gap for example), companies that market their own brands but do not have their own retail outlets (like Nike or Reebok) or international trading companies that have an intermediary role between producers and retailers. Buyers supply designs and specifications to producers with their market power determined by their brand name and their ability to manage the various stages of the chain. Here, profits are determined principally by product design, branding and marketing that allow the creation of product niches in global markets. This pattern is found typically in consumer goods sectors, in which labour is a significant proportion of costs, such as garments, footwear, toys, some electronics and a range of handcrafted items. Developing country firms are major participants in this form of chain although typically only a small proportion of the final sales price accrues to the developing country suppliers.

Firms from outside the NIEs, wishing to participate in global chains, will have to commence initially with the production of labour-intensive components and inputs. International production with both forms of chain is highly competitive, since where wage costs are the key determinant of the competitiveness of a location, there is always a risk that a lower cost supplier will emerge. Hence, for example, Japanese firms started in the 1980s to source inputs from their subsidiaries in Thailand, shipping them back to Japan for further processing, because wage costs in Thailand were lower than in Japan. However, in the 1990s, China emerged as a cheaper cost location than Thailand, causing some firms to relocate from Thailand to China. In turn, in the new century, Vietnam emerged as a lower-wage location than China, causing further shifts in foreign investment. This competitive process puts downward pressure on wages and is likely to have contributed to the worsening terms of trade for developing country exporters of manufactures noted in Chapter 1. The implication is that export success based on low-wage costs alone will inevitably be transitory and sustained competitiveness requires an improvement in productivity, so that unit costs can be held down if wages rise, as well as an upgrading of export composition and a shift into higher-value goods.

Success for individual countries in the export of higher-value goods requires that its firms acquire the ability to produce finished goods in the chain (as opposed to parts and components) and to establish alliances to sell these through international distributors. Where firms do this using the design and brand name of a transnational firm, this is termed *own equipment manufacture*, since the developing country firm is a producer not a designer or innovator. Where in a further step the developing country firm develops its own brand name this is termed *own brand manufacture*. As yet, success stories of firms in this latter category are limited to the NIEs. However, the fact that there are some shows the potential for penetrating the global market. Well-known examples of own brand goods from the NIEs include Hyundai and Kia cars and Samsung electricals from Korea, Acer computers from Taiwan, Corona and Sol beer from Mexico and Brasilia aircraft from Brazil. However, the risk for the majority of lower-income countries is that they remain operating in the highly competitive low-wage, labour-intensive segments of value chains, where profit margins are low and success may be transitory. Production as part of such networks is often influenced by agglomeration effects as firms concentrate in specific locations to obtain the external benefits of close proximity discussed in Chapter 2.

Attracting global networks

There is broad agreement on the conditions necessary for economies to attract transnational firms to establish such networks or for the emergence of local firms as suppliers and in some instances as lead firms.

Stability in both a macro-economic and political sense appears an essential prerequisite, as it reduces uncertainty and the perceived risk of project failure. High inflation and currency fluctuations make long-term financial planning difficult and frequent change of political regime casts doubt on how long current policies, for example, on tax, will remain relevant. In addition, for export success trade policy should allow imported inputs required for export production to enter the country at low or zero tariffs and without quota barriers.

However, preconditions for successful integration in these networks go much further and include high-standard physical infrastructure covering reliable power supplies, and good-quality transport and communication links (so goods can be produced and shipped to other parts of the network with minimum disruption), a well-functioning legal system (so contracts can be enforced speedily) and an efficient public administration (so delays in customs clearance can be reduced and informal payments to officials minimised). These conditions are now termed *the investment climate*.[7] Tax incentives, typically in terms of holiday periods often of five years or more during which no tax is paid on profits, may make a difference to the location decision of firms, but only after these basic preconditions are met.

Requirements for labour costs and skills and supporting networks of local supplying firms will vary between manufacturing industries. In clothing, relatively low-cost, low-skilled labour is needed but not technologically sophisticated inputs or service activities. This is why clothing tends to be the most footloose of the networks with new suppliers emerging in response to rising wage costs in others. Automobile networks, however, require labour of medium skill levels and a relatively sophisticated set of support services. Electronics is somewhere between these two extremes, with a wide range of discrete activities involving different skill and technology levels.

To assess the standing of countries in terms of the investment climate, and hence their attractiveness as production locations as part of global chains, it is now common for surveys of enterprises to be conducted which aim to highlight operating conditions in a country to do with aspects like:

- The quality of infrastructure (e.g. the days power supply is unavailable and the length of time it takes to move goods to a market for sale to consumers).
- The efficiency of government bureaucracy (e.g. the number of days for goods to pass through customs, the length of time it takes to get a permit to start a business or the number of visits made by officials to a premises).
- The legal framework (e.g. the length of time and cost to enforce contracts and the days notice or redundancy payments granted to employees).

The idea here is that obstacles to new investment can be created by the business environment for enterprises, with poorly functioning infrastructure, an intrusive or possibly corrupt bureaucracy and a slow or weakly implemented legal framework acting as key disincentives to invest. From this perspective, a good industrial policy is one which listens to and addresses the complaints of firm, where such obstacles exist.

Table 4.1 summarises some of the data from such investment climate surveys for a selection of countries. Here, information is averaged across firms in the country samples. As these are averages in some cases across very large countries (such as China, Brazil and India), they may be misleading as a guide to specific local circumstances. Box 8.3 shows how more detailed studies have been compiled in China. Some aspects of the investment climate relating to government bureaucracy and the legal framework have been held up as key factors holding back manufacturing in low-income environments like sub-Saharan Africa. However, an examination of the relevant data, such as that in Table 4.1, suggests that whilst improvements terms of streamlining the system may be justified, they are unlikely to be the simple solution to the region's problems in terms of a low level of integration into global networks. In Table 4.1, relative to the United Kingdom, no country included does particularly well by these indicators. At the regional level, on average, sub-Saharan Africa appears to be a more difficult location than elsewhere for accessing imports in terms of delays in customs and

Table 4.1 Investment climate indicators: selected countries

Country	*Customs*	*Starting a business*		*Redundancy payments*	*Enforcing a contract*	*Infrastructure index*
	Time to import days	*Time in days*	*Cost (as % of average income)*	*Weeks of salary*	*Time in days*	*Country ranking*
China	24	37	5	91	406	30
India	20	30	66	56	1420	42
Pakistan	18	20	6	90	976	71
Ghana	29	33	26	178	487	91
Kenya	25	34	37	47	465	100
Tanzania	31	29	37	18	462	132
South Africa	35	22	6	24	600	26
Brazil	16	120	7	46	616	49
Mexico	17	13	12	52	415	53
United Kingdom	8	13	1	22	399	6
Average sub-Saharan Africa	39	46	100	68	644	na
Average Latin America and Caribbean	21	62	37	53	707	na
Average South Asia	20	28	27	76	1052	na

Source: Doing Business Indicators 2010 available from www.doingbusiness.org.

Notes

The infrastructure ranking comes from the connecting to World Bank Compete: The Logistics Performance Index and its Indicators, 2007 available from www.worldbank.org.

Na is not applicable.

a relatively expensive place to start a business. Its labour legislation offers relatively strong worker protection, with high redundancy payments for those in jobs to be balanced against as a perceived high barrier to new job creation; the Ghana case is an extreme example of this. However, on average, redundancy payments are less than those offered in South Asia and in of terms of the legal system, as reflected in the time for contract enforcement, African countries appear to have a less difficult operating environment than that in countries in South Asia or Latin America. Critically in terms of links with global networks the final column gives the country ranking for expert perceptions of the quality of the infrastructure required for foreign trade. Here, the difference between African economies and others is clearer with the former clustered towards the bottom of the country ranking.

Regional differences

East and Southeast Asia is the region where integration into global networks has been carried furthest, as evidenced by its share in world manufactured exports, particularly for clothing and electronics, although trade data cannot distinguish adequately between total exports of a good and exports of components of the good that are part of a network or chain. The first-tier NIEs (Korea, Taiwan, Singapore and Hong Kong) were followed by the second tier (principally Malaysia and Thailand, but also Indonesia and the Philippines) in establishing links with global networks. The routes were not always the same in that Korea and Taiwan relied relatively little on direct investment by foreign firms preferring to import foreign technology. This was applied by national firms as suppliers to the networks controlled by lead transnational firms, but over time national firms (like Samsung and Hyundai) themselves developed into lead firms. Elsewhere in the region, foreign direct investment, particularly from Japan, played a key role as Japanese firms established subsidiaries in lower wage locations like Thailand and also subcontracted work to local suppliers. This reliance on foreign direct investment as the route to integration in global networks has been followed in more recent years by China and to a lesser degree Vietnam, as they have emerged as manufacturing suppliers to the world market. Trade in manufactures within East Asia is very substantial with networks, particularly in electronics linking the different countries in often complex chains. Much of this trade is in parts and components with the finished goods in which they are embodied exported to the United States.

There is no single explanation as to why this region seized the opportunity of integrating with global networks much earlier than others have. In the 1960s, the first-tier NIEs looked to export opportunities to offset their relatively small domestic markets and to pay for the food and raw materials they could not produce themselves. They also had relatively low-cost and well-educated workers and invested heavily in acquiring and adapting foreign technology. In contrast, despite its much longer history of industrialisation, Latin America in the 1960s and 1970s pursued relatively inward looking policies and in the 1980s underwent a traumatic period of macro-economic instability and adjustment linked with foreign debt repayment. It was also a higher wage location and productivity differentials were not high enough to offset this disadvantage. Where networks have emerged in Latin America, they are largely country- or activity-specific. Mexico and some of the small Central American economies are closely linked in networks with US firms, which in Mexico's case was stimulated by the North America Free Trade Agreement (NAFTA) treaty signed in the early 1990s. This means that Mexico participates in networks in sectors like electronics, clothing and automobiles sending both parts and finished goods to the US market tariff-free (provided a minimum level of value is added in Mexico). It also means that Mexico is the economy in Latin America most vulnerable to rising competition from China.

The sector where Latin America has developed strong network links is automobiles with major production centres in Mexico, Brazil and Argentina, and the exchange of parts and components and assembled cars between these countries and the United States. For example, the regional trade agreement (MERCOSUR) has fostered exchange of auto parts between Brazil and Argentina as NAFTA did for Mexico–United States trade. In automobiles, networks are stronger and more extensive in Latin America than in East Asia. Possible explanations for this difference are first, the fact that automobile networks in Latin America emerged from the previously well-established but domestically oriented automobile sectors in these economies, in which all of the main transnational firms were already involved (including Ford, General Motors, Volkswagen and Fiat). These sectors built up behind protection, but also subject to industrial policy interventions, were able to emerge as internationally competitive in a more open foreign trade environment in the 1990s. Second, because of their lower value-to-weight ratio automobiles and some of their components, like engines, are less attractive for shipping over long distances than are electronic goods. Hence, US firms looking to locate assembly or component production overseas looked to Latin America (particularly Mexico) rather than East Asia.[8]

South Asia (particularly India, Pakistan and Bangladesh) also missed the initial waves of networks partly because of what was perceived as a less welcoming attitude towards foreign investment and a tighter regulatory regime. Despite low wage costs, skill levels were also low. This has meant that this region has lagged behind the Eastern part of Asia in network development with the major exception in recent years being the growth of clothing and textile exports from Bangladesh and Pakistan and the software exports from India.

Manufacturing in sub-Saharan Africa

Sub-Saharan Africa is the main part of the world left out from the spread of global networks and industrialisation more generally. Macro-economic policy reforms in the form of reduced budget deficits, greater flexibility in exchange rate management and much reduced import barriers have been introduced widely in Africa since the early 1990s. This has meant that previous protected import substitute industries have declined in importance or disappeared. The key problem, however, is that new competitive export-oriented producers have not emerged in sufficient numbers to replace them and create a dynamic industrial sector. This is in large part due to Africa's weak links with the global production networks. The absence of a skills base and the poor infrastructure facilities of these economies have meant that international lead firms have not seen Africa as an attractive location in which to invest, with unit costs often well above those in competing locations.

In addition, a weak financial sector has meant that the banking system is unable to provide adequate long-term credit for domestic investors in industry. This is a particular problem for smaller firms making it difficult for them to grow and thus contributing to an unbalanced industrial structure with a shortage of medium-sized firms (see Chapter 6). Skills and education levels remain low by international standards, affecting not just productivity of workers which is typically low relative to competitors, but more generally this reduces the technological capability of economies, which in turn manifests itself in the limited ability of enterprises to apply and adapt modern technology. Domestic markets are typically small, reducing the incentive to invest and making it difficult for domestically oriented firms to grow to achieve a size of production necessary to achieve any scale economies that are available and to cover the fixed costs of entering export markets. Regional free trade arrangements are a means of widening markets for an enterprise since tariff-free access to the markets of a neighbour is equivalent to expanding the home market. However, even where members of such a free trade area share common borders, high transport and logistics costs can create serous non-tariff barriers to trade.[9]

The absence of sub-Saharan Africa from world exports of manufactures is illustrated by the fact that in 25 countries, manufactured exports were less than 10 per cent of national income and in 21 less than 5 per cent.[10] On a per capita basis, manufacturing export value in sub-Saharan Africa (excluding South Africa) is only about 10 per cent of the developing country average and the share of manufacturing value-added in GDP was around one-third of the average.[11]

The level of manufacturing activity must be related to an economy's factor endowments, history and international economic relations. What is a high or a low share cannot be determined without consideration of these characteristics. Africa is relatively well endowed with land and natural resources relative to its population size and still has relatively a low educational attainment and stock of skilled and highly educated personnel. Both of these conditions suggest it should not be expected to have as high a level of manufacturing in GDP as low-income economies with lower land–labour ratios or higher education attainments. Nonetheless, the extremely low and, in a number of countries, declining share of manufacturing is cause for concern, because it denies African economies the potential dynamic productivity gains that a competitive manufacturing sector can create. Out of the UN LDC group of poor countries, those in Africa have an average manufacturing share in national income of close to half that for Asian countries in the same group.[12]

Most manufactured goods made in Africa come either from South Africa or North Africa (Algeria, Egypt, Libya, Morocco, Tunisia) with other sub-Saharan economies producing very little. The only really significant network links are in buyer-driven chains in textiles and clothing under the preferential access to the US market for sub-Saharan economies through AGOA.[13] The main sub-Saharan exporters of these products under AGOA in order of sales have been Lesotho, Madagascar, Kenya, Mauritius, Swaziland and South Africa with foreign investors (many from East Asia) attracted to take advantage of the low labour cost combined crucially with preferential access to the US market. This access has been critical in creating a competitive advantage for exporters since the global structure of the sectors means that oligopolistic buyers in the major consuming markets source (often though trading company intermediaries) globally. Economies of scale mean that suppliers with large-volume plants can price more competitively, and this favours producers who can work on the basis of large production runs (as do many Chinese firms). This makes it difficult for smaller-scale suppliers in much of sub-Saharan Africa to compete.[14]

A number of detailed studies of firms in different countries of sub-Saharan Africa have shed considerable light on the difficulties faced by manufacturing firms there.[15] In a number of activities, despite its low wages, sub-Saharan Africa is shown to be a high-cost location, since low wages are offset by low productivity and higher input costs than elsewhere. In garment production, for example, Bangladesh and Kenya have similar incomes per capita and by implication wages. A comparison of plants using a similar technology and scale of production shows costs in Kenya to be three times as high as in Bangladesh. Similarly, comparisons between Kenya and Thailand for food processing and textiles show total factor productivity to be three times higher in Thai firms. Within sub-Saharan Africa, differences are also significant with large firms in Mauritius (the leading manufactured export economy in the region outside South Africa) more able to export than similar firms in Ghana, since although wages were three times higher in Mauritius labour productivity was four times higher.

As well as relatively high wage costs per unit of output (due to low productivity) African firms are disadvantaged relative to firms in Asia by high costs for infrastructure like power, transport, telecommunications and water, as well as services like security, and accounting and in some countries the requirement to make unofficial payment to obtain permits or licences. Firms from sub-Saharan Africa suffer disproportionate losses from power outages, crime and losses of goods in shipment. Intermittent power supplies are usually addressed by firms by installing their own generators at much higher unit costs. Slow customs clearance and poor road and port infrastructure can delay export shipments and raise trade costs. Shortage of credit particularly for smaller firms is highlighted in many discussions. This appears less of an issue for larger firms, but the bulk of African manufacturing is small-scale and the progression rate for individual firms from the small to large category is low. There is strong evidence that the vast majority of manufactured exports from sub-Saharan Africa are from firms of more than 100 workers (which is large scale by African standards). Part of the reason for this may be scale economies at the plant level, so longer production runs are needed to reduce unit costs of operations. However, there is also a high fixed cost of exporting due to the need to invest in acquiring market information, establishing an alliance with a lead firm as part of a network and in complying with international technical and environmental standards. These high entry costs to export markets coupled with the difficulty of small firms to attract long-term credit are a partial explanation for the failure to expand into global networks. However, those African firms that do manage to break into export market tend to remain as exporters, so that past export success at the firm level is a good predictor of future sales.

Poor infrastructure is a critical factor in addition to the fact that transport costs to markets in North America and Europe tend to be higher from Africa than from other developing regions. This is of particular concern, because analyses of firm level data have concluded that in Africa firms tend to learn through exporting, as they are exposed to foreign markets and technologies rather than as found elsewhere the more efficient firms deciding to export.[16] Hence, this route to higher productivity and mastery of technology is blocked. The *learning by exporting* phenomenon for the region, but not elsewhere, may be due to the fact that the technology gap between sub-Saharan Africa and technology leader economies is greater than for other regions.

Some aspects of the investment climate relating to government bureaucracy and the legal framework have been held up as key factors holding back manufacturing in low-income environments like sub-Saharan Africa. As noted in relation to Table 4.1 whilst improvements in various indicators of the investment climate may be useful in their own right, they are unlikely to be the simple solution to the region's problems in terms of a low level of industrialisation. By some indicators, such as time to enforce contracts the African countries appear to have a less difficult operating environment than countries in South Asia or Brazil.

Global competitiveness and the China factor

In response to falling trade costs and greater international capital mobility China has emerged as a major exporter at both the labour-intensive low technology and at the knowledge-intensive, higher-technology end of the product spectrum. For the former goods, the large labour surplus in rural China has ensured a plentiful labour supply for the export sector at what has been a relatively constant real wage set by the low opportunity cost of rural labour. The consequence has been that in wide range of activities China has been the marginal supplier of low-technology goods to the world market and its productivity and wage level have set world prices for these goods. China's productivity has improved fast enough to offset increases in rural wages to ensure its competitiveness in labour-intensive goods. For higher-technology goods, export growth has been based on a combination of growing domestic capability and the activities of transnational firms in relocating segments of their production networks to China to take advantage of low labour costs.

China's strategy has been a pragmatic combination of a heavy reliance on foreign investment attracted by favourable tax status and other incentives to a range of Special Economic Zones within the country and attempts to raise the economy's technological capability by insisting that foreign investors transfer their technology to local joint venture and supplier firms, as well as conduct more of their applied R and D activity within China rather than in their headquarters or at production sites in other countries. Other initiatives, encouraged by local and city governments but essentially firm-driven, include the emergence of very large vertically integrated firms that bring together the different parts of the supply chain – designers, suppliers and manufacturers – under one large company with the different stages of the chain conducted in the same locality in China. These *supply chain cities* aim to take advantage of economies of scale, to minimise transaction costs and to foster more flexible and effective supply chain management. They represent the polar opposite of product fragmentation based on supply chain links between Chinese firms and suppliers in other countries. These supply chain cities have become important in some of the more traditional manufacturing activities like clothing and footwear.[17]

The speed, magnitude and range of China's export expansion have raised worries that competing countries were losing their overseas markets and that inflows of foreign investment that would have come to them were being diverted to China. This raised the issue of a 'competitive threat', where trade becomes a zero-sum game so one country gains at the expense of another; the loss of markets thus means a loss of jobs, incomes and growth. Hence, it became common at the start of this century for a serious policy discussion in many countries on whether the rapid growth of China was a 'threat' or an 'opportunity' for lower and middle-income countries.

In principle, it is possible to see both positive (complementary) and negative (competitive) aspects of the rise in global significance of China (and also but to a lesser degree India) for other economies. International trade theory based on resource endowment explanations of trade points to demand growth and the potential for specialisation along the lines of comparative advantage as the key factors. In static trade models this leads to a welfare improvement for both trading partners and a shift in relative prices and the distribution of factor income (see Box 4.3 for an analysis of this complementarity). Here all countries benefit from trade, since the loss of markets in one industry does not imply that a country as a whole is less competitive, as given factor mobility resources can shift from declining to expanding activities. The rise or fall of particular activities is irrelevant and the opening up of trade (or the entry of a new player) leads to a new equilibrium in which again all participants are better off. In this model, the pattern of specialisation does not matter, since there are no externalities and adjustment is instantaneous and costless.[18]

Box 4.3 Trade theory and China–Africa trade

Recent trends in world trade showing increased specialisation in trade between developing countries and China are illustrated in the emerging importance of China as a market for primary exports from Africa. China takes around 10 per cent of Africa's export (whilst India takes about 3 per cent). However, these exports are precisely those predicted by resource–endowment explanations of trade. Over 60 per cent of Africa's exports to China are oil and natural gas, with the bulk of the remainder being ores, metals and agricultural raw materials. In return, Africa imports manufactures from China, whilst Africa's manufactured exports to China are very small.[19] The implications of this trade pattern can be analysed using the standard concepts of international trade theory.

The trade between China and an African developing country can be analysed in a simple two-country, two-factor model taking land and labour as the two factors. China has the higher labour–land ratio, so in resource terms it is the labour-intensive, land-scarce economy, whilst the African country is the land-intensive, labour-scarce economy. Two goods are produced by both countries – a manufactured good s (shirts) and a primary good w (wheat). Both countries use the same technology but at each set of factor prices shirts always have a higher labour–land ratio than wheat, so they are the labour-intensive good and wheat is land-intensive. If there is no trade in each country relative prices (P*s*/P*w*) will be determined by the wage–land rental price (*w/r*). The wage–land rental price ratio will be lower in China than that in the African country, because in relative terms China is labour abundant and the African country is labour scarce. As the two goods are produced only with the two factors, relative factor prices determine relative product prices. This means that relative to wheat shirts will be cheaper in China than in the African country. Thus, using the superscripts *c* and *a* to denote the two countries, we have

$$(w/r)^c < (w/r)^a$$

and

$$(Ps/Pw)^c < (Ps/Pw)^a$$

This is the rationale for comparative advantage based on resource endowments. If trade now takes place for both parties to gain the relative trading price must settle somewhere within the range set by the two pre-trade relative prices (somewhere between $(Ps/Pw)^c$ and $(Ps/Pw)^a$.

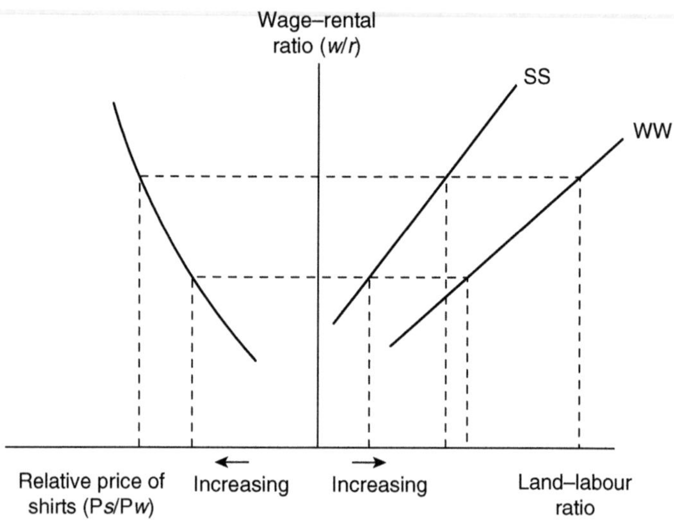

Figure 4.3 Relative prices and factor intensity.

Figure 4.3 illustrates the inter-relationships. The left hand side of the figure shows the land–labour input combinations for different wage–land rental ratios. SS refers to shirts and WW to wheat. Shirts are labour-intensive since at every wage–rental ratio production uses a lower land–labour ratio than does wheat. Similarly, wheat is land-intensive since at every wage–rental ratio it uses a higher land–labour ratio. The right-hand side of the figure shows the relative price of shirts to wheat rising with the wage–rental ratio.

Opening to trade has lowered $(Ps/Pw)^a$ – that is reduced the relative price of shirts in Africa and raised $(Ps/Pw)^c$ – that is raised the relative price of wheat in China. As we can see from Figure 4.3 a change in the relative price is matched by a change in the factor price ratio. This means that in the African country as P*s*/P*w* has fallen and so too does *w*/*r*, the wage–land rental ratio. This reduces the land–labour ratio in production of both goods. Similarly, in China as P*s*/P*w* rises, *w*/*r* rises also which raises the land–labour ratio in production.

The generalisation of this result is the *Stolper-Samuelson theorem* of international trade which states that opening to trade raises the return to the factor in which an economy is abundant. A similar analysis can be applied to the trade of China with a higher-income economy by replacing the two factors labour and land with two labour categories unskilled and skilled labour. Now for the developed country, abundant in skilled labour relative to China, the wage for skilled labour will be raised relative to that for unskilled labour.

Broadly speaking, the predictions of this simple model match recent trends in prices on the world market, where manufacturing prices have fallen relative to prices of primary commodities, as China has exported manufactures in return for the land-intensive primary resources that it requires. Within China, there has been a rise in wages relative to farm incomes. There is also evidence of a fall in the price of unskilled-labour-intensive manufactures relative to skilled-labour-intensive manufactures on the world market.

Source: Krugman and Obstfeld (2003, Chapter 4).

However, if the assumptions of standard trade models are relaxed to allow for greater realism, involving scale economies, differentiated products, uncertainty, externalities and agglomeration effects the outcome can be quite different. There remain benefits from specialisation and trade remains a non-zero sum game, but the realisation of the benefits from trade depends on the ability of each economy to create or attract competitive capabilities and to move into activities that offer the best opportunities for growth, technological development and external benefits. Here the structure of comparative advantage matters, since the composition of exports influences growth prospects (see Box 2.1).

Therefore, a more dynamic interpretation of comparative advantage based on the accumulation of skills, mastery of new technology and positive external benefits, lays greater stress on the potential for competitive effects. Where *first mover* advantages are important, it is possible that economies characterised by inflexibility in markets will lose out to competition from China either in their domestic markets (as domestic firms that compete with Chinese exports are forced to close) or in third country markets. This may be a particular concern where countries are blocked by Chinese competition from establishing production in sectors that have strong export demand prospects and potential for productivity growth. From this perspective, the entry of a large, efficient low-wage competitor like China into new export markets can involve significant adjustment costs for its competitors and, where rapid adjustment is not attained, can lead to welfare losses. Countries most vulnerable to Chinese competition are those with similar trade structures to China and those with inflexible markets and institutions, which make adjustment to greater competition more difficult.[20] The policy implication which has been drawn by many countries is the need to improve *competitiveness*, defined as the ability of the firms of an economy to sell goods competitively both domestically and on the world market. The package of measures designed to improve competitiveness covers both those that address the cost of doing business (the investment climate discussed before) and more specific policies designed to generate learning and improve training, skills and technological capacity. These latter measures are normally considered aspects of industrial policy to encourage manufacturing. The experience of the East Asian NIEs with these measures is discussed in Chapter 7.

China's impact on trade and investment

There are several alternative approaches to assessing the impact of competition from China on the trade, investment and growth prospects of other countries, which are illustrated in the following section. One uses macro-economic modelling techniques to capture the inter-relationships between countries. A second approach looks at trade data and seeks to describe the changes in market shares for various countries and links these with Chinese competition. A third approach uses econometric analysis to explain patterns in trade and investment data, whilst isolating a separate China effect.

For example, an authoritative modelling exercise at the World Bank poses the question of what are the implications for the rest of the world by 2020 of China and India (the *Asian Giants*) growing by 2 percentage points higher than in their baseline run of the model based on best estimate consensus forecasts at the time of the study (hence, this baseline does not incorporate the financial crises and global downturn of 2008). With this strong growth in the Giants, there are gainers and losers relative to the baseline scenario. The mechanism is the terms of trade effects, with lower prices for Chinese and Indian goods as their production expands and higher demand for natural resource imports both in the Giants and the world as a whole. The world as a whole (including sub-Saharan Africa) gains from the higher growth in the Giants, although the overall welfare effects are modest, but there are losers (relative to the baseline) who are principally the Southeast Asian economies (like the Philippines and Singapore whose trade structure overlaps significantly with China) and some South Asian economies.

At the manufacturing sector level, higher growth in the Giants and the consequent terms of trade effects lowers manufacturing output (relative to the baseline) in clothing and textiles in most countries and in electronics in Mexico and in Southeast Asia (apart from Singapore and Thailand). Over all of the neighbouring countries, the Philippines is the biggest loser, principally because of the high share of assembled electronic products in its exports, which suffer a large terms of trade loss due to Chinese competition. The exercise is an illustrative 'thought experiment' and the losses noted here are not absolute reductions in income, but reductions relative to the scenario where China and India grow at the baseline prediction. The overall message of the study is there is much to gain from high growth in the Giants and that losses in other countries need not be major if economies can compete through innovation and adjust flexibly in line with changes in relative world prices.[21]

The optimistic view of the generally positive impact of competition from China found in this and other economic modelling exercises are questioned in studies that examine trade data to describe how exports of manufactures from different regions are adapting to Chinese competition. These examine what has happened to the export market shares of countries for different manufactured goods in large markets like the United States and European Union and compare these with changes in China's share. How far countries are vulnerable to Chinese competition will also depend on how similar their structure of exports is to that of China. For example, the East Asian NIEs and China export many similar electronic products to the United States and the former have been losing market share there in these goods since the late 1990s.

Clearly, a fall in a country's market share and a rise in that of China need not imply that the latter causes the former, but there is often a plausible case for an association. Equally, as noted earlier, in economies that are characterised by flexibility a decline in one market need not be a problem if the resources involved can be shifted to produce for another market. The extent of a competitive threat can be illustrated by taking a country's manufactured exports and dividing them into various categories depending on how the country's share of the world market is changing relative to China. An approach along these lines conducts this exercise for the main Southeast Asian economies, as well as Korea and Taiwan. It identifies five categories:

1 *Direct threat*: where China gains world market share and the other country loses it;
2 *Partial threat*: where both gain, but China gains more;
3 *No threat*: where both gain world market share, but China's exports grow more slowly;
4 *Reverse threat*: where the country gains world market share and China loses it;
5 *Mutual withdrawal*: where both the country and China lose world market share.

Table 4.2 China threat in the world market: selected countries 2000 (% of total exports)

Category	*Singapore*	*Taiwan*	*Korea*	*Malaysia*	*Thailand*	*Indonesia*	*Philippines*
Direct threat	23.5	22.9	26.2	28.7	15.1	19.9	5.8
Partial threat	40.4	34.0	28.0	56.5	61.6	48.3	44.0
No threat	32.0	39.3	42.2	5.0	15.9	10.7	44.3
Reverse threat	3.4	3.4	2.9	6.3	6.1	8.9	3.6
Mutual withdrawal	0.7	0.4	0.7	3.5	1.3	12.2	2.4

Source: Lall and Albaladejo (2004, Table 6).

Taking the change over the 1990s selected East Asian countries' exports in 2000 can be classified into these five categories (see Table 4.2).

This analysis reveals how competitiveness of different countries, as measured by changes in their world market share, compares with that of China. All of the economies covered have a majority of their exports in categories in which China has an increasing world market share relative to the economies concerned (in other words, the categories of direct and partial threat are 50 per cent or more of total exports by value). For all but the Philippines and Thailand, the direct threat category (where China is gaining market share and the economy concerned is losing it) accounts for at least 20 per cent of exports and in the case of Malaysia nearly 30 per cent. The countries with the technologically most sophisticated export structures are those where proportionately the direct threat category is largest, reflecting the very fast growth of China's high-technology exports from a small base over this period. In all cases, the reverse threat category, where the country is gaining relative to China is small, at less than 10 per cent and in several instances less than 5 per cent.

This analysis gives the broad perspective on overlapping patterns of trade but it is at a fairly aggregate product level and cannot reveal the detailed nuances of shifting specialisation and competitiveness. A more disaggregate approach examining changes in market share at the 4-digit level of trade classification shows changes in import share in the US and Japanese markets for Chinese and Southeast Asian exports over 1995–2000. Whilst ASEAN exports grew over this period, for several of the important categories there was loss of market share, particularly in the United States; the important exception is the case of electrical machinery where market share continued to grow, but at a slower rate than for China (a partial threat in the previous terminology). This analysis shows that for all Southeast Asian economies, loss of market share has been greatest in the most specialised and therefore the most established lines of activity. This pattern holds across the full spectrum of products from the labour-intensive to high-technology end of the range.[22]

In Latin America as a whole, the similarity in export structure with China is much less than in East Asia, with the important exception of Mexico. Prior to

China's entry to the WTO at the end of 2001 most of Mexican exports had not been losing ground to China in the US market. However, since then competition from China has accelerated rapidly, so that by 2004 around 70 per cent of Mexican exports to the United States were losing market share relative to China (as compared with 11 per cent in 2002). In one sector in particular, television receivers, Mexico has experienced a dramatic loss. The only two major products in which Mexico has increased its market share relative to China are the automotive products, lorries and piston engines, where transport cost is important as the value-to-weight ratio is relatively low and Mexico's geographical proximity gives it a natural advantage. More concerning on a regional scale is that across Latin American economies there is a correlation between scale of loss of market share relative to China and the growth of world exports, so that Latin American economies, even where losses were relatively modest, were losing proportionately more in the fastest-growing products.[23]

Sub-Saharan Africa has not been a region from which there has been much growth in manufactured exports. Competitive pressure from China in third country markets has not been a major issue aside from the case of clothing and textiles under the trade preferences granted by the United States under the African Growth and Opportunities Act (AGOA). The Act allowed tariff-free entry for Southern African produced goods and for the lower-income participating countries (Kenya, Lesotho and Swaziland). The requirement for a 35 per cent minimum value-added component generated within the exporting country was waived to allow producers to import their materials from non-AGOA and non-US producers. This latter waiver allowed the purchase of low-cost textile inputs from China and Southeast Asia and had a big impact on competitiveness of African firms. In the small economies of Lesotho and Swaziland textile and clothing exports to the United States under AGOA came to dominate the manufacturing sector and in Lesotho at their peak were equivalent to half of total GDP. However, the ending of the quota system that governed international trade in clothing and textiles at the end of 2004 saw a major inflow of clothing and textiles from China into the United States and a consequent decline in the value of exports under AGOA. Total sales to the United States under AGOA fell by about 25 per cent from 2004 to 2006, with Mauritius and South Africa the countries suffering the largest declines in exports.[24] Detailed survey data from clothing firms in Kenya and Madagascar reveal how far behind African producers are in cost terms in comparison with firms in both China and India. Hence, without preferential market access, sales were bound to decline (see Table 4.3).

How far these falling market shares should be a cause for concern for the countries involved rests on what is assumed about the use of the resources that would have been allocated to producing the goods that are now supplied by China. As noted earlier, in economies that are characterised by flexibility a decline in one market need not be a problem if the resources involved can be shifted to produce at the same return and with the same future demand for another market. This is likely to be a strong assumption in some cases.

Finally, as a third approach, econometric analysis has been applied to test for competition between other countries and China in the context of foreign

Table 4.3 Clothing firms: comparative costs

Cost item	*Kenya*	*Madagascar*	*China*	*India*
Export finance (% per annum)	13	18	5.5	10.5
Materials (US$/sq ft)	3	4	1.5	2.5
Transport costs to US East coast (US$/item)	0.29	0.29	0.33	0.23
Labour productivity[a] (pieces/day)	18	16	25	21

Source: Compiled from data cited in Kaplinsky and Morris (2007).

Note

a with equivalent machines.

direct investment (FDI) flows. China has been a major recipient of foreign direct investment since the early 1990s. The question of whether these flows to China have been at the expense of other countries (a competitive effect) or whether they encourage further flows to others (a complementary effect) has been examined using econometric tests. There can be different types of foreign investment: to exploit natural resources in an economy (*resource seeking*), to serve the domestic market of the economy (*market seeking*) or to exploit low costs in an economy as part of a global production network (*efficiency seeking*). Competition between China and other locations for foreign investment is likely to be strongest for this latter category, based principally on competition in relation to wage costs. There may be some competition in relation to foreign investment to serve the domestic market (e.g. should a transnational firm invest in the large countries of China, Brazil or Nigeria?). However, given the geographical distance and differing income levels, this type of competition is likely to be relatively modest. In general, other things being equal, for geographical reasons, US firms tend to invest in Latin America in preference to China and Japanese and Korean firms to invest in China rather than in Latin America, for example. Competition over resource-based investment is likely to be even weaker as exploitable natural resources are specific to a limited number of locations.

Econometric analyses of this issue normally explain FDI to a country or region by a series of factors reflecting the characteristics of the countries concerned (like income level and income growth and aspects of policy) plus a variable measuring foreign investment to China. The sign and significance on the coefficient on this latter variable then determines whether or not there is a competitive (a significant negative sign) or a complementary (a significant positive sign) relationship. There are now a number of studies available and these generally show that at least at an aggregate level in terms of total FDI flows there is either no relationship (so investment to China is unrelated to investment elsewhere) or a positive relationship (so investment to China may stimulate investment elsewhere). The positive relation found in Southeast Asia, for example, can be interpreted as the spread of global networks through foreign investment, so that, for example, investment in an assembly plant in China is linked to investment in supplier firms in another country to provide inputs to the plant in China. Given what is known about the spread of networks in East Asia this result is highly plausible.

The network links between Latin America and China are weak because of the distance involved and consequently there is less evidence of a complementary relationship. In general, there is little evidence of a competitive relation, with China diverting foreign investment in manufacturing away from other countries, with the exception of one study that has found a negative relation for Mexico.[25] Again, this is plausible, as Mexico is the country in the region with the export structure that is closest to China and where networks links through foreign direct investment, principally from the United States, are important. However, most of these studies are at an aggregate level and there needs to be further work done to assess such relationships within different branches of manufacturing before conclusive judgements can be made on the impact of China on foreign investment inflows to other countries.

The potential negative impact of competition from China highlighted in these various empirical studies must be contrasted with the potential gains for countries that can succeed in expanding their exports to the large and growing Chinese market. The overall impact will depend on the balance of these effects, and as noted earlier, modelling work that tries to capture the range of possible effects generally comes to positive conclusions.

Manufacturing and the environment

The impact of manufacturing on the environment is an important negative side of the externality story discussed in Chapter 2. A key feature of industrialisation is that as it proceeds it creates rising pollution levels due both to the generation of the energy needed as well as the process of transforming materials and components into finished goods through production within manufacturing itself. The direct pollution impact of manufacturing is typically estimated using a pollution intensity measure showing toxic releases – whether effluent, atmospheric or solid – per dollar of output. These toxic substances will create water, air and land pollution with local consequences for health and various forms of production. In addition, with the accumulation of evidence, we now know that there are potentially highly serious global consequences from the emission of so-called greenhouse gases (principally carbon dioxide) as a result of their effects on temperature levels. Climate change in the form of rising global temperature is predicted to cause serious economic and social effects, through, for example, the impact of higher temperatures on land use, cropping patterns and sea level rise.

Empirical studies have examined the trends both in pollution intensity from manufacturing and pollution intensity relative to GDP as economies develop. There is clear evidence that as economies start to industrialise, emissions rise by both measures, with the rise in pollution relative to GDP greater, where economic growth is associated with a rising share of manufacturing. Some studies find evidence that beyond a certain income level emissions relative to GDP start to decline. The reasons are likely to be a shift in economic structure, as manufacturing becomes relatively less important and as more pollution-intensive manufacturing

Table 4.4 Classification of industries by pollution intensity

Ranking	*Air emissions*	*Water emissions*	*Metal emissions*	*Overall*
1	Iron and steel	Iron and steel	Nonferrous metals	Iron and steel
2	Nonferrous metals	Nonferrous metals	Iron and steel	Nonferrous metals
3	Non-metallic minerals	Pulp and paper	Industrial chemicals	Industrial chemicals
4	Petroleum coal products	Miscellaneous manufactures	Leather products	Petroleum refineries
5	Pulp and paper	Industrial chemicals	Pottery	Non-metallic minerals
6	Petroleum refining	Other chemicals	Metal products	Pulp and paper
7	Industrial chemicals	Beverages	Rubber products	Other chemicals
8	Other chemicals	Food products	Electrical products	Rubber products
9	Wood products	Rubber products	Machinery	Leather products
10	Glass products	Petroleum products	Non-metallic minerals	Metal products

Source: Cited in Copeland and Taylor (2004, Table 1).

activities grow more slowly than the average combined with the introduction of better environmental regulation and control as economies develop.[26]

What is clear is that pollution intensity varies considerably within manufacturing. US data on emissions have been used to define 'clean' and 'dirty' industries in relation to the environmental damage they cause. Table 4.4 sets out the ten dirtiest manufacturing sub-sectors by three separate types of emissions and overall. The important point is that globally as part of the industrialisation process ongoing in low- and middle-income countries, their relative share of dirty or pollution-intensive industries has increased and that of higher-income economies has declined. This is despite the fact that the developed world remains by far the greatest source of total global pollution and that some of the NIEs have made significant progress in reducing their own pollution intensity.[27] What remains in dispute and has been the subject of extensive testing is the cause of this shift in production of dirty industries to the developing world. It may be due to increasingly stringent environmental regulations in developed countries, what has been termed the *pollution haven* hypothesis as firms are forced to relocate to countries with less stringent regulations to avoid the cost of investing in pollution abatement. On the other hand, the shift may be due to rising wage and material costs in the higher-income countries of North America, Europe and Japan which mean that the NIEs have developed a comparative advantage in these pollution intensive or dirty activities.[28] The decline of the steel industry in the United Kingdom (and its growth in countries like Brazil and China) is an example of an industrial migration away from a high-income economy that preceded recent concerns over environmental impact.

Climate change and globalisation

Global problems with climate change driven by CO_2 emissions are recognised as a key policy challenge. Manufacturing firms – particularly in energy-intensive heavy industries are major energy users – and their energy demand impacts strongly on global emissions. It is now accepted that CO_2 emissions are contributing to rising global temperatures creating a serious negative externality, in the sense that energy-users are not being charged for the damage created by climate change. Without policy intervention, firms have no incentive to alter their behaviour in a less polluting and less carbon-intensive direction. A central policy question has become how to stimulate adaptation to a more energy-efficient growth path. Central to this adaptation will be ensuring that the price system reflects the full cost of emitting CO_2 into the atmosphere, which requires estimating the damage per marginal unit of gas emitted.[29] Incorporating these costs into pricing can be done in a trading system that gives permission to emit above a certain level only if a permit is purchased from someone who has reduced their own emissions thus keeping overall emissions within the specified ceiling. A price for carbon will thus emerge in this market and if the market works well, a system of emissions trading will be expected to minimise the cost of keeping within the ceiling. Alternatively, countries may opt for a national tax that approximates the social cost of carbon emissions.[30]

The details of what global regulatory regime will emerge in the coming years to address the carbon emissions issue are unclear. Precisely what low- and lower-middle-income countries, most of which are low emitters on a per capita basis, will be expected to do under such a regime is equally unclear. What is obvious is that they will not be major innovators in most of the frontier energy-saving technologies and will require access to these technologies at a price that reflects the marginal cost of transferring the technology, not the full cost of its development. At some point in the future, they may agree to join regional trading schemes so that permits to emit can be can exchanged between neighbouring countries or they may agree to harmonise their taxes on carbon on a regional basis.

In the short term, the expectation is that it will be developed higher emitter economies that will make the largest adjustments and either impose an emissions trading system with a tight overall ceiling or a relatively high carbon tax. There is general agreement that a significant emissions reduction will require a relatively high carbon tax of at least US$50–70/ton. This has raised the possibility that energy-intensive carbon emitting industries may relocate to middle-income countries (like the NIEs) where wages are lower, infrastructure is reasonably good and carbon taxes are either non-existent or still low. Empirical work has generally found that the impact of the stricter environmental regulations introduced in developed countries in the 1990s has had at most only a weak impact on foreign trade and foreign investment. However, a new carbon tax or a relatively tight trading permit regime may create a much stronger impact (see Box 4.4).

The discussion of the potential impact of environmental policies on trade is not confined to theoretical possibilities. The Stern Review on the economics of

Box 4.4 Environmental policy and foreign trade

The trade theory involved in analyzing this effect of a stricter environmental policy on the global location of industry can be illustrated simply in Figure 4.4, which uses the technique of relative demand and supply curves to show how pollution can impact on trade and production.

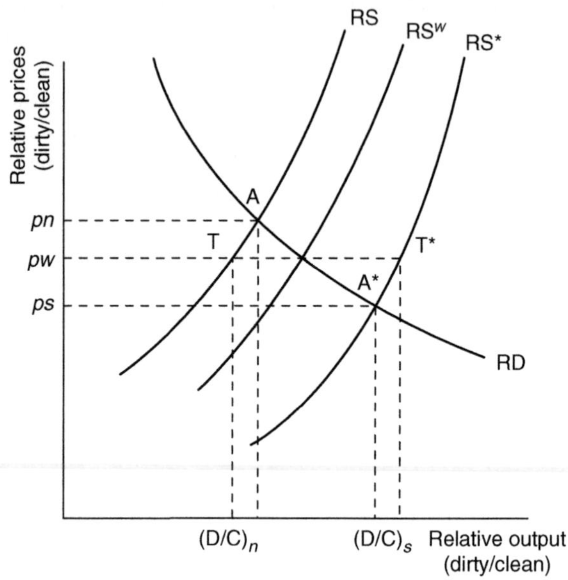

Figure 4.4 Pollution tax and international trade.

Two industries are included to reflect 'clean' (C) and 'dirty' (D) manufacturing activities and there are two countries a developed country (N) and a developing country (S). Unlike normal price–quantity relationships, which are in absolute terms (with a price of 10 demand is 100), the relationships are relative (so that, for example, if the relative price is 10/12 the relative quantity will be 100/80). For simplicity, countries N and S are assumed to be the same in every way and therefore have no reason to trade. This means they have the same relative supply (RS) and relative demand (RD) curves. Initially, they both have the same carbon tax. However, if it is removed in country S, this will shift the relative supply in country S outwards in comparison with that of country N since for every relative pre-tax price ratio (*p*) more of the polluting good D will be produced there. This new relative supply curve is shown as RS*. Since the curve has shifted, there will now be two different relative prices in the two countries (*pn* and *ps*) before any trade takes place (*autarky prices*).The existence of two different relative prices gives the possibility of gains from trade. The relative price of the dirty good D is now higher in N since its relative supply is lower than in country S. Conversely, the relative price of the clean good is higher in S since its relative supply is lower there.

With trade between the two countries, the world relative supply curve is RS^w and the relative world price is *pw*. Country N will import the dirty good from S, whilst S will import the clean good from N. It can be seen that in country N the production of the dirty good has contracted relative to the pre-trade case (A is greater than T), whilst the production of the dirty good has expanded in S (T* is greater than A*). Thus, trade has created a specialisation in a polluting activity in response to a change in environmental policy. Whether this will be a welfare improvement for country S cannot be answered until the increase in income is compared with the damage costs from pollution. N, however, has unambiguously gained from trade since its pollution has been reduced.

Source: Copeland and Taylor (2004).

climate change policy devotes a chapter to the issue of how far production of energy-intensive industries that would suffer most from a carbon tax might be diverted to countries without such a tax.[31] Table 4.5 lists the most energy intensive and thus vulnerable manufacturing branches in the United Kingdom, as far as possible taking direct and indirect energy use into account. It also shows the estimated percentage increase in cost created by a carbon tax of US$30/ton CO_2. The results show that whilst in a few cases there are substantial cost increases (defined as more than 4 per cent) these are only a minority. The manufacturing activities that appear most sensitive are petroleum products, iron and steel, chemicals, plastics, fibres and non-ferrous metals (particularly aluminium).

The conclusion of earlier research on the impact of environmental policy on trade and investment was that it has had only a modest impact. Since the cost of compliance with earlier policies appeared only a relatively small part of total costs, environmental considerations were not treated as a major factors in firms' decisions on where to produce. The Stern Review reached similar conclusions in relation to carbon taxes. However, this does not mean that the shift of pollution and energy-intensive manufacturing to developing countries that has occurred over the last 30 years will not continue. There are likely to be other factors at work in this process reflecting changing factor endowments and growing technological capability in the NIEs and these may be considerably more influential than environmental policy in causing the relocation of industries. This can also be reflected in Figure 4.4 where the relative supply curve in country S shifts not because of environmental policy, but because of an accumulation of factors in S (such as physical or human capital) that are used intensively in product D.

Table 4.5 Energy intensity of UK manufacturing and cost increase due to a carbon tax of US$30/ton CO_2

Sub-sector	*Energy as % of total cost*	*Percentage point change in variable cost*
Non-ferrous metals	1.32	2.36
Plastics	1.85	4.57
Textile finishing	1.95	3.34
Industrial gases	2.03	4.31
Man-made fibres	2.21	4.60
Sugar	2.37	3.20
Organic chemicals	2.38	6.27
Pulp, paper and paperboard	2.42	4.23
Inorganic chemicals	2.58	5.64
Iron and steel	2.69	7.02
Structural clay products	2.73	6.61
Fertilisers	4.61	13.31
Cement	9.00	5.00
Refined petroleum	23.44	72.83

Source: Stern (2007, Annex Table 11.A).

This factor accumulation has the same effect as the environmental policy in that both result in S specialising in the dirty product. This trend has occurred in the NIEs and appears set to continue.

The role for policy in this context is to manage the expansion of energy and pollution intensive industries in the NIEs and lower-income developing countries in a way that gradually introduces the use of more energy efficient technologies.

Conclusions

The era of globalisation has been characterised by falling costs of moving goods across national frontiers, lower policy-created barriers to trade and falling costs of doing business globally leading to growing trade and investment in manufactures. This growth of trade has been linked with the spread of global production networks dominated by lead firms, typically from the developed economies, but some firms from the NIEs are also beginning to play this role. There has been a tendency for concentration of new manufacturing centres in a relatively small number of countries, but nonetheless for many lower- and middle-income economies, manufactures are now an important part of their exports and hence their competitiveness in manufacturing has become a critical aspect of their economic prospects. Sub-Saharan Africa has particular problems that are holding back manufacturing there. If manufacturing is to play the role of leading sector, stimulating growth in other parts of the economy (as Chapter 2 suggests it might) it must be internationally competitive. This requires improvements in the investment climate – defined broadly to cover all aspects of investing and doing business – as well as improvement at the firm level, including learning to operate and adapt existing technology as well as applying new technologies. The following chapter takes up the issue of technology and technological capability as the basis for the competitiveness of firms. Finally, globalisation has been linked with the migration of polluting industries from developed economies to other parts of the world. In the past, this has had relatively little to do with tighter environmental policy, but high carbon taxes or tight emissions ceilings may contribute to this process in the future.

Further reading

Two alternative perspectives on globalisation – one generally positive and the other generally critical – are Wolf (2004) and Stiglitz (2002). Krugman and Obstfeld (2003) set out alternative theories of international trade and the predictions of these theories on globalisation. On the technical issue of trade costs, see some of the chapters in Brooks and Menon (2007). In relation to the debate on competitiveness, see the special issue of Oxford Review of Economic Policy (1996) and Lall (2001). On the impact of China and India on other countries, Winters and Yusuf (2007) give considerable detail, whilst Boardman (2007) focuses on the impact on sub-Saharan Africa. The Special Issue of World Development (2008) reports detailed country and regional studies on the consequences of trade competition from China. Stern (2007) is a definitive analysis of the economics of climate change and globalisation.

5 Technology and industrialisation

There is widespread agreement that technical change – the introduction of new ways of producing things – and the technology that lies behind it are critical for growth and industrialisation. However, technology remains something of black box, frequently discussed but not always fully understood. Technology can be defined broadly as both the processes for transforming inputs into outputs and the knowledge and skills necessary for their application. Hence, it has both a codified and reproducible form as designs and blueprints that can be transferred in goods or in documents and a more intangible dimension which exists in the minds of those who apply it. Both dimensions are needed for the successful application of technology in industrialisation. This chapter commences with a discussion of some key concepts related to technology. It then addresses the role of technology in developing countries, before turning to case-study examples of technological development.

Some technology concepts

To use or master technology requires a set of skills and information (*technological capabilities*) many of which will be specific to individual enterprises. *Technological development* at a national level is the accumulation of these capabilities within enterprises in the country. Technological capabilities can be categorised in different ways; a common distinction is between:

- *Production capability* (covering aspects of product design, production management and operations, repair and maintenance, input sourcing and marketing).
- *Investment capability* (covering project selection, design and engineering).
- *Invention capability* (covering capacity to adapt, improve and develop technology).

Within these different categories there will be different levels of mastery between knowledge of how things work (*know-how*) and of the key concepts that lie behind production processes (*know-why*). Once invention moves beyond basic adaptation, this latter understanding will become critical.

Technological effort in the creation and application of technology can be conducted at different levels. A simple categorisation distinguishes between:

- Basic research into the theory underlying production processes.
- The commercial application of new theory in new products or processes.
- Improvements in existing products or processes in the light of local conditions.
- Copying of existing products or processes new to a firm.

Basic research requires significant investment in Research and Development (R and D) and expenditure under this heading is one of the direct measures used to gauge the extent of technological effort across countries. However, it will typically fail to reflect the efforts made at the other levels noted here and in addition the needs of different industries for R and D expenditure will also vary with the potential for improvement through innovation. Within the R and D category some expenditure will be for pure research, some for applied commercially oriented activity and some will be of a military nature not intended to have commercial implications. Table 5.1 gives a classification of industries in terms of R and D intensity based on the share of R and D in the value of gross output.

Types of industrial organisation also influence the type of technological effort required. In the early twentieth century, much of industry was organised on a mass production basis in the manner pioneered by the Ford Motor Company. This form of production was characterised by long production runs, single products and a continuous flow of production based on the synchronisation of all activity. The key production technological capability was the ability to synchronise production of a single product. This system (often termed *Fordism*) spread to

Table 5.1 R and D-intensity of manufacturing industries

Category	*R and D-intensity (%)*	*Industries*
High technology	Above 5.0% of output value	Aircraft, pharmaceuticals, office and computing equipment; television and communication equipment; medical and precision equipment.
Medium–high technology	1.5–5.0% of output value	Electrical machinery, motor vehicles, chemicals, railway and other transport equipment; other machinery and equipment.
Medium–low technology	0.7–1.5% of output value	Coke, refined petroleum products, rubber and plastics, non-metallic mineral products, ships and boats, basic metals, fabricated metal products.
Low technology	Below 0.7% of output value	Manufacturing not classified elsewhere, wood and paper products, printing, food, beverages, tobacco, textiles, clothing, leather, footwear.

Source: Cited in UNCTAD (2005, Table 111.3).

well beyond the automobile sector and was the dominant form of large-scale industrial activity until the 1980s. The challenge to this system of mass production came initially from developments in another automobile firm Toyota, who pioneered the *just-in-time* flexible system. This was based on a multi- rather than a single-product system and was organised in production cells rather than in a single assembly line. The aim was to minimise stocks (hence the name *just-in-time*) whilst at the same time introducing flexibility by focussing on production of small batches of goods. This system copied initially by other car producers spread to other sectors, where long runs of standardised products are not required.

A new range of technological capabilities is required for this more flexible form of production, since flexibility requires the ability to adjust the number of workers in a cell, rapid changeover in the tasks of machines and multi-skilled workers. The spread of global production networks in many industries means that batch production can be spread across countries and high levels of managerial capacity will be required in co-ordinating these inter-country flows. In addition, the application of micro-processor computer technology has created further flexibility with a continuous product redefinition and improvement.[1] An example of this redefinition in recent years is the innovation, introduced initially by Canon, of converting a camera into a computer with a lens. Companies in high-technology sectors require the capability to manage this continuous innovation by introducing the results of applied research into production. Many of these more demanding capabilities will be beyond firms in lower-income economies, but not beyond many firms in the NIEs.

Technological efforts at a national level have been analysed using alternative concepts of *national innovation systems* or *domestic knowledge systems*. These are similar with the latter a broader version of the former. Both are intended to stress that the application of technology and the creation of knowledge are the result of wide ranging social processes and not simply the result of expenditure on narrowly focused research, education and skills training. A knowledge system, for example, is a set of institutional arrangements within a country and between the country and other countries, which generates technological effort and the creation of knowledge.[2] In simple schematic terms, a knowledge system can be represented as in Figure 5.1.

Three blocks are shown – suppliers of knowledge (including public research and training institutes, research and training departments of firms, universities, standards institutes, and foreign licensors), users of knowledge (including enterprises and the government as an economic agent) and intermediary institutions that bridge the gap between the first two (including technology and business support services, business associations, public extension services, financial institutions and venture capitalists). The links between all three operate through a variety of mechanisms from the very formal such as research contracts or technology licensing, to inter-firm linkages through supply contracts and to the very informal such as the movement of skilled workers between firms and product copying. All of these mechanisms operate within an institutional environment

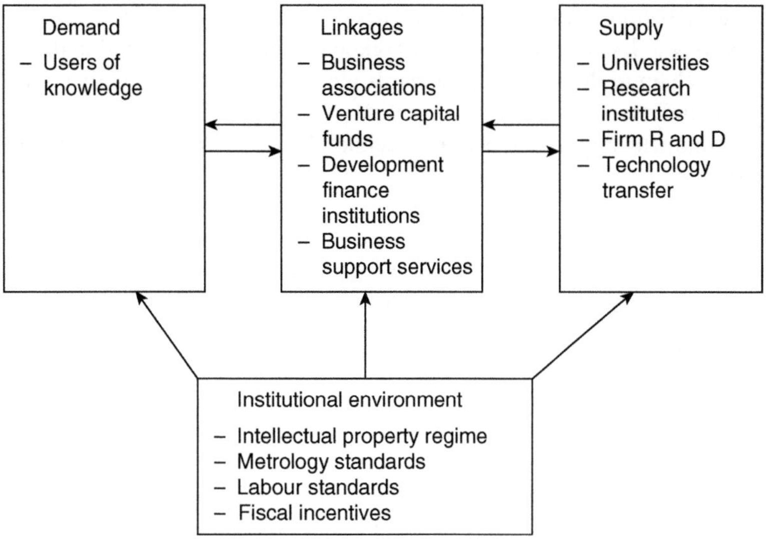

Figure 5.1 Domestic knowledge system.

Source: Adapted from UNCTAD (2006) Chart 52.

based on legislation, principally on patenting, formal technical standards, and fiscal incentives for research and training. How far knowledge creation will be turned into innovation and product development will be determined by the institutional environment and the degree of entrepreneurship of investors who see the opportunities created by new knowledge.

Low and lower-middle-income economies are followers as far as international technological progress is concerned. They are not creators of original knowledge and rely on imports of technology developed elsewhere for the key aspects of their technological development. However, this follower status is potentially an advantage since these countries can avoid the cost of developing new technologies themselves and can industrialise on the basis of foreign technology that is new to them, but not to the world. This is the main mechanism of the *catch-up growth* referred to in Chapter 1.

Follower economies have various channels through which they can access foreign technology:

- Direct licensing from the innovating firm, which requires regular royalty payments and normally excludes modification and adaptation during the duration of the licensing agreement.
- Foreign direct investment through which the innovating firm exploits its technology advantage in the local market; in some cases, this may lead to knowledge gains for local firms either through imitation by local competitors (*a technology spillover*) or through information on supply processes provided by the foreign investor to local suppliers (*a technology linkage*).

- Participation in global production networks whereby lead firms provide technology to local firms to produce component products required in the production chain to the technical standards required for internationally competitive production.
- Equipment imports embodying technology that is new to the country with training on how it is to be used.

Sustained industrial success requires firms to move beyond importation of foreign technology to its adaptation and modification. Success here requires a supportive *national innovation system*, with a well-educated labour force, applied research bodies of an international standard, entrepreneurial attitudes amongst the owners and managers of enterprises and a supportive institutional environment. Japan and the East Asian NIEs grew rapidly on the basis of high levels of technology imports and their subsequent adaptation and modification in the final 40 years of the twentieth century (see Box 5.1 for a formal model that illustrates this process). However, as yet the capacity for technological development in most low- and lower-middle-income economies remains no more than modest.

Two different views of the high-growth experience of East Asian economies in the latter part of the twentieth century (*the East Asian Miracle*) have been put forward. One sees it as due primarily to the accumulation of physical and human capital with high investment rates and high education enrolment. The other argues that *assimilation* – in the sense of the importation, adaptation and improvement of foreign technology – although accompanied by high investment, was the driving force. In this latter view, the entrepreneurship of the private sector in seeing the profitable opportunities created by the availability of foreign technology, accompanied and helped by supportive government policies, plays a key role.

Box 5.1 East Asian NIEs and the assimilation of technology

A relatively simple model based on a change in industrial structure and the application of new technology in the modern sector of the economy explains the stylised facts of development in Korea and Taiwan from the 1960s onwards. The model has two sectors: a craft sector c using traditional technology and a modern sector m using new foreign technology. Both produce the same output at a given price (e.g. set on the world market). The cost of capital is also the same for both sectors. Capital per unit of output (K/Q) is the same in both sectors, while factor proportions defined as a capital–labour ratio (K/L) are fixed within each sector, but differ between them. Output per unit of labour (Q/L) is higher in the modern sector, so K/L must be higher in the modern sector as well. The modern sector requires skilled or educated labour that is not needed in craft production.

If at the start of a development spurt both sectors co-exist, at any time output per unit of labour (Q/L) for the economy as a whole will be a weighted average of labour productivity in the two sectors with weights determined by employment shares. If Q/L is rewritten as a then as labour is more productive in the modern sector $a_m > a_c$, where the subscripts m and c refer to modern and craft.

For the whole economy, the overall level of labour productivity (Q/L) will be

$$Q/L = a_m.L_m/L + a_c.L_c/L \tag{5.1}$$

where L_m and L_c are the labour force in the craft and modern sector, respectively.

Since $L_c/L = (1 - L_m/L)$, Equation 5.1 can be rewritten as

$$Q/L = a_m.L_m/L + a_c.(1 - L_m/L)$$

which reduces to

$$Q/L = a_c + (a_m - a_c).(L_m/L) \tag{5.2}$$

Hence, from Equation 5.2, total labour productivity in the economy rises as the share of modern sector employment (L_m/L) rises. The overall capital–labour ratio (K/L) will also rise with the increased employment share of the modern sector.

The difference in the wage per worker is the only price difference between the two sectors, but as workers in the modern sector are more skilled or educated there is a skill premium to be paid to employ them. Thus, if w is the wage in the craft sector, the wage in the modern sector is $g.w$, where g is greater than 1.0 and reflects this premium. However, in the model, g is never so large as to offset the productivity advantage of modern technology.

Since the price of output and the capital per unit of output is the same in both sectors, the difference in cost between them is a function of the difference in labour productivity and the wage rate. The difference in cost ΔC between the sectors is

$$\Delta C = w.(1/a_c - g.1/a_m) \tag{5.3}$$

where $1/a_c$ and $1/a_m$ give labour per unit of output (L/Q) in the craft and modern sectors, respectively. Thus, the first term in Equation 5.3 gives wage cost per unit of output in c and the second term gives this cost in m.

The higher profitability in the modern sector (as labour productivity a_m is sufficiently high not to be offset by the wage premium g) provides investors with an incentive to shift investment from the craft to the modern sector (i.e. from c to m). In the model, the degree to which this happens (for a given cost advantage) depends on the strength of entrepreneurial drive denoted by *e*.

Writing the change in capital in the two sectors as ΔK_m and ΔK_c, respectively, the relative shift in capital between the two sectors $\Delta\ (K_m/K_c)$, is given as

$$\Delta(K_m/K_c) = e.w.(1/a_c - g.1/a_m) \qquad (5.4)$$

The higher is *e* the more will investors respond to the cost advantage in the modern sector in the economy created by the use of new foreign technology.

Since capital in the craft sector (K_c) is total capital (K) minus that in the modern sector (K_m)

$K_c = K.(1 - K_m/K)$ and by substituting in Equation 5.4 gives

$$\Delta\ (K_m/K) = e.w.(1/a_c - g.1/a_m).(1 - K_m/K) \qquad (5.5)$$

Equation 5.5 shows that the share of capital in the modern sector depends positively on entrepreneurial drive (e), the wage in the craft sector (w) and the productivity advantage of new technology ($a_m > a_c$) and negatively on the skill premium (g).

The parallel with East Asian experience is that a fast-growing modern sector based on highly productive imported technology (creating a high a_m) grew rapidly through the activities of a highly entrepreneurial investor class (with a high e) backed by strongly supportive government policies, including heavy investment in education and skills training (keeping down g).

The investment rate and the share of profits in income over this period were very high, but this was an enabling factor not the driving force in the growth process. In the model, capital share in national income grows most rapidly when output and capital per worker are growing rapidly in response to the shift of resources to the modern sector. This latter point is explained in the model by further manipulation. The share of capital in total income is a weighted average of its share in the two sectors. Setting the product price at unity, the share of capital in income will be $(1 - w.1/a_c)$ in the craft sector and $(1 - gw.1/a_m)$ in the modern sector. Weighting these by the income shares of the two sectors gives

$$Sk = (1 - w.1/a_c).Q_c/Q + (1 - gw.1/a_m)Q_m/Q \qquad (5.6)$$

where Sk is the capital share, Q is total income and Q_c and Q_m are incomes in the two sectors, respectively. Qc is $Q\ (1 - Qm/Q)$; hence, we have $Qc/Q = (1 - Qm/Q)$. Substituting into Equation 5.6 gives

$$Sk = (1 - w.1/a_c).(1 - Q_m/Q) + (1 - gw.1/a_m)Q_m/Q$$

or

$$Sk = 1(1 - Q_m/Q) - w.1/a_c.(1 - Q_m/Q) + (1 - gw.1/a_m)Q_m/Q$$

which reduces to

$$Sk = (1 - w.1/a_c) + w.1/a_c.Q_m/Q - gw.1/a_m.Q_m/Q$$

or

$$Sk = (1 - w.1/a_c) + w.(1/a_c. - g.1/a_m.).Q_m/Q \tag{5.7}$$

The term before Q_m/Q in Equation 5.7 determines the cost advantage of the modern over the craft sector and from Equation 5.4 determines the shift of capital towards the modern sector for a given *e*. Hence, the share of capital in income *Sk* will be high whenever the shift of resources towards the modern sector is high. *Sk* is not driving the process of growth but simply reflecting the structural change in the economy. In turn, structural change is determined by the opportunities created by imported technology and the drive or entrepreneurial spirits of investors.

Source: Nelson and Pack (1999).

Measuring technological effort and capability

Several alternative measures of the concepts of technological effort and capability are available using similar data in slightly different combinations. All agree that the group of developing (essentially low- and lower-middle-income) countries continues to lag far behind richer economies in terms of both the creation of knowledge and its application in new technology. Most measures are based on a combination of input and output indicators. As noted earlier the most basic input indicator is expenditure on R and D, usually as a share of national income. This measure is inadequate, since it does not capture adaptation to technology which in these countries is more important than research into new technology or products; in many countries it also contains a large military component. Commonly used output measures of knowledge creation are the number of patents (usually those registered in the United States) relative to population and the number of published scientific journal articles relative to population. Again, these latter measures are biased against the type of technology activities developing countries are likely to pursue. For comparison, Table 5.2 gives a summary of this data for groups of countries. The gap between the developed countries and developing

Table 5.2 Indicators of technological effort

	Least developed countries[b]	*Other developing countries*	*Developed countries*
R and D as % of GDP 2003	0.2	0.3	2.2
Scientists per million of population	176	662	7144
Scientific publications: total 1990–99	7788	479,837	4,841,762
Patents[a]: total 1991–2004	20	14,824	1,823019

Source: UNCTAD (2006, Table 36).

Notes
a Patents for inventions.
b Country groupings follow the UN definitions.

countries is very wide and is particularly wide for the poorest and most vulnerable least developing countries.

A composite index combining measures of technological activity and skills developed for UNCTAD World Investment Report confirms the technological gap between poor and rich countries (see Box 5.2 for details). The index covers 117 countries which are grouped into high, medium and low categories on their scores by the index in 2001. The top group contains three of East Asian NIEs – Taiwan, Korea and Singapore – plus Argentina which scores relatively high due to its good education and skill system not because of its technological performance. The medium group contains the other NIEs and China. The low group contains most of sub-Saharan Africa (the exceptions are South Africa and Mauritius which are in the medium group) and all of South Asia. India is included in the low group, despite its large scientific base, because this is scaled by population, as is Indonesia for the same reason. Latin American economies (with the exception of Argentina in the high and Paraguay in the low groups) are included in the medium category. Scores on the index are linked closely with income per capita, although there are outliers. China and India both have higher scores on the index than would be predicted by their income and Hong Kong has a lower score than predicted. Broadly, these deviations can be interpreted as reflecting government policy on supporting innovation and education within these economies, as well as their industrial structure.

Box 5.2 Innovation Capability Index

A number of different indicators of technological and innovation capability are available.[3] All have variables for innovation inputs (R and D spending or personnel), outputs (patents nationally or in the United States, scientific journal articles) and human capital (various measures of education enrolment). Some also include infrastructure variables (such as power availability or Internet connections). The UNCTAD index is a simple average of two sub-indices: a Technological Activity Index and a Human Capital index. Each sub-index is in turn based on three components. The components for the Technological Activity Index are not weighted, while those for Human Capital are weighted to reflect the role of higher education in innovation.

Components of the Innovation Capability Index

Indices	*Components*	*Weights*
Technological Activity Sub-Index	R and D personnel US patents Scientific publications all per million of population	All components have equal weight
Human Capital Sub-Index	Literacy rate as % of population	Weight of 0.17
	Secondary enrolment as % of age group	Weight of 0.33
	Tertiary enrolment as % of age group	Weight of 0.5
Innovation Capability Index	Technological Activity Sub-Index Human Capital Sub-Index	Both Sub-Indices have equal weight

Using 2001 data the top five economies by this index are the Scandinavian countries plus the United States and as expected developed economies dominate in the group of the top 20 countries as measured by the index. An indication of the range of performance by this indicator is given by the un-weighted averages for different regions of the world.

Un-weighted Regional Averages by the Innovation Capability Index

Region	*1995*	*2001*
Developed economies (excluding new EU members)	0.876	0.869
New EU members	0.665	0.707
Southeast Europe	0.602	0.584
Southeast and East Asia	0.492	0.518
West Asia and North Africa	0.348	0.361
Latin America and the Caribbean	0.375	0.360
South Asia	0.223	0.215
Sub-Saharan Africa	0.157	0.160

Between 1995 and 2001 Latin America, and the Caribbean fell slightly behind West Asia and North Africa and that in four regions (including Latin America and the Caribbean and South Asia) the index fell between these years. Sub-Saharan Africa and South Asia are the weakest performing developing regions with an index score less than half that of the East and Southeast Asian economies (which are predominantly NIEs). In sub-Saharan Africa and South Asia, technological and innovation capability remains low.

Source: UNCTAD (2005).

Firms and technical change

Many firm and plant level studies have been conducted on manufacturing firms in developed economies and the NIEs, as well as a smaller number of such studies in low and lower-middle-income economies. Several broad conclusions have been drawn from these studies.

- First, it is clear that technical change can occur in a variety of ways and that investment in formal R and D, whilst critical for breakthroughs in product or process technology, is not the only mechanism. Incremental change based on wide range of minor adaptations and modifications to products and processes has been important in many instances. However, the emergence of these adaptations and modifications is rarely costless and is normally based on conscious investment to achieve these improvements. This means that the concept of technical change as an automatic process of *learning by doing* is rarely applicable.
- Second, location specific factors have been important in the transmission of knowledge about new technologies (*technology spillovers*). This has been documented in the case of major breakthroughs in developed economies where the proximity of firms to the source of an innovation (whether other firms with research departments, public research institutes or universities) appears to have been important in stimulating further breakthroughs or in fostering imitation. The movement of highly skilled professionals between firms has been an important part of this process. The clustering of high-technology firms in science parks and in specific locations (of which Silicon Valley in California is the best-known example) is explicable in these terms.
- Third, in developing countries, foreign sources of technology have been critical in cases of successful technological development. Foreign technology has been provided through not just licensing agreements, but also through new equipment imports, the movement of individuals between firms and foreign direct investment, where the investor brings new technology to an economy. In addition, it is often argued that foreign firms raise the technology level of local firms through externalities created by technology spillovers. The mechanisms involved will vary with the relationship between the foreign and local firms. If the latter are suppliers of inputs to the foreign firm, as part of a supply contract, the local firm may be given product specifications and information on process technology to ensure that its production meets the standards required by the foreign firm. Alternatively, if the local firm is a competitor, through the pressure of competition, it may be forced to seek out comparable technology to that used by the foreign firm. The empirical significance of these effects has been the subject of considerable debate and testing (see Box 5.3).
- Finally, most plant level studies in lower-income economies (e.g. in much of sub-Saharan Africa) find manufacturing firms operating relatively old technology and frequently not operating this technology at maximum efficiency.

Technological capability at the different levels of production, investment and invention capability identified earlier is generally deemed very low, although in these economies there is normally a range of efficiency between existing plants. This is partly a function of the relative lack of attractiveness of this region for foreign investors.

Foreign technology and the development of electronics in East Asia

The emergence of East Asian firms from the NIEs as major producers and exporters of electronics is widely attributed to the successful, gradual and incremental assimilation and application of foreign technology, described as a 'hard slog' as opposed to a more dramatic 'leapfrog'.[4] Historically, firms moved from the assembly of relatively simple products (such as transistor radios and non-colour televisions) in the 1960s to the manufacture of these and other newer products (such as colour televisions, calculators and digital watches) in the 1970s. The 1980s saw a major move forward into the technologically more sophisticated product range of professional electronics (including computers and related equipment, video recorders, camcorders and semi-conductors), with the 1990s and beyond seeing a further shift to information technology systems with some NIE firms (such as Samsung of Korea and Acer of Taiwan) becoming world leaders. Over the period, the competitive advantages of NIE firms changed from the low-cost, relatively skilled labour necessary for assembly in the 1960s to the precision engineering skills necessary for more technologically advanced production in the 1990s and more recently to the R and D capability necessary for production at the world technology frontier. There has also been production relocation within the East Asian region with successful firms from the NIEs relocating labour-intensive elements of production to lower-cost locations initially to the second-tier NIEs (Thailand, Indonesia and the Philippines) and more recently to China and Vietnam.

The acquisition of the foreign technology required for this process came through a variety of channels. In addition to foreign investment in local subsidiaries and joint ventures, contacts with buyers in high-income economies, who provided both product design and the assistance of their engineers, was important. Links to export markets were developed through sub-contracting under *Own Equipment Manufacture*, whereby local firms provided goods to the design specification of international buyers. The buyers then marketed the product under their own brand name. Often, this involved the foreign buyers in the selection of equipment and in the training of engineers and technicians. As technological capability developed in the NIE firms, a system of *Own Design Manufacture* evolved in which the firms themselves captured a higher share of value added by undertaking the bulk of product design to the general specification provided by the buyer and still marketed under the buyer's brand name. Ultimate mastery of foreign technology allowed NIE firms to sell under their own brand names under *Own Brand Manufacture*, although even currently this process remains more limited than the other forms of exporting. Once this stage is reached in a sector where technical change is rapid, such as electronics, a firm's own R and D activity, rather than reliance on foreign technology imports, becomes critical for continued competitiveness.

The Samsung and Acer cases are well known, but success along this path has been achieved by many smaller, less-well-known NIE firms such as RJP (Hong Kong) and Microelectronics Technology Inc (Taiwan).[5] RJP, a consumer electronics manufacture was founded from family savings in 1971 with only nine employees. This number had risen to over 3,200 by the early 1990s, located mostly in mainland China. In its early years, RJP learnt to manufacture a range of products, such as pocket and desktop diaries, pagers and electronic games, through assistance from the US retailer J.C.Penney. By the mid-1980s, RJP controlled the design of most of its key products and in 1986, it launched its own brand of electronic diaries and pocket computers, followed in 1993 by its own palmtop computer. Microelectronics Technology Inc was a supplier of integrated circuits for telecommunications founded in 1983 by Taiwanese engineers previously employed in the United States. Early work was under the design specification of US manufacturers, who provided parts for US television satellite broadcasters; however, by the early 1990s, around half of output was under the company's own brand.

Technology spillovers from foreign direct investment

It is now well documented that across all countries and sectors, relative to their local counterparts foreign-owned firms tend to be larger, have higher productivity, pay higher wages, export more and use technology that is closer to the international best practice. This raises the possibility that foreign investment can be a transmission mechanism for raising the technological level of an economy. A long-standing argument relating to the presence of foreign-owned firms is that they bring new technology to an economy, which will benefit not only the foreign firms themselves and their local partners, but also both local competitor and supplier firms. Any such effect will be an externality provided the originator foreign firm does not receive an equivalent monetary payment for this technology spillover from the local firms involved.

In principle, there are four broad mechanisms through which foreign investment embodying new technology and management practices could impact on firms not directly owned by the foreign investor. The first three relate to effects on firms within the same industry as the foreign investor (*intra-industry effects*) and the fourth to supplier or user firms in another industry (*inter-industry effects*).

- The first mechanism is imitation (sometimes referred to as *reverse engineering*). Here, local firms operating as competitors to the foreign investor copy product design, management practices and with more difficulty, process technology. Clearly, the scope for imitation will vary with the nature of the product and the complexity of the technology involved, with simpler manufactures and processes offering greater scope. Managerial and organisational innovation is likely to be the easiest to copy. The transfer of Japanese organisational techniques (the *just-in-time* system that minimises the holding of stocks and work-in-progress and allows flexibility in production in response to changes in orders) to relatively unlikely operating environments in sub-Saharan Africa is an illustration of this.[6]

- The second and related mechanism for spillover is skill acquisition through labour mobility. Here, workers employed and possibly trained by the foreign investor move to work with local firms taking their skills and knowledge of new technology with them. This effect is more than merely a labour training externality as mentioned in Chapter 2, where benefits to the local firms are savings in training cost. The tacit knowledge of the workers involved allows the local firm to copy the new technology and without this labour mobility imitation may not be effective. The clustering pattern found in many industries, whereby firms making similar products tend to concentrate in a fairly narrow geographic location, is partly explicable in these terms, as mobile workers can take their knowledge and skills to different employers.
- The third mechanism is industry competition, whereby the arrival of new foreign firms operating best practice technologies, puts pressure on competing local firms. This competitive pressure may force local firms to either use existing technology more efficiently or to seek out new technology at or close to the international frontier. Competition may also stimulate exports with local firms faced with a shrinking domestic market imitating the export marketing strategies of foreign-owned firms. Exporting in turn may expose local firms to best practice technology.
- Finally, the fourth mechanism relates to local supplier and user firms. Here, the foreign investor may provide technological information to its input supplier firms to ensure that their inputs meet the quality standards required by the foreign firms. Even insisting on higher quality without providing technical assistance may induce local supplier firms to seek out new technology. Similarly, foreign firms producing goods that are themselves inputs used by local firms downstream may provide technical information to their customers on how their goods can be used most effectively. Where the respective information flows are not charged for (or are charged at below their full cost) an external benefit will be created in the form of a technology spillover.[7]

Empirical evidence on technology spillovers

These mechanisms are widely understood, but they do not rule out the possibility of negative effects, if local firms lose market share due to competition from foreign firms and consequently, either operate at higher unit cost or downgrade their production to technologically simpler segments of the market. Despite extensive empirical work, the evidence on the quantitative significance of technological spillovers from foreign investment is often ambiguous. There are two broad approaches in this literature, one based on detailed firm-level case studies of the links between foreign-owned and local firms and the other involving econometric analysis of data across sub-sectors of manufacturing or of data from individual firms over time (see Box 5.3). There is some evidence of positive spillovers from

Box 5.3 Testing for technological spillovers from foreign investment

Early empirical efforts in this direction were hampered by lack of sufficiently detailed data often relying on aggregate sub-sector level data at a point in time. More recently, the availability of detailed time series data on individual firms has allowed the application of panel data techniques. These are seen as the best-practice means of testing for spillovers, since they allow the analysis of productivity over time and allow firm or sub-sector specific factors that do not vary over time to be incorporated in the regression model. The problem with cross-sectional analysis at a point in time is that these time-variant factors are not allowed for adequately. Thus, foreign firms may be strongly represented in high-productivity sectors without themselves creating the high productivity.

The simplest regression approach is to explain productivity (either simple labour or total factor productivity) by a number of standard variables plus a measure of foreign firm presence (such as share in employment or sales in a sub-sector). If the analysis finds a positive and significant coefficient on the variable for foreign presence this is taken as evidence that domestic firms operating in the same sub-sector have benefited from the presence of foreign firms (through horizontal spillovers) with higher productivity used as a proxy for a move to a higher technological level.

Sjoholm (1999) examines spillovers in Indonesian manufacturing in the 1980s in an example of a detailed cross-sectional approach. Its main interest is that it makes a clear effort to understand the market and firm-specific circumstances under which positive effects from foreign investment are likely to arise. Data are utilised on all manufacturing establishments with more than 20 workers at two points in time. The basic model that is tested explains labour productivity in each firm (i), in each sub-sector (j) in a production function framework, which can be represented as

$$Yij = Aij.(Lij^{\alpha}.Kij^{\beta}) \tag{5.8}$$

where Y is value added, L is labour input, K is capital input, α and β are the elasticities of value added in relation to labour and capital, respectively, and A is a parameter reflecting the increase in output not due to additional labour and capital inputs (i.e. total factor productivity).

Aij will be due to a number exogenous factors (Zij) plus it is hypothesised the presence of foreign investment in sector j (Fj). Thus:

$$Aij = f(Zij, Fj^{p}) \tag{5.9}$$

where f represents a function of, and p is the elasticity of value added with the respect to foreign firm presence.

Equation 5.8 can be converted to per worker terms through division by total labour L to give

$$yij = Aij.(kij^{\beta}) \quad (5.10)$$

where y is value-added per worker, and k is capital per worker.

By inserting Aij from Equation 5.9, Equation 5.10 can be rewritten as

$$yij = (Zij, Fj^{p})(kij^{\beta}) \quad (5.11)$$

Testing Equation 5.11 requires a model that makes value added a function of the capital–labour ratio $(ki)j$, foreign firm presence in a sector (Fj) and other variables included in Z reflecting a firm's characteristics (like scale of production, or age of firm). Hence, the regression model estimated is

$$yij = aij + b.kij + c.Fj + d\,Zij + eij \quad (5.12)$$

where aij is a constant and eij is the error term. The test for spillovers is the sign and significance of the coefficient c on Fj, with positive spillovers requiring a significant and positive coefficient. A positive and significant c implies that allowing for other things, the greater is foreign firm presence in terms of market or employment share the higher will be labour productivity.

Equation 5.12 is used by Sjoholm (1999) to test for level effects; in other words whether, controlling for other factors, the level of value added per worker is affected by the presence of competing foreign firms in the same sector. Here, the only Z variable used is the scale of output in firm i relative to the sector average.

In addition, a dynamic version looks at whether the growth of value added in firms is affected by foreign presence. This test requires differentiating Equation 5.12, so that

$$Y^{1}ij = A^{1}ij + \alpha L^{1}ij + \beta K^{1}ij \quad (5.13)$$

where Y^{1}, A^{1}, L^{1} *and* K^{1} are growth of value added, total factor productivity, labour and capital, respectively.

From Equation 5.9 growth of total factor productivity is determined foreign presence and other factors. If the other factors in Z do not change, they can be excluded in an analysis of rates of change, so combining Equations 5.13 and 5.9 we have

$$Y^{1}ij = \acute{\alpha}ij + \alpha L^{1}ij + \beta K^{1}ij + \rho F^{1}j + \varepsilon ij \quad (5.14)$$

where $\acute{\alpha}$ is a constant picking up excluded factors, $F^{1}j$ reflects the change in foreign presence by sector and εij is an error term.

In the practical application of this test, a slightly different version of Equation 5.13 is estimated that includes the level of foreign presence not its change (*Fj* rather than F^1j) and in the absence of data on the growth of capital stock (K^1ij), the share of investment in gross output is used. Foreign firm presence is measured as the share of foreign firms in sector output.

Equations 5.12 and 5.13 are estimated both for all firms and for segments of the sample. To test for the impact of domestic market structure and absorptive capacity the sample is split into firms operating in high- and low-competition sectors and into firms with high and low technology gaps. For the level estimates, results are unambiguous that foreign firm presence is associated with higher labour productivity across all firms. In the dynamic specification, however, a positive and significant impact on growth of value added from foreign firm presence is only found in the high-competition segment of the sample and in firms where the technology

Tests for spillovers: Indonesia

Dependent variable	*Level estimation: VA per worker 1991 (yij)*	*Dynamic estimation: growth of VA 1980–91 (Y^1ij)*			
	All firms	Low competition	High competition	Low technology gap	High technology gap
Constant (*aij*, *ἀij*)	8.01***	30.43***	31.43***	28.03***	34.22***
Investment per worker (*kij*)	0.02***				
Investment share in output (proxy for K^1ij)		0.16***	0.10**	0.21***	0.09**
Growth in employment (L^1ij)		1.17***	1.04***	1.13***	1.01***
Scale (*Zij*)	0.09***				
Foreign firm presence (*Fj*)	0.03***	0.34	0.70***	0.34	0.68***
Adjusted R^2	0.15	0.41	0.34	0.39	0.31
Number of observations	15,760	816	2076	1279	1542

Source: Sjoholm (1999, Tables 4, 5 and 6).

Notes
***coefficient significant at 1% level; **coefficient significant at 5% level.

gap is high. This is illustrated next with the signs on *Fj*, which are always positive, but are only significant in the growth estimation for the high-competition and high-technology gap equations.

The finding that a high-technology gap is needed for local firms to benefit from spillovers contradicts earlier results and is rationalised in terms of a varying (i.e. non-linear) relationship at different levels of the gap and with different impacts in different parts of manufacturing. There may be some sub-sectors, with relatively complex technologies at which a large gap is too large to bridge. In others, with simpler technology, a large gap may be easier to overcome, so that imitation and demonstration effects on local firms from foreign investors stimulate technology upgrading. The results illustrate the difficulty of generalising about technology spillovers given the fact that no universal effect on productivity growth is found.

Source: Sjoholm (1999).

case studies principally through the backward linkages between foreign firms and their local input suppliers. The difficulty here is in generalising from a limited number of cases. In principle, consistent econometric evidence should allow generalisations to be made. However, the evidence is far from consistent with results ranging from support for positive spillovers, to no evidence of any impact, to negative effects. Again econometric results from firm or plant level studies imply that spillovers may be more common between a firm and its suppliers (*vertical spillovers*) than that between a firm and its competitors (*horizontal spillovers*).[8]

Part of the ambiguity in results is that in theory there is no reason why all domestic firms will benefit equally in terms of improvements in technology due to foreign investment. In particular, the ability of a firm to respond to the potential information on technology arising from the foreign firm presence (its *absorptive capacity*) and the gap between the existing technology of a local firm and the best practice international frontier (the *technology gap*) will have a major influence on whether in the presence of foreign firms the local firm can upgrade its technology. Common hypotheses are that other things being equal, the greater is absorptive capacity (often approximated empirically by a firm's R and D expenditure relative to sales) and the smaller is the technology gap (often approximated by the difference in productivity between the local firm and the foreign firm) the more a local firm will be able to benefit from a technology spillover. In other words, to benefit from spillovers local firms cannot be too far behind the international technology frontier and must have a minimum level of in-house expertise.

Detailed firm level empirical studies have found support for the view that only firms with a 'moderate' technology gap and a minimum level of technological capability will benefit. However, this result is not universal with other studies finding the reverse, that a larger technology gap gives greater scope for catch-up.[9]

This particular empirical disagreement remains unresolved. The general conclusion is that in principle, spillovers from foreign investment may occur, but empirical testing does not suggest that they are always either important or positive. This conclusion should perhaps not be surprising since technology spillovers from foreign investment represent the failure of foreign investors to capture all of the extra income or rents created by their technological advantages over local firms. Foreign investors themselves can be expected to try to minimise such losses and may be helped in many instances by patent protection and intellectual property legislation, the effectiveness of which will vary between countries and sectors.

What can governments do?

The market for technology, whether embodied in equipment or disembodied in the form of designs, blueprints or the knowledge of individuals, is one that is highly imperfect, and hence, in terms of conventional economic theory, there is a strong case for government intervention. Three features of *market failure* in the technology market are normally identified.

- The first is *lack of information*. Technology suppliers cannot reveal the full information on their product, since this would undermine the basis for trade and buyers cannot assess the full value of technology, since they do not have the information to do so. This can limit the size of the market for technology.
- The second feature of the technology market is that suppliers typically have *market power* incurred by their technological lead over other suppliers and by intellectual property protection (normally through patents). This market power allows technology suppliers to set prices often well above the marginal cost of supplying the technology, which generates monopoly profits. These profits are the return on investment in product development, but the higher the price charged for technology the lower is the benefit to users.
- The third feature is the fundamental one that technology creation frequently creates *external benefits*; that is extra income for others apart from the technology innovator, for which the innovator is not compensated. These are the technology spillovers discussed earlier, which can arise from both foreign and domestic innovation. Furthermore, spillovers are not restricted to innovation. Firms who import new technology, rather than create it themselves can also generate spillovers, as others watch and learn from their example. In the presence of positive externalities from an activity, it is well known that if left to itself the market will produce a sub-optimal level of output. This can be illustrated in a simple competitive demand and supply framework, which ignores the first two features of the technology market and focuses solely on externalities (see Figure 5.2).

The demand line DD represents the demand for technology from users and reflects the benefits they expect to obtain. The supply line SS reflects cost of supply (and ignores the monopoly power of suppliers). If left to itself the market

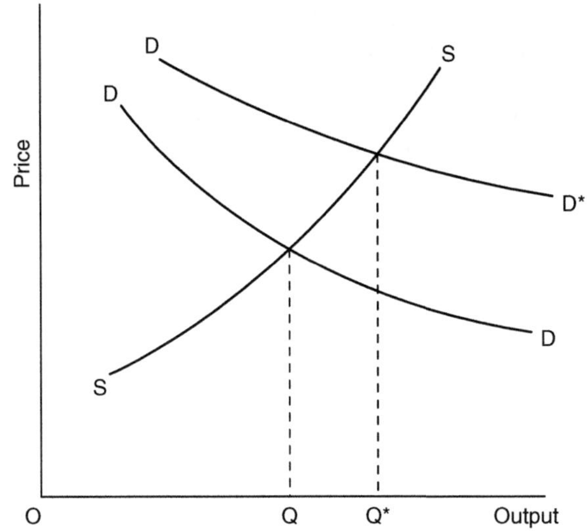

Figure 5.2 Market failure in technology.

will settle at an 'output' for technology of OQ, where private demand and supply are in balance. Introducing external benefits means that the true or social value of the technology is given by a higher demand line DD* where the difference (DD* – DD) reflects the external benefit at each output level. In social terms, the preferred output level is OQ* and the market will under-supply technology by OQ* – OQ. Market failure means that, in theory, government intervention can improve the situation. For example, in Figure 5.2, a subsidy equal to the difference between DD* and DD at output OQ* would equate private and social benefits from technology and give a signal to the market to produce the optimal output.

Technology policy can be and has been implemented in differing ways by different countries; however, broadly speaking, it can be seen as aiming to address the three features of market failure identified in the preceding section – external benefits, market power by suppliers and lack of information by users.

Product and process innovation requires investment in R and D and it is widely argued that competitive economies need to have high levels of R and D relative to GDP. A focus on R and D is relevant to both developed economies at the technology frontier and for middle-income NIEs moving into technologically sophisticated activities.[10] Other low- and lower-middle-income economies lag far behind by this indicator and for them pure innovation is much less important than minor modification to products and processes. However, simple comparisons of the success of technology policy using this indicator require qualification. As noted earlier, different sectors have very different needs for R and D and hence very different levels of such expenditure. The structure of an economy will therefore have an influence on the overall R and D to GDP ratio. For OECD economies, the range of R and D investment expenditure ranges from a low of 0.2 per cent of value-added in publishing and printing to 25 per cent in pharmaceuticals and 27 per cent in office and computing machinery.[11] Clearly, economies with a specialisation in these latter two sectors will have high R and D-to-GDP ratios, whilst economies for which low-research-intensity sectors are important will have low ratios. Similarly, some countries may have low ratios, because overall investment to GDP is low, not simply because there is low R and D activity. Meaningful country comparisons need to allow for these aspects.

Nonetheless, the level of R and D is treated as an important parameter and because of the externality argument, most countries provide public funds to support R and D. This is either directly through grants or subsidised loans for R and D or indirectly though tax credits (so that R and D expenditure is used to offset tax liability) or through the provision of subsidised technical and scientific higher education. In addition, public sector research institutes and universities can collaborate with enterprises in developing research that can be commercialised in new products or processes. Support for science and technology through subsidies and non-financial measures is compatible with WTO regulations provided it does not infringe patents or copyrights and provided it is not offered on a selective or discriminatory basis to favoured firms. Venture capital (short-term funds for investment in new technology areas) has been provided by many governments, including those in the NIEs. A key to the success of such funds in the NIEs is likely to be the development of an effective stock market in which shares in the new companies can be traded. Such trading allows the venture capital funds to be invested for only a short period, until the new high-technology companies are profitable. By selling the shares held in the new company, the initial venture capital funds are increased and can be reinvested in other new companies.[12]

Governments of several of the NIEs have made considerable efforts in the support of local R and D with Singapore frequently seen as a world leader in the development of a technology-intensive, knowledge economy. It has been particularly successful in attracting international firms to use Singapore as a base for their own R and D work, which is then disseminated globally to their affiliates and partners. This success has been achieved through a combination of generous subsidies to R and D expenditure made within the country and the provision of a world-class technology infrastructure of institutes and universities. Surveys of executives of multinational companies reveal consistently that the decision to locate R and D activity in their Singapore operations rather than the normal pattern of using their home country headquarters was taken principally because of this government support.[13] However, no other NIEs can match Singapore's achievements and in lower-income, developing economies, R and D levels remain low, and technical change is principally through minor changes and incremental modification (see Table 5.2).

Mindful of the imbalance in information and market power in the technology market in the past some governments have tried to operate controls over the import of technology, both in terms of disseminating information on technical alternatives and in screening proposed licensing deals. Japan of the 1950s provides a clear case of intervention to restrict duplication of technology imports to reduce negotiated royalty payments to foreign suppliers and to conserve foreign exchange used for this purpose. This form of intervention also played a role in other countries during the import substitution era (including the NIEs Korea, Taiwan and Mexico), but it has been criticised for blocking access to a key source of technology by dissuading foreign firms from licensing their technology. Even the highly efficient Japanese bureaucracy was known to make errors in this area, and was reported to have turned down one of Sony's initial requests to import technology on the grounds that the then small company was not yet ready to assimilate the relatively sophisticated foreign technology it wished to purchase.[14] Other less-well-informed bureaucracies are likely to have made far greater errors.

Intellectual property protection

Today thinking is very different with considerable efforts made to encourage, not to restrict, technology licensing. Central to these is the introduction in importing countries of *intellectual property rights* (IPR) legislation. This gives patent protection to registered innovations, which cannot then be copied and applied in a commercial operation for the duration of the patent (typically 20 years), although in return innovators have to divulge technical details of the innovation. Hence, some firms prefer not to take out patents to avoid this divulging of information. Firms from NIEs are making increasing use of patents, although in most other developing economies patent levels are low.

In 1994, the Agreement on Trade Related Aspects of Intellectual Property Rights (TRIPS) became obligatory for all WTO member countries. It obliges members to grant patents for inventions in all fields of technology provided they are novel and have a commercial application, regardless of the place of invention. Exceptions are allowed in sensitive areas, such as through *compulsory licensing* where a government allows production without the consent of the patent holder or *parallel importation* where imports come from a source abroad where the patent has lapsed. These flexibilities are applied principally in the field of public health allowing access to cheaper non-patented generic pharmaceuticals.

The TRIPS agreement strengthens the market power of technologically innovative firms, partly by protecting their technology, but also by allowing them to use patents as a tool to block innovation by competitors. However, by raising the cost of imitation and easing the enforcement of technology contracts in local markets, it may also make innovating firms more willing to license their technology and to undertake foreign investment utilising this technology. This potential benefit to developing country technology importers must be set against barriers to imitation created by patenting. At present, it is not clear empirically which of these effects is greater outside the NIEs. Amongst the NIEs, where technological capability is higher and scientific infrastructure more developed, IPR legislation is more likely to be an important force for technological innovation, although even here its impact is likely to vary between manufacturing activities, with chemicals, pharmaceutical and parts of electronics more likely to use patents (rather than trade secrecy) to protect their innovations. However, the patent legislation required of countries after 1994 on its own is unlikely to be a major driver of technology policy, and it will only work if accompanied by broader efforts to improve the knowledge and education base of an economy and to provide the financial incentives for investment in technological improvement.

Distortions in technology choice

An aspect of policy that received much negative comment in the past relates to the impact of controls on prices in factor markets leading the selection of technologies that do not use intensively the factors which are abundant in a country. This distortion in technology choice, it was argued, encouraged producers to follow an *anti-comparative advantage* path. For example, a policy to fix the exchange rate of local to foreign currency at an artificially high rate (e.g. to keep down inflation) will reduce the price of imported capital equipment in local currency. With an exchange rate of 10 pesos/US$ a piece of equipment costing US$0.1 million, will cost a million pesos. However, if the exchange rate is controlled at an artificially high level of 7.5 pesos/US$ (so the peso is overvalued by 25 per cent) the same equipment will cost 0.75 million pesos (or 25 per cent less). The cost of equipment will also be reduced if it is purchased with a trade credit whose interest rate is controlled at a rate that is below the real cost of using the funds (which is their opportunity cost elsewhere in the economy). In a number of countries in the past macro-economic policy included both fixed and overvalued exchange rates and controlled interest rates, which combined to reduce capital costs below what they would otherwise have been.

Similarly, in relation to urban labour employed in manufacturing in some countries minimum wage legislation protected those in work and maintained their wages at levels well above what could be earned in agriculture or the informal sector. These twin effects of reductions in the cost of capital and increases in the cost of labour, it was argued, created an incentive to shift technology choice in a capital-intensive direction and thus weakened the impact of a given growth of output on job creation. It also worked to alter technology in a direction contrary to the resource endowments of low-income countries (which are typically capital-scarce and labour-abundant). Comparisons between East Asia and Latin America sometimes suggest that the latter followed a labour-intensive production path and the former one with greater capital-intensity, which partially explains the greater success of East Asian NIEs in developing manufactured exports.[15]

Although the discussion was conducted most frequently in terms of a simple capital–labour choice, it applies whenever the price of a resource to a firm is reduced or raised due to taxes, subsidies or controls. Steel, for example, can be produced with a coal-based blast-furnace technology or an electricity-intensive, natural-gas-based direct reduction technology. Any measure that influences the price of coal, electricity or natural gas may impact on the relative attractiveness of the two alternatives. For example, an implicit subsidy to natural gas (where it is sold domestically at a price below its export price for example) can shift choice in favour of the direct reduction technology. Alternatively, a subsidy to coal will favour the blast furnace. Box 5.4 illustrates the technology choice issue.

Not all of the capital-intensity noted in the manufacturing sectors of the NIEs and other developing countries can legitimately be put down to distortions in factor markets and their impact on technology. In some sub-sectors of manufacturing the scope for major technology choice may be limited; for example, in

Box 5.4 Technology choice

The argument relating to choice of technology is illustrated diagrammatically using the concept of a production isoquant, which is a curve showing the different combinations of resources (here capital and labour) that can be used to produce a given output. In Figure 5.3, this curve is drawn as convex to the origin due to the assumption of diminishing returns, so if one factor is reduced, proportionately more of the other is needed to keep output constant (*a rising marginal rate of substitution*). Here, three alternative technologies are illustrated – *A*, *B* and *C* – and the respective isoquants – *aa*, *bb* and *cc* – show how once a technology is installed there is only a modest scope for substituting one factor for another. Where firms operate the technology inefficiently they will only be able to substitute along the higher isoquants aa^1, bb^1 *and* cc^1 where the same output as produced by the lower isoquants now requires higher inputs of both factors.

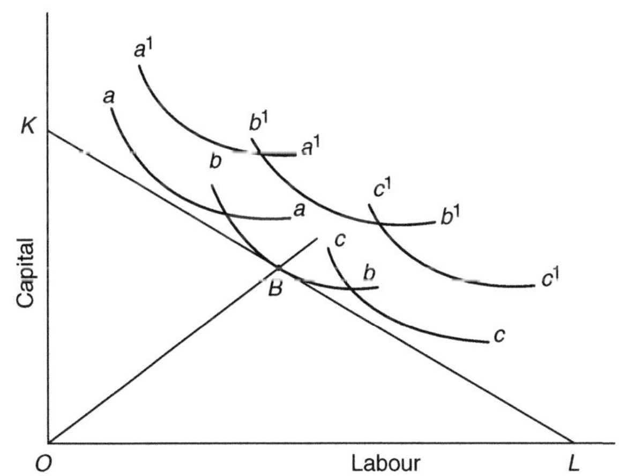

Figure 5.3 Technology choice.

The key decision on which technology to apply will be determined by cost, which in turn will depend on the relative prices of capital and labour. The factor price line (or *wage–rental* ratio) shows the combinations of each factor that can be purchased for a given expenditure. Hence, if all of the budget goes on labour, *OL* will be purchased, and if all goes on capital *OK* will be purchased. The slope of *KL* therefore gives the relative factor price ratio. A cost-minimising firm will select the lowest possible isoquant for a given factor price line and assuming it is available this will be the isoquant that is a tangent to the price line. As drawn in Figure 5.3, it is technology *B* which minimises cost.

Factor distortions enter the analysis if they alter the factor price ratio (e.g. an interest rate subsidy lowers the relative cost of capital so that all of the given expenditure now buys OK^1). This is illustrated in Figure 5.4. If the wage for labour remains unchanged, this will shift the price line to K^1L and as drawn the more capital-intensive technology A now becomes the more cost-effective technology than B and production shifts in a capital-intensive direction.

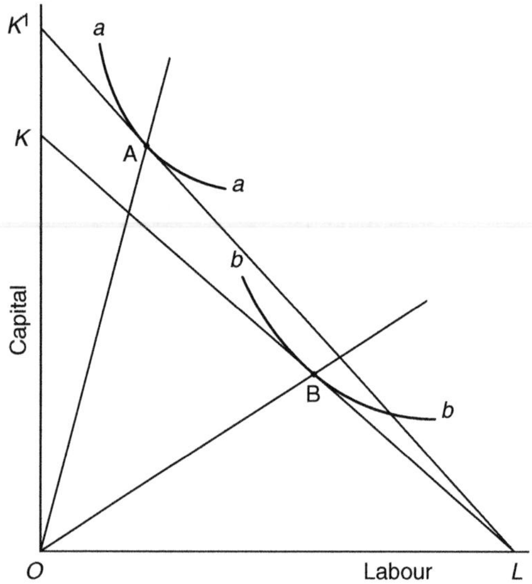

Figure 5.4 Distortion in technology choice.

textiles, a variety of looms (such as automatic, semi-automatic and water jet looms) may be available, but whilst there will be differences in the employment–capital assets ratio between these three the differences will not be dramatic.[16] Similarly in steel the choice between blast furnace and direct-reduction technology is principally in terms of energy source not in terms of high or low employment–capital ratios. Hence, in some sub-sectors, once a decision to expand output is taken the scope for technology choice in a labour or capital-intensive direction may be limited. Nonetheless, the output expansion decision itself could be influenced by the impact of controls in factor or product markets, so that capital-intensive sectors (like steel) are favoured by an interest rate subsidy relative to more labour-intensive sectors (like textiles).

Recent thinking has argued for a removal of factor market controls like interest rate ceilings or wage controls and they are now much less common. Removal of such controls is now a starting point for discussions of economic reform and freeing factor market prices is one of the key macro-economic recommendations of investment climate studies. Hence, in this area, technology policy links with wider discussions of economic reform.

National firms and technological capability

As noted before, a typical sequence for successful manufacturing firms in the NIEs is the import of foreign technology and its gradual adaptation and modification. Firms themselves are the drivers of this process sometimes using imported licensed technology and sometimes in partnership with foreign investors. Most NIE governments have attempted to influence this process by offering finance, sometimes at subsidised rates, tax credits for R and D, an improved technology infrastructure in research institutes and universities and the supply of a skilled and educated workforce. Some governments have gone further and actively championed the development of large national firms. Support for large diversified firms (the *chaebol*) in Korea in the 1970s and 1980s is the clearest example of this, but the strategy has been followed elsewhere, including recently in China. These large national firms, it is hoped, will have the capacity and finance to master existing and develop new technology. Success has been mixed, however, and the range of experience can be illustrated with reference to the aerospace industry. Airplane technology is relatively sophisticated but some NIEs with a large defence industry have attempted to break into this market. Brazil and Indonesia provide contrasting experiences (see Box 5.5).

Box 5.5 Aerospace industry in Brazil and Indonesia

Aircraft production is characterised by long lead times in production, large economies of scale and the need for high R and D. It is dominated by a few firms globally, although both the Brazilian and Indonesian governments gave significant support to their own national firms in an attempt to break into the segment of this market for smaller planes. In Brazil, national security concerns were used by the military to support the creation of a national aircraft producer *Empresa Brasileira de Aeronautica* (EMBRAER) in 1969. This government-owned company used foreign licensing of technology to build up production of small turbo-prop commuter planes. It received financial support in the form of low-cost loans both for itself and its customers and benefited from export subsidies. Despite initial export success in the 1980s, by the early 1990s the company was partly privatised with the government retaining only a very small stake and foreign investment limited to 40 per cent. Production shifted in the 1990s to smaller civilian regional jet aircraft with exports taking around 95 per cent of sales. By 2000, the company had become the second largest regional jet-maker in the world. Government support both in the early days and more recently was critical. R and D initiatives were outsourced to a specialist publicly funded aeronautical research centre and export subsidies in lower interest rates were offered by state banks (these were subject to a challenge at the WTO by the government of Canada in support of Bombardier, the Canadian rival firm to EMBRAER).

The origin of the aircraft industry in Indonesia was quite different, being the idea of one individual Bacharuddin Jusuf Habibie, who had worked in the industry in Germany. He argued that a national industry was essential in an island-based country like Indonesia and would have a range of technology spillovers. A national public sector company *Industri Pesawat Terbang Nusantara* (*IPTN*) was formed in 1976 with Habibie as its President, and it focused initially on assembly of helicopters and turbo-prop aircraft under licence. Despite the mastery of some complex technology, sales were not strong and were mostly on an uncompetitive basis to the armed forces and government-owned companies. The company could not survive financially without government budgetary support. The Asian Financial Crisis of 1997 and the subsequent resort to IMF loans meant that a decision was taken to end all subsidies to aircraft manufacture and without these *IPTN* was not viable. Aircraft assembly was run down with a new focus on operating as a sub-contractor for the supply of parts to aerospace and other activities.

A key difference in these experiences lies in the degree of exposure to market forces and international competition with EMBRAER experiencing significant productivity gains through learning based on competition. It also benefited from a strong network of local suppliers. On the other hand, given its protected environment *IPTN* was managed in such a way as to give pre-eminence to technology development over financial and marketing issues. Furthermore, because of the weaker technological base in Indonesia, as compared with Brazil, a network of competitive suppliers and sub-contractors did not emerge. The overall experience indicates, however, that global success in high-technology activities, like aerospace, is possible if a market niche can be found and if sound government support is available.

Source: Goldstein (2002).

Conclusions

Follower economies have the potential advantage that industrialisation based on imported and adapted technology is possible. The application of foreign technology and its later modification and improvement in the NIEs and earlier in Japan shows what can be achieved. However, success in technological development is very mixed. In general, low- and lower-middle-income economies operate well behind the global technology frontier using old technology, often inefficiently. Firms in these economies conduct little R and D. Foreign direct investment offers one route to technology upgrading, but its impact in terms of technology spillovers is uneven, and foreign firms will not invest in new technology areas in such economies without an improvement in their skills and education bases. Government technology policy has been important in some of the NIEs, but both the resources and the capacity for intervention in this area are limited in poor countries. However, there is widespread agreement that improvement in technological capability is essential for successful industrialisation.

Further reading

On technology concepts Lall (1992) and (2001) and UNCTAD (2006) have useful data and many references to studies on these issues. Gorg and Greenaway (2004) is a useful survey of the impact of technology spillovers from foreign investors. Studies of technological capability in East Asia are in Yusuf (2003).

6 Small-scale industry

Sink or seedbed?

Industrialisation is not just about large-scale production involving long production runs, large investments and many workers. In all countries, small firms are important, particularly as a source of employment, and in low-income countries, some of these are very small (*micro-* or *cottage* firms) with production taking place in the home of the households running the business. However, what is small in one country is not necessarily small in the context of another. In lower-income countries, small firms tend to be classed as those employing 20 persons or less, although in some countries the small classification goes up to 50 or even 100 workers. Micro-firms tend to be those with five workers or less although again some studies class them as up to nine workers. Large firms are generally defined as those with more than 100 workers, although in some richer countries a firm with 100 workers would be treated as no more than medium scale. Very small firms are also often informal in that they are not registered with the relevant government authorities and as registration would mean they become part of the tax net, they often have little incentive to do so.

Small firms can play dual roles in most economies, but this is particularly so in poor countries. On the one hand, they can offer a means of additional, possibly only subsistence, income. This is their *sink* role in absorbing unemployed or underemployed labour. On the other hand, under the right conditions, they can offer the opportunity for risk-taking and new investment to create jobs and raise incomes. This is their role as a *seed bed* for new entrepreneurship. Which role predominates will vary with country circumstances. This chapter discusses these alternative roles. It begins with a brief discussion of trends over time, and then focuses on very small micro-firms, which often represent the sink element. The issue of relative efficiency and economies of scale is also addressed, before a discussion of small but technologically dynamic firms, which have become important sources of entrepreneurship in some sectors in developed economies. The strategy of cluster development, discussed in Chapter 2, is also addressed here. Although it is not the exclusive preserve of small firms, as a means of compensating for any disadvantage of small size arguably they have more to gain from location in clusters than do large firms.

International trends

In poorer countries, very small firms dominate in terms of numbers of manufacturing enterprises, as well as in manufacturing employment. However, it is a well-established pattern that as national income per head rises the share of micro- and household enterprises in employment and output declines. The unusual feature of developing countries is that both very small (below 20 workers) and fairly large firms (over 100 workers) have a significant share of output and employment, whilst firms in between are under-represented as compared with the size distribution of firms in developed economies. This phenomenon of the 'missing middle' is usually interpreted as due to the difficulties small firms have in a developing country environment of growing and thus graduating to a medium-size category.

It is dangerous to generalise too much about small-scale manufacturing given the diversity of experience. However, a few stylised facts about representative small firms and how they change as economies evolve and average per capita income rises can be identified. At very low income levels (e.g. in much of sub-Saharan Africa today) the typical small firm is likely to be a household-based firm, using the labour of family members as necessary. Activities might include tailoring and knitting, woodworking or metal working, basket or mat weaving and simple repairs. Such firms will be financed almost exclusively by the savings of the family or their friends, are more likely to be rural than urban-based and in some countries may be more likely to be run by females than by males. Markets served are highly local, based in either the village or urban location of the households.

At a slightly higher income per capita, the representative small firm may become a micro-enterprise, perhaps employing non-family labour and possibly based in a workshop rather than the household home. The activities undertaken may be similar to that at the first stage, but at a slightly larger scale and possibly using a less traditional technology. In addition, simple manufacturing involving a larger scale of operations, like baking, brewing and the creation of building materials may also take place. Some external savings may be drawn on, principally from moneylenders or where they operate from microfinance or development finance institutions. Markets will be less local and an increasing proportion of enterprises are likely to be urban-based.

At a more advanced stage, at higher income per capita, the representative small firm is more likely to be modern manufacturing unit engaged in making things like clothing, metal and simple engineering products, processed foods, chemicals and paints. Firms will operate as small factories with hired labour. Some external credit will be obtained either from banks, suppliers or customers. Markets will cease to be totally local and in some cases a portion of output may be exported. Production locations are now more likely to be in urban areas or where more sophisticated production is involved in special factory zones or industrial parks. At low income levels, firms may still use older technology, but in higher-income economies small firms may operate in dynamic technologically sophisticated markets. In Taiwan, and to some extent Korea, for example, small and medium firms contributed significantly to the growth of new export products in the period after 1960 and continue to do so today. Thus, as economies grow, the small- and medium-scale sector will become increasingly sophisticated.

The imprecise empirical data that we have show no clear trend in terms of whether small firms have increased or decreased their share in manufacturing employment in the last fifty years with considerable variation between countries and time periods. Comparative statistics on the importance of small and medium enterprises are relatively rare but one detailed database compiled for the World Bank suggests a clear trend from the 1990s that, as economies progress and incomes rise, the share of small and medium enterprises (SMEs) increases. The definition of SMEs is very wide (formal sector enterprises with up to 250 workers) and as we have pointed out in low-income countries, some of these may be relatively large firms. In the sample of up to 76 countries for the 1990s for the low-income group manufacturing SMEs take 32 per cent of total employment, as compared with 54 per cent in the middle-income and 64 per cent in the high-income countries. Formal regression analysis of this data controlling for country characteristics and the starting level of income per head finds that the size of the SME sector is positively associated with economic growth. However, there is no support for the interpretation that it causes higher growth. What appears to have happened in the 1990s is that a rising share of SMEs in employment and income was a characteristic of fast-growing economies. The same database provides estimates of informal (i.e. unregistered economic activity) which shows a clear tendency to decline as a proportion of national income as economies grow. Thus, the rising share of SMEs is in part a result of the decline of informal activity as previously unregistered firms shift into formal manufacturing. Perceived obstacles to the expansion of small firms, like lack of access to credit, and cost of business start-up, when measured at the country level are associated with smaller shares of SMEs in economic activity. However, the size of the SME sector as measured here is not associated with direct reductions in poverty or inequality over the 1990s, that is over and above any contribution arising from the association between SMEs and economic growth.[1]

These relationships referred to here are averages and hide considerable country variation. Table 6.1 shows the shares of manufacturing SMEs (by the definition

Table 6.1 Share of manufacturing SMEs in employment and informal activity in GDP: selected economies 1990s.

Region/country	*SMEs in employment %*	*Informal sector in GDP %*
East Asia		
Indonesia	79	na
Korea	79	38
Philippines	66	50
Singapore	44	13
Thailand	87	71
Vietnam	74	na

Table 6.1 (Cont'd)

Region/country	*SMEs in employment %*	*Informal sector in GDP %*
Latin America		
Argentina	70	22
Brazil	59	33
Chile	87	28
Colombia	67	30
Costa Rica	54	29
Mexico	48	38
Nicaragua	34	na
Peru	68	51
Africa		
Cote Ivoire	19	na
Cameroon	20	na
Ghana	52	na
Kenya	33	na
Nigeria	17	na
Tanzania	32	32
South Africa	82	na
Zambia	37	na
Zimbabwe	15	na
Transition economies		
Albania	9	na
Azerbaijan	5	47
Belarus	5	17
Georgia	7	53
Kazakhstan	13	na
Kyrgyz Republic	63	na
Ukraine	5	39
Developed economies		
UK	56	10
US	52	12

Source: Ayyagari *et al.* (2003, Table 1).

Note
na is not available.

of below 250 workers) in employment in selected countries from this data source. It can be seen that whilst in Latin America and East Asia SMEs by this definition are normally well above 50 per cent of total employment, in Africa and the transition economies of Europe they are a much smaller share of total employment. Here, firms of up to 250 workers will be large for the countries concerned and in these cases, the data reflect the output and employment of 'large' small and medium firms. In these latter economies, informal activity is much more important, although accurate estimates are often not available.

Micro-firms and job creation

Small firms have been seen as 'appropriate' for poor countries in the sense that they use relatively labour-intensive ways of producing simple products. This means that the investment cost per job created is relatively low, start-up costs are also low and they can cater to local demand for low-cost products. They, thus, offer job opportunities for those who lose their previous jobs, for example, in manufacturing, retailing or the civil service, and can also provide supplementary forms of income to households by drawing on family labour. On the other hand, they also offer the opportunity for those with business acumen or entrepreneurial initiative to set up their own businesses at relatively low cost. In all countries, the vast majority of firms (in terms of numbers) are very small. Even in the United States, nearly 80 per cent of firms have five workers or less and two-thirds of registered firms are owner-only.[2] In developing countries, and particularly in the poorest of these, small firms show high entry into and exit from an industry. In other words, over a period, there is a significant level of turnover (or *churning*) with a relatively large number of very small firms starting up and nearly as many closing down, to create only a modest net effect. Some small firms succeed in growing in size but a majority remain small and in some instances the growth in size in some existing firms is offset by a contraction in others.

Detailed surveys of small enterprises in Africa usefully shed light on this process (see also Box 6.1).[3] In most country cases studied, enterprise start-ups as a proportion of the total of existing small firms was as much as 20 per cent, but was usually matched by a similar closure rate. Start-ups were well above the 10 per cent average rate normally found in developed countries. Explanations for high start-ups distinguish between high- and low-profit activities. Where potential profits are high, the level of start-ups is likely to be negatively related to the initial investment needed and positively related to the business experience of the owner. However, in low-profit activities, start-ups are closely linked with macro-economic conditions, so that slow growth and job losses elsewhere encourage start-ups where new small firms act as a sink to absorb displaced workers. Closures tend to occur in the early years of a firm's life (e.g. up to three years after starting up) when owners are learning about the business. However, not all closures need be due to business failure since firms are in some cases reported as closing for personal reasons (e.g. changes within a family such as illness, retirement or migration making family labour unavailable) or due to better options for the owner (e.g. obtaining a better paying job working for someone else).

Employment growth is restricted to a minority of small firms who succeed in surviving and growing. In the African context, only around 5 per cent of the expanding small firms succeeded in growing enough to graduate to the employment category of more than 10 workers. Analysis of causes of growth amongst small firms suggests that it is the surviving younger and smaller (within the range of up to 30 workers) firms that are most likely to grow and that small firms located in urban areas tend to grow more rapidly than similar rural firms do. However, these relationships can also be slightly more complex in that age and

Box 6.1 Small firms in Ghana

Most of manufacturing in Ghana is conducted by small firms. In the late 1990s, a detailed survey was conducted on small firms operating simple manufacturing in the central region. Production covered bakeries, block-making, blacksmithing, woodwork, pottery, oil processing, salt extraction, tailoring, soap making and the manufacture of roof tiles. The services of hair-dressing and dressmaking were also included to allow coverage of female-run or -owned activities. Of the 175 firms sampled, most were established in the previous ten years with an average age of nine years, indicating the high entry and exit in the sector. The vast majority (86 per cent) were owner-run and a majority (67 per cent) employed five workers or less. Virtually none of the entrepreneurs had a tertiary level education, but a majority (62 per cent) had completed primary school. A significant number of owners (44 per cent) had other work in addition to the firm surveyed and this proportion was higher in rural areas, where agriculture provided the main alternative activity. The majority (69 per cent) of workers hired by firms were apprentices, with many firms (apart from those in salt making and block making) preferring to use this cheaper source of hired labour. Of the hired workers, few were employed permanently with most engaged as casual labour, but at daily wage rates up to 50 per cent above the national minimum wage.

There was evidence of small firms doing similar things *clustering* in certain localities. In separate locations, there were groups of oil processors, of salt makers, of aluminium potters and of clay potters. Co-operation amongst these firms was principally in sharing equipment and collaboration in marketing. Nearly one-third of firms shared equipment. Firms with specialised equipment (such as knitting and milling machines) were also willing to undertake tasks for neighbouring firms for a fee. Most firms (93 per cent) received no credit from banks or investment promoting financial institutions. Even the small number of owners who received credit did not judge it to be very useful due to the small amount and relatively high costs in time and effort that were involved. Most firms drew initially on the savings of family and friends.

Two main measures of the performance of these firms were estimated. The first is capacity utilisation defined as actual output to maximum possible output. Small firms, particularly those related to agro-processing, typically operate seasonally, sometimes producing little or nothing in the slack season. In this case, the working year was divided into peak, medium and slack periods and firms were asked the length in weeks of each period, as defined by them and their average weekly output and maximum possible output in each period. The average capacity utilisation rate derived in this why was 33 per cent, which is comparable with that found in similar studies. It was significantly higher for urban (39 per cent) as compared with rural-based firms (28 per cent).

The second performance measure is annual net profit. This was defined in two separate ways. The first definition was value added minus wage costs for hired labour. However, there should also be an allowance for the cost of the owner–operator's own time, so that the second definition of net profit was value added minus the cost of hired labour plus the cost of the owner's time, with the latter valued at the national daily minimum wage. All firms showed a positive net profit under the first definition, meaning that they were able to generate sufficient revenue to cover raw material costs and the cost of any hired labour. Labour costs were kept low due to the fact that most firms used apprentices, seasonal workers or unpaid family labour. However, when owner's time was included as a cost a majority of firms (approximately 75 per cent) showed a negative net profit, meaning that they did not generate an income sufficient to cover the cost of the owner's time at the minimum wage. The main activities with positive profits by this definition were block-making and salt extraction. The smaller firms (below 5 workers) were more likely to generate a loss than firms in the size range of 5 to 30, rural firms were more likely to generate a loss than were urban firms and firms with owners who had another job or source of income were also more likely to make a loss. This latter set of profit results implies that owners cannot obtain alternative full-time employment at the minimum wage (since if they could, they would be better off doing so) and confirms the view of the small-scale sector as only a modest source of income and part of a household *coping strategy*. Many firms in the sample were a supplementary source of income with a significant proportion of owners (29 per cent in urban and 58 per cent in rural areas) engaging in other income generating activities such as farming, trade or formal sector employment. Nonetheless, despite their low profitability a majority of firms in the sample (55 per cent) took on more workers in the two years prior to the survey, suggesting the importance of such firms as a low-income source of employment.

Source: Mensah *et al.* (2007).

size of firm can interact. Hence, for example, there is evidence that the negative relation between size (within the small firm category) and growth may be weaker for older small firms. Thus, a small firm may initially grow rapidly, but this growth may tail off, as the firm gets older and ultimately may turn negative.

Constraints on the growth of small and micro-firms

It has now become common to undertake surveys of firms to identify their perceptions of the key problems they face. Initially these *investment climate* surveys focussed on relatively large, usually urban-based firms, but in many countries they are now being extended to smaller firms engaged in manufacturing, trade or other service activity in rural areas. These surveys of small firms (including trading as well as manufacturing firms) have highlighted factors that owners themselves perceive as key constraints on their ability to grow. Common findings from small firms are difficulty in accessing credit, and poor-quality rural infrastructure, particularly intermittent or non-existent power supplies, poor road links and lack of access to communications, either as fixed phone lines or cell phones. In some countries and at some points in time lack of demand for the products of small firms may also be an issue. Infrastructure facilities can also vary markedly within countries, so what is a problem in one region may not be in another (see Box 6.2 for the results of such a survey).

Box 6.2 Barriers to small firms in rural Sri Lanka

In Sri Lanka, rural non-farm enterprises account for as much as 40 per cent of employment in rural areas, largely in very small firms of 1–5 workers. From the survey data within simple manufacturing about one-third of enterprises are based in the home. Poor infrastructure emerges as the key constraint when owners or managers of enterprises are asked to identify the most important barrier to their development; 30 per cent of manufacturing firms identified poor electricity supply as the key constraint, followed by 9 per cent for lack of road access. However, there were important regional differences electricity being a particular problem in the north and east of the country, where road access was not perceived as a barrier. In the north and east, poor road quality was perceived as an issue rather than road access. As in many other countries, access to credit and its cost are also perceived as a problem with 8 per cent of manufacturing firms reporting poor financial infrastructure as the key barrier they face.

The impact of aspects of the investment climate and particularly the role of poor infrastructure on the likelihood of small rural firm growth is examined econometrically in a model that makes whether or not a new firm is started up a function of household characteristics (like its size, assets and the education level of the household head), the various possible barriers in the operating environment for new firms (like poor infrastructure, weak demand and government regulatory controls) and the region in which the household is located. A similar analysis is conducted on the likelihood of existing firms expanding through new investment. In relation to new firm start-ups, infrastructure variables dominate compared with all other factors. For example, the propensity to start up a new firm is 14 per cent lower in areas where electricity is perceived as a major constraint. Since this result is derived from an analysis of all firms the impact of removing the electricity barrier on small manufacturing firms, that are higher electricity users than, for example, trading firms, would be even greater. Overall, eliminating electricity constraints alone would raise the start-up rate by about 3.5 percentage points and by about 4.3 percentage points for manufacturing firms only. On the other hand, the analysis of the probability of firms investing once they have been established suggests that lack of road access and poor financial infrastructure are bigger barriers to investment than poor electricity supply. Removing the constraint posed by road access would increase the number of firms investing by 13 per cent and removal of the credit constraint would increase the number by 15 per cent. This analysis of obstacles to the growth of small firms in rural areas of Sri Lanka suggests that the barrier posed by the overall regulatory environment (the need for licenses and payment of taxes, for example) is much less important for firms than lack of good infrastructure facilities, particularly electricity and roads, since these infrastructure constraints dominate all others.

Source: Deininger *et al.* (2007).

Lack of access to credit is a problem that is common to many countries. Small firms in developing countries lack access to credit for a number of reasons.

- First, as they are small, the loans they seek will also be relatively small. This means that the transaction or administrative cost of processing these loans will be high relative to the amount involved. They are therefore less profitable for commercial banks than loans to large firms.
- Second and most fundamentally, small firms typically lack the assets or collateral that can be used as a guarantee against the loan they take out. This means they are perceived as high-risk borrowers who are either denied credit or only offered it on expensive terms.
- Third, and related to the lack of collateral, is the point that they will also lack the relationships that larger firms can establish with commercial banks that allow their need for credit both for working capital and investment to be met on a regular long-term basis.
- Fourth, they rarely can draw on trade credits provided by supplier firms who offer finance to allow the purchase of their products. Small firms are far less likely than larger firms to receive this form of credit because the small size of their orders makes it less attractive for suppliers to offer it.

These problems can be illustrated drawing on data from the previously cited surveys of small enterprise in Africa, a region where the problem is particularly acute. Survey data on manufacturing firms in six African countries have been used to identify the nature of funding constraints amongst firms of varying size. This reveals that most firms did not apply to formal financial institutions for funding in the year before the survey, although amongst micro-firms the proportion is even higher (at 92 per cent). Among those applying for external funds, overall a

Table 6.2 Formal credit market participation by firm size (%)

	Micro	*Small*	*Medium*	*Large*	*All*
Did not apply	92	82	80	75	82
Applied and did not receive	6	11	9	5	8
Applied and received	2	7	11	20	10

Source: Bigsten and Soderbom (2006, Table 1).

majority of firms obtained funding, although the picture varies with firm size. For the categories of micro- and small firms, a majority of those applying did not receive credit with only 2 per cent of micro-firms and 7 per cent of small firms receiving credit, as compared with 20 per cent of large firms (see Table 6.2).

The fact that most firms did not apply for credit does not mean that they were not constrained by a lack of credit, since they might not have applied because they did not expect to be successful in their application. Questions in the surveys shed light on this issue by asking why firms did not apply, whether because of their own lack of need for credit or because they thought they would be rejected. Here, only a minority of micro-firms (33 per cent) stated they had no demand for credit, with half of small firms saying the same thing. Nearly two-thirds of micro-firms either did not apply for credit because they expected the application to be rejected or applied and were rejected. For small firms the proportion is 42 per cent. This suggests that for the smallest firms, lack of credit holds back growth (*a credit constraint*) in roughly two-thirds of the firms surveyed. The comparable proportion for large firms is only 10 per cent (see Table 6.3).

Where small firms cannot obtain finance from the commercial banking sector, there are only a limited number of alternatives. As discussed in the foregoing section, the savings of family and friends is often used to finance the start of operations, but typically this will allow only a modest amount of financing. Moneylenders offer an alternative, but this typically covers only small sums at high interest rates well above those in commercial banks. Finally, there are various forms of developmental lending – through governmental or non-governmental (NGO) financial institutions targeted specifically at the small scale sector and often lending at concessional interest rates. Where these organisations are deliberately non-commercially-oriented, they must rely significantly on external

Table 6.3 Credit constraint by firm size (%)

	Micro	*Small*	*Medium*	*Large*	*All*
No credit demand	33	50	67	66	55
Applied and rejected/did not apply due to expected rejection	64	42	21	10	33
Received loan	3	8	12	23	12

Source: Bigsten and Soderbom (2006, Table 2).

funds, either from national government budgets or from aid donor funding, to finance their lending programmes. Furthermore, even where profitability is their key objective, many such organisations have found great difficulty in covering their costs, largely because of the high rate of loan defaults (or *non-performing loans*). These problems have been due to a combination of poor initial scrutiny of borrowers, the intrinsic difficulties faced by small enterprises and lack of an adequate mechanism to enforce repayment.

An interesting development in recent years has been the spread of microfinance organisations targeting the small enterprise sector. These offer relatively small loans either to individuals or to groups of lenders who assume collective responsibility for the loan, so that if one defaults all lose their right to borrow further under the programme. These institutions typically charge relatively high interest rates that are aimed at allowing them to cover their costs and generate a financial surplus for re-lending and their interest charges are usually somewhere between the rates charged by money lenders and those charged by commercial banks. Microfinance has become popular as a poverty reduction mechanism but in Latin America, in particular, it has focussed principally on the small enterprise sector and filled a gap in financial markets by offering loans to small producers, who would otherwise have been excluded from access to credit. However, the spread of this type of small-scale lending across countries has been very varied with Bangladesh and Indonesia in Asia and Bolivia and Peru in Latin America being some of the countries with the largest outreach. Box 6.3 illustrates the case of microfinance in Pakistan.

Box 6.3 Khushhali Bank and Micro-enterprise in Pakistan

Microfinance remains relatively little developed in Pakistan, although there has been rapid growth since 2000 starting from a low base. The potential market for microcredit is very large and the microfinance strategy of the State Bank of Pakistan targets a total of three million borrowers by 2010. The Khushhali bank was founded in 2000 as the first initiative of the Microfinance Development Program sponsored by the Asian Development Bank. It was an early version of a commercially oriented microfinance intervention with its share capital drawn from 16 commercial banks. Whilst operating alongside more conventional aid funded microfinance institutions, it has become the largest provider of microfinance in Pakistan, at the time of the survey providing a range of loan products to over 360,000 active borrowers (nearly 25 per cent of the national total borrowers), whilst focusing on the core objective of operational self-sufficiency. The bank targets clients who are 'poor' and 'very poor', but not those who are 'destitute' (living off charity or *zakat*) or the 'non-poor', who receive enough income to pay income tax. Loans are offered for investment in micro-enterprises to establish a new business or purchase assets or working capital for an existing business, at interest rates above those in commercial banks, but well below estimates of the cost of borrowing from moneylenders.

In 2005, a detailed survey of borrowers was undertaken to establish whether this bank is making a difference to the income and welfare of borrower households, who would otherwise not have access to credit. This type of impact study requires a comparison of borrowing households with a *control group* of similar households in the same location who have not borrowed. There are complex econometric issues in relation to isolating the impact of a loan from all other factors at work, which may bias the results. This study used as the control group households who had been approved for a loan, but had not yet received it, so as far as possible similar groups are compared with the key difference being that one has already received loans from the bank whilst the other has been approved for loans, but has not yet received them.

Following this approach, impact is estimated with a single equation

$$Y_{ij} = \beta_1 X_{ij} + \beta_2 V_j + \beta_3 M_{ij} + \beta_4 M_{ij}.T_{ij} + \varepsilon_{ij} \quad (6.1)$$

where Y_{ij}, is a vector of impact variables (such as profits), X_{ij} is a vector of household characteristics (such as education of the heads of the household and family size), V_j represents dummy variables for different village and urban locations, M_{ij} is a membership dummy variable equal to 1 for any household that is a member of the bank and thus able to borrow under the program, T_{ij} is a dummy variable equal to 1 for bank members who have already received a loan and ε_{ij} is an error term.

In this analysis, micro-credit will make a difference to household welfare if the coefficient on the interaction term $M_{ij}.T_{ij}$ is positive and significant. Various measures of impact are examined but in urban areas, households accessing loans were found to have statistically significant higher sales and profits from their micro-enterprises than those who have not yet received their loans. Sales of urban micro-enterprises in the previous 12 months before the date of the survey were over US$800 higher than expected given other relevant factors, resulting in profits that were higher by about US$250 annually for borrowing households relative to the control group. These are not large amounts in absolute terms, but for the sort of low-income borrowers reached by the bank the se are substantial impacts and suggest that access to micro-credit can make a large difference to micro-enterprise success.

Source: Montgomery (2005).

Small firms, efficiency and scale

Micro-firms normally operate in different market segments producing different types of product to larger firms. However, small firms (employing say 10–50 workers) can produce similar product ranges to larger firms. There has been considerable discussion on whether, in low- and lower-middle-income countries, small firms (however small is specified) are as economically efficient and dynamic as larger firms. The greater labour-intensity of these firms has already been noted, but this in itself is no guarantee of superior performance. In theoretical terms, what is needed is to establish that one size of firm has a higher economic return to the resources committed to it than a different size of firm. A higher return to a small firm can be expressed as

$$(VA_s - L.w_s)/Kr_s > (VA_l - L.w_l)/Kr_l \qquad (6.2)$$

where VA is value added, L is units of labour, K is units of capital in monetary terms, w is the economic cost of employing a worker (the *opportunity cost of labour*), r is the expected economic return on capital (the *opportunity cost of capital*) and the subscripts s and l refer to small and large firm, respectively. Each variable is expressed per unit of standard output (so, for example, VA is value per unit of output, L is number of workers per unit of output and K is value of capital per unit).[4]

Equation 6.2 can be rewritten as

$$(VA_s/Kr_s - Lw_s/Kr_s) > (VA_l/Kr_l - Lw_l/Kr_l) \qquad (6.3)$$

We are fairly sure that small firms are more labour-intensive (which means that $L/Kr_s > L/Kr_l$). Hence, for Equation 6.3 to hold, we need this labour intensity to be offset by either higher capital productivity in smaller firms (so $VA_s/Kr_s > VA_l/Kr_l$) or lower economic wage rates ($w_s < w_l$) or a combination of both.

Although wage rates tend to be higher in larger firms, there is no guarantee that this or a capital productivity differential will be sufficiently high to offset the larger labour to capital ratio in small firms. Insofar as this type of economic return calculation has been carried out, it has yielded ambiguous results as to the advantages of a particular size of firm.[5]

Economies of scale

Generalisations about the impact of size on efficiency and growth prospects must be qualified by reference to the different sub-sectors of manufacturing since the impact of production scale on unit costs (*economies of scale*) can vary between types of activity. Table 2.1 in Chapter 2 identifies sectors characterised by differing degrees of scale economies, with activities with heavy initial capital investment like petroleum and coal products, nonferrous metals, transport equipment and chemicals, having the largest scale effects. However, formal tests of the existence of economies of scale in developing countries have often found that in some sectors their effect is only modest.

A common way of testing for economies of scale is to fit a production function where

$$Qi = A.K^{\alpha}.L^{\beta} \qquad (6.4)$$

and Qi is output for firm i, A is a constant, K is capital input, L is labour input and α and β are the elasticities of Q with respect to capital and labour, respectively.

If Equation 6.4 is differentiated with respect to time, it gives a growth version, where growth is explained by a constant A (capturing total factor productivity) and the growth of capital and labour. Where Q responds more than proportionately to the growth of capital and labour inputs there will be increasing returns scale; where it responds less than proportionately there will be decreasing returns. This is tested empirically by estimating the equation

$$lnQi = A + \alpha lnK + \beta lnL + ei \qquad (6.5)$$

where ln refers to natural logarithms and e is an error term.

In Equation 6.5 the coefficients α and β are elasticities and if they sum to more than one ($\alpha + \beta > 1$) this demonstrates the existence of economies of scale, as output responds more than proportionately to the growth of inputs. If they sum to unity, there is constant returns to scale and if they sum to less than unity, there is diminishing returns to scale.

There are empirical difficulties in conducting this type of exercise, particularly in getting an accurate value for capital, but it has been carried out within and across a number of manufacturing sub-sectors in many countries. Usually very small or micro-firms are excluded as data on their operation is not available, so the analysis typically starts at a firm size of 20 employees. Although there are differences between country and sector, the results generally suggest that if one excludes very small firms, returns to scale are either constant (so $\alpha + \beta = 1$) or only mildly increasing (so $\alpha + \beta = 1.05$ to 1.10).[6] Hence, scale effects may not be as dramatic as they are sometimes pictured.

Broadly speaking, it appears that very small firms may see a decrease in their unit costs of production if they can survive long enough to reach the small-size category (say up to 20 workers); furthermore, in some sectors, moving from small to medium size (say from 20 to 100 workers) may also make a difference to average unit cost. However, beyond a certain output level (*the minimum efficient scale of production*) which varies between sub-sectors, further expansion may have little effect on unit costs. Thus, scale effects will vary, depending on what size of firm is being considered and the branch or sub-sector in which it is located. Box 6.4 illustrates this with data from Taiwan, an economy in which small- and medium-sized enterprises are known to have played an important role in industrialisation.

Box 6.4 Economies of scale in manufacturing in Taiwan

Taiwan is an economy with a significant and dynamic small and medium enterprise sector, although in its statistics, small firms are defined as those with 5–99 workers and medium firms as those with 100–299 workers. Manufacturing Census data for the period 1981–91 have been analysed to capture the effect of firm size on productivity. For each firm in the Census an individual indicator of total factor productivity (TFP) was estimated using data on output and all measurable inputs, so that TFP is output not attributable to the inputs. Estimated firm TFP is then regressed on dummy variables to reflect different size categories (small equals 1.0, medium equals 2.0 and large equals 3.0) and a variable capturing the age of each firm to reflect experience in production. Firm data are grouped by two-digit manufacturing branch to allow for differences across sub-sectors. The reference group with which the three other size categories are compared are the very small micro-firms (defined as those with below five workers). Hence, the regression can be expressed as

$$Pij = a + \beta.Dsij + \gamma.Aij + eij \qquad (6.6)$$

where *Pi* is total factor productivity for firm *i*, *Ds* is a dummy variable for the three different size categories, *Ai* is the age of firm *i*, *j* refers to the sub-sector in which *i* is located, *a* is a constant and *eij* is the error term.

The constant term *a* gives the average level of TFP in the reference group of micro-firms for the relevant sub-sector *j*, and coefficient on the three dummy variables β gives the proportionate increase in average TFP in each of the three size groups for the sub-sector concerned relative to the average for micro-firms in that sub-sector. For all sub-sectors, the β coefficients are positive indicating higher productivity (and lower unit cost) in the size categories relative to micro-firms. The largest gain in efficiency (and therefore reduction in unit cost) occurs in moving from the micro- to the small-size category, that is from less than five to somewhere between 5 and 99 employees. The gain from moving from the small- to the medium-size category is slightly less and for all but two sub-sectors (paper and publishing and transportation equipment), there appears no significant gain in moving from the medium (100–299 workers) to the large category (more than 300 workers). The implication is that there are increasing returns to scale but these weaken after a firm size of 100 workers and largely disappear (for all but the paper and publishing and transportation equipment sub-sectors) beyond a size of 300 workers. Hence, in most sub-sectors, minimum efficient production scale is around 300 workers and, beyond this, there are relatively few gains to be had by expanding scale alone. The β coefficients that compare average TFP in micro-firms and the other firm sizes are given next for the different sub-sectors examined.

Scale effects: coefficients on size dummies[a]

Sub-sector	*Small*[b]	*Medium*[c]	*Large*[d]
Textiles	0.222	0.409	0.438
Clothing	0.197	0.376	0.389
Paper and publishing	0.151	0.370	0.471*
Chemicals	0.163	0.278	0.271
Plastics	0.146	0.304	0.337
Basic metals	0.137	0.217	0.232
Fabricated metal	0.138	0.296	0.313
Machinery	0.137	0.304	0.338
Electricals	0.145	0.226	0.238
Transportation equipment	0.158	0.287	0.382*

Source: Aw (2002, Table 4).

Notes

a Figures give proportionate increase in average TFP for the size category of firm relative to the average of micro-firms.

b 5–99 workers.

c 100–299 workers.

d 300+ workers.

*Sub-sectors where the difference in coefficients for large- and medium-sized firms is statistically significant.

Small-firm technological dynamism: what can explain it?

The degree of economies of scale in a particular branch are likely to have an influence on the chances of survival of new firms, since if they cannot capture an increasing share of the market, they will be penalised by their low output level as their cost will be above that of larger firms operating at the minimum efficient scale. However, we know that whilst many small firms do not survive and grow, some do, playing the role of seedbed for new entrepreneurs and proving a source of dynamism both in terms of productivity growth and technical change. Furthermore, in some countries, principally in East and Southeast Asia, small and medium firms have emerged as participants in global production networks and significant exporters of high-technology manufactures. Where small firms have become important exporters this is often because they have found product niches and have adapted with to the changing demands of the world market (e.g. with flexible clothing designs adjusted to changing seasons and fashions and mobile phone specifications changing with the development of telecommunications technology). In such cases, their production organisation is typically the opposite of the lengthy production runs and standardised goods offered by larger firms.

To understand fully the phenomenon of dynamic small firms, it is necessary to look at recent developments in the theory of industrial organisation and technical change in the context of higher-income economies like the United States and European Union. There, it is recognised that in some parts of manufacturing small firms have become key agents of change through technical innovation. Data from the United States suggest that small firms dominate in number of innovations in key high-technology sectors including computing equipment, electronic components, and precision and scientific instruments.[7]

The role of firms of different size in particular industries can be related to the life cycle of an industry. One form of classification distinguishing broadly between high-innovation and low-innovation industries and different stages in their life cycles is given in Table 6.4. Small firms are important sources of innovation at the early stage of dynamic high-innovation activities and at the late or declining stage of low-innovation activities.

To explain this phenomenon a widely used concept is the knowledge production function. In broad terms, this makes innovation and technical change by firms a function of their own expenditure on R and D aimed at generating new knowledge, the research expenditure by research institutions like public laboratories and universities and the R and D activity of other firms. Small firms may be able to afford only small R and D budgets of their own. However, recent work has stressed the development of innovations within specific geographic locations, so that R and D by institutes and other firms in the same geographic area can also have a positive effect on the innovation of any individual firm. This is the process of *knowledge spillover* discussed in earlier chapters. In this interpretation, the knowledge production function should be viewed at the level of a geographic area not an individual firm and the fact that a firm has only a modest R and D budget of its own need not hold back innovation if spillovers are important.

This theoretical development has been in response to the observation that many of the small-firm innovations in the United States and European Union have been concentrated in narrowly defined areas (such as those around San Francisco and Boston in the United States). This localisation of innovative activity in fairly small geographic areas has been put down to the critical importance of knowledge that is tacit – that is not embodied in designs or blue prints. This type of

Table 6.4 Innovation, life cycle and firm size

Stage in life cycle	*High-innovation industries*	*Low-innovation industries*
Early stage	Innovation predominantly by small firms (for example, electronics)	
Growth stage	Innovation predominantly by large firms (for example, pharmaceuticals)	
Mature stage		Innovation predominantly by large firms (for example, photographic equipment)
Late stage		Innovation predominantly by small firms (for example, optical instruments)

Source: Adapted from Audretsch (2002).

knowledge exists in the minds of scientists, specialist workers and industry entrepreneurs. Accessing it requires direct contacts that are only feasible where firms are located in close proximity to each other. Tacit knowledge is more important in some industries than that in others, but is typically important in the early stages of highly innovative industries before product and process designs become codified and standardised (see Table 6.4). Key mechanisms for the transmission of tacit knowledge include new firm start-ups by researchers or employees of other firms, labour mobility between firms, joint research initiatives and information sharing. This focus on localised knowledge spillovers as an explanation for small-firm innovation has led to the paradoxical conclusion that at the same time that globalisation as a process has weakened greatly the impact of national borders, technical change in at least some high-innovation activities has become more, not less, localised.

The groupings of firms in particular localities (or *clusters*) can derive initially from different types of advantages. Some clusters have been formed around a large lead firm which sub-contracts work to smaller suppliers in the same geographic area. This is a relatively common pattern in Japan, where, for example, firms like Toyota set up links with specialist suppliers. These suppliers may be provided with know-how from the lead firm as part of the contractual arrangements. Alternatively, some clusters may be based in an area around research institutes and universities, such as the grouping around Stanford University in California, United States. The availability of a pool of specialist or highly qualified workers in an area may also explain why firms group together in an area; for example, the location of some fashion and footwear clusters in Italy may also be explained in this way.

Small-firm clusters

This explanation of small-firm dynamism is largely a developed country story, although it finds some parallels in the development of science parks in the NIEs, such as Korea, Taiwan, Thailand and China. However, even in activities that are not highly innovative, small firms in some developing countries have found it advantageous to group together in *clusters*. The motive again is principally to draw on mutually beneficial externalities as well as benefits that are obtained as market transactions; in other words, benefits which firms have to pay for rather than receive as external benefits. The gains from clustering have been referred to as *collective efficiency*, since firms operate with greater efficiency in proximity to each other than they would in isolation.[8] The two key mechanism of this process are:

- *External economies* arising from the local interaction of firms including the transfer of skilled workers as they move between firms, technological adaptation as ideas are copied and shared and the communal use of facilities such as power generators or specialist machines.
- *Joint action* as firms deliberately co-operate, for example, in the sharing of information on markets and technology, by specialising in different production lines and in training and recruitment.

The key difference is that by definition, the former is unplanned and is a by-product of production, whilst the latter are explicit attempts at co-operation, sometimes involving payments between firms.

The number of such clusters have been documented in a range of sectors and countries, although chiefly in Asia and Latin America rather than in Africa, where progress in cluster development has been slower. The sectors involved include footwear (in Brazil and Mexico), metalworking, simple engineering and electronics (in India), textiles (in India and Korea), surgical goods (in Pakistan), furniture (in Indonesia) and software development (in India and various other countries, including Uruguay) (see Box 6.5).

Empirical work reveals a wide variety of experiences within clusters in low and lower-middle-income countries. Collaboration between firms varies greatly from casual exchange of tools and information to direct collaboration in sharing orders and training. In some cases, clear specialisation emerges with some firms emerging as suppliers of parts and components to other firms in the cluster. In others where firms grow, they cease to rely on external suppliers but start to make some of the components they need themselves. In some clusters, social networks and cultural cohesion remain important, whilst in others, these are replaced by impersonal market relationships with external agents or traders playing a key role in stimulating links between firms.

Clusters have been important for different types of firms; for the small they may offer a means of overcoming key marketing or technology weakness, whilst in other cases they may offer medium-size firms the chance to grow and export. In technologically simple activities, advantages for small firms also include a reduction in start-up costs, where machinery can be shared and in working capital since where specialist local suppliers are close by there is less need to hold large stocks. For small firms links with international buyers, often through agents and local traders acting as intermediaries, will be critical if such firms are to break into export markets. As discussed in Chapter 4, in this type of buyer-driven global production network, buyers will often provide the design and process technology needed for small firms to produce to international standards (see Box 6.6).

Even relatively large and technologically sophisticated firms may benefit from location in a cluster. None of this is automatic, however, and there are examples of stagnant as well as dynamic clusters, with success in part depending on the more general economic climate (see Chapter 4).

Box 6.5 Software cluster in Uruguay

Computer software is a hybrid activity in that where it involves product development of new software packages it is comparable to manufacturing, whilst where it involves consultancy services to apply or explain existing packages it is comparable to a service. A number of countries have created an expertise in software product development and much of this is highly localised in a narrow geographic area. As a small, middle-income, developing country with a well-educated population, Uruguay has developed an expertise in software with virtually all software firms concentrated in the capital city, Montevideo. This software production is based predominately on small- and medium-sized firms. A recent survey covering the majority of these found most were below 100 workers, with an average size of around 25 workers. Many of these firms were found to be relatively innovative with over half having been the first to introduce a new product to the market and over two-thirds having upgraded existing products in the five years preceding the survey. Nearly half of sales value; on average was accounted for by product innovation in software development.

The subsequent analysis of the data generated by the survey casts light on how far this technological innovation can be attributed to the benefits of clustering. The role of the three key potential mechanisms for knowledge spillover between firms are examined:

- New firms start-ups (where employees of an existing firm leave to set up their own small firm);
- Labour mobility (where employees move from one firm to another taking their skills and knowledge with them);
- Informal interactions (where firms share knowledge or simply learn from the example of other firms).

Basic data from the survey suggests that all these effects might be important. Almost half of the firms were spin-offs from other firms and labour turnover was relatively high, with roughly one-third of workers having joined their current firm in the five years preceding the survey. However, firms' own internal efforts at generating knowledge (as opposed to receiving it from others) were also likely to be important as roughly one-third of the workforce was classified as being engaged in research and development.

The importance of knowledge spillovers arising from being part of a cluster is tested formally by econometric analysis. Measures of the innovative output of firms (based on the share of sales generated by innovative products or on whether a firm had been the first to introduce a new product) are explained by variables reflecting, respectively.

- The benefits of clustering (measures of labour turnover, new firm spin-offs and a subjective assessment by firms themselves of the importance of informal interactions as a source of knowledge).
- Extra-cluster sources of knowledge (assessments by firms themselves of the importance of technology purchase).
- Internal learning effort (measures of the education level of the workforce and of R and D activity).

In addition, the age and size of each firm is also controlled for, as these might be expected to have an additional influence. The results indicate clearly that the three measures of the benefits of clusters are each significant and appear more important for these firms than external transactions, that is purchases of technology. In this cluster, the three mechanisms of labour turnover, firm spin-off and informal interaction are thus the key external sources of knowledge that complement firms' own internal efforts. It is thus no surprise that internationally software development is an activity characterised by clusters of producers working in close proximity to each other.

Source: Kesidou and Romjin (2008).

Box 6.6 Furniture cluster in Indonesia

A widely studied and relatively successful cluster in a technologically simple branch of manufacturing is the furniture cluster in Jepara district of central Java, Indonesia. Firms range from the very small to the large (over 300 workers) and there is extensive sub-contracting with small firms providing parts for larger firms as well as producing finished goods to order for traders. Many of the larger firms concentrated on a few stages of production whilst contracting out others, such as the kiln drying of wood, to the small specialist firms. Clustering allowed this division of labour and the use of sub-contracting created the flexibility to respond to changing orders. The furniture is of a specialist carved variety produced by skilled artisans, who are mobile between firms moving in response to offers of improved wages. Although production was initially for the domestic market since the late 1980s the majority of sales are for export. Foreign buyers and agents provided most of the impetus for export sales seeking out local suppliers, providing new designs and imposing quality and scheduling requirements. They also arranged export credit finance and developed marketing links in export markets. Foreign investors have also set up larger firms and these foreign-owned firms take a disproportionate share of total exports from the cluster. Government policy is seen as significant in fostering the cluster. Initially, a ban on the export of logs in the early 1980s provided a key incentive to set up furniture production. The upgrading of the provincial port of Semarang to international standards reduced the time and cost of exporting and improvements were also made to road and telecommunication facilities by the local government. The participation of small firms in trade fairs has also been supported by the local authorities.

A recent survey of the current state of the cluster confirms its continued growth and argues that previous estimates of its size have been serious underestimates. The new estimates suggest a total of over 15,000 production units, and the employment of as many as 170,000 workers, roughly two-thirds of these on a permanent basis. The vast majority of firms are small workshops and sub-contracting and other links between firms remain close, with nearly 80 per cent of firms reporting they have at least one firm with which they collaborate closely. Exports remain important but in recent years, there is evidence of an increasing proportion of sales to the domestic market, as national income rises.

Source: Yusuf (2006) Chapter 6 and Roda *et al.* (2007).

What can governments do?

The issue of whether governments should have special policies for small firm development has been debated for a long time. Clearly, some of the obstacles to the growth of large firms may be even more important barriers to small firms. Government requirements, for example, on enterprise registration, environmental standards, or health and safety regulations, whilst they may be necessary, can impose a greater burden on small firms, since the cost of meeting them will often be a much lower proportion of sales turnover for larger firms. Similarly, where there are delays in customs clearance or in the issuing of investment licences, these may impact more seriously on smaller firms for whom delays in starting production create a cash shortfall that is difficult to cover. The general message of streamlining bureaucratic procedures and of focusing only on necessary regulation is one that is widely accepted and underlies arguments about improving the investment climate.

In addition, as discussed earlier, infrastructure deficiencies, whilst remaining a cost for all firms may be a greater burden for many smaller ones. The most obvious example relates to interruptions in power supply, which larger firms can avoid by investing in their own power generators. Similarly, for exporters, poor domestic road or rail links and slow-functioning ports can be circumvented by sending goods abroad as airfreight. These options are typically not open to small firms, at least those facing a shortage of credit. Hence, the general policy advice on the importance of improvements to infrastructure as a means of supporting manufacturing industry holds particularly in the case of small firms.

However, suggestions on ways of supporting small firms go much further. The importance of a credit constraint for many small firms has been highlighted already. Small firms may be high-risk borrowers, with relatively few assets that can be offered as security against a loan, and often with what is perceived as a lack of managerial expertise. In addition, where only small amounts of money are required the administrative cost of processing a loan will be a higher proportion of its face value than is normal with larger borrowers. In many countries, governments have tried to address these problems, for example, by variously mandating banks to lend a proportion of their portfolio to small firms (as *directed credit*), establishing specialist financial institutions to cater for small firms (either as *development banks* or more recently as *microfinance institutions*) and additionally in support of these initiatives by providing training in management, entrepreneurship and marketing to the owners of small firms.

Experience suggests that a policy of providing loans to small firms on subsidised terms, with interest rates below commercial levels, whilst it is superficially attractive as a means of supporting the small-scale sector and redistributing income, can promote inefficiency, with the risk that relative low return activities receive funding, whilst at the same time not providing a revolving fund to allow the future expansion of finance to small firms. In recent years, it has become conventional for aid donors, for example, who often provide the finance to support this type of directed lending to small firms, to insist that the funds are lent out on commercial terms to avoid these problems. This is part of the more general critique of the use of interest rate subsidies in a policy of *financial repression*. Theoretically there is a case for such subsidies either on income distribution or externality grounds (where the recipients of the subsidy provide benefits for others), but even where these conditions hold, there are financial limits on how far subsidised finance can be made available.

The specialist training and advice offered to small firms as part of a package of support has been of highly variable quality, particularly where it is difficult to recruit specialist staff. Frequently, the success stories of small-firm development stress the roles of either foreign or national buyers who prove information on markets, design and credit (in buyer-driven production networks) or of larger firms who subcontract work to smaller firms and who provide similar advice and funding (in producer-driven networks). This is in contrast to the disappointing results of government support programmes. This is illustrated in assessments of small-firm support in Indonesia in the 1990s, for example, which highlight its limited outreach and classify it as a supply-side approach in contrast with the more dynamic demand focus of linking small firms with markets via production networks.[9]

Given the potential role of clusters in supporting small firms, the role of government in encouraging cluster development has also been examined extensively. Governments have in the past provided an array of incentives to induce the development of clusters including:

- Infrastructure investment in transport, telecommunications and factory space,
- Fiscal incentives such as profits tax holidays and the waiving of import tariffs in duty-free zones.
- Funding for standards and testing centres, applied research and higher education.

Whilst the success of low-technology clusters appears to be driven principally by private sector initiatives through sub-contracting and links between small firms and buyers, public policy may have had a greater impact in the successful high-technology clusters in the NIEs, such as Hsinchu Park, outside Taipei, Taiwan, Pudong, Shanghai and the Penang area of Malaysia (see Box 6.7).

Box 6.7 Computer components clusters in Malaysia: different government roles

Computer components (part of the *information hardware* sector) are produced in a number of clusters in Malaysia and a cluster approach to high-technology development was adopted formally in the Second Industrial Master Plan in 1996. Different states within Malaysia have implemented a cluster support policy with varying degrees of government involvement. The most active state has been that of Penang and surveys of firms in Malaysia have contrasted the relative success of firms there in establishing themselves as part of global networks and in developing linkages with smaller local sub-contractors, with the much weaker development in other states, such as Johor. It has been argued that the state government in Penang adopted a successful interventionist approach with the Penang Development Corporation playing a key role in filling information gaps on local sub-contracting capacity and in putting multinational investors in touch with small local sub-contractors. Similarly, the Penang Skills Development Centre, established with strong government support, was rated highly by foreign and local firms as a source of labour training.

Part of this greater state involvement in Penang has been explained by the political configuration there as compared, for example, with Johor. Historically, ethnic Chinese have dominated small and medium enterprises in Malaysia, and this group found it easier to work with the Penang state government than with governments in other states, so the Chinese Chamber of Commerce worked closely with the state leadership in Penang. However, government intervention cannot resolve all issues and the Penang computer components cluster has been criticised for its lack of R and D activity, with multinational firms preferring to undertake R and D in their home country or Singapore. Lack of R and D capacity is a national issue relating to investment in education and scientific research and there is little that individual state governments can do to overcome national limitations.

Source: Oyelaran-Oyeyinka and Rasiah (2009, Chapter 4).

Conclusions

Small manufacturing enterprises are important sources of employment and output in most economies. At lower levels of income per capita, they tend to offer an alternative source of employment to workers displaced from larger enterprises and often are household-based. This type of activity tends to expand counter-cyclically in that as an economy slows down and jobs are lost, small informal enterprises increase in number in response. Small firms can be a source of dynamism. In higher-income economies and in the East Asian NIEs, they have played a dynamic role in innovative activities, for example, in electronic parts and components and computer software. Poor-quality infrastructure and lack of credit have been highlighted in surveys as key constraints on the growth of small firms. However, they can benefit considerably from establishing sub-contracting relationship with larger firms and in some instances from clustering in specific locations to undertake joint activities and to take advantage of interactions with similar firms.

Further reading

Useful surveys of firms in developing countries are Tybout (2000), Bigsten and Soderbom (2006) and Iqbal and Urata (2002). An analysis of the scope for local technology development in developed countries is given in Audretsch (1998). For an analysis of progress of high-technology small firms in East Asia see Yusuf (2006).

The special issue of World Development (1999) has a number of articles on clustering in developing countries; see also the discussion on agglomeration in Collier and Venables (2007).

7 Industrial policy and the East Asian miracle

The last fifty years or so have witnessed a remarkable pace of economic growth and structural change amongst countries that were previously seen as poor and under-developed. The original four newly industrialised economies (NIEs) – Hong Kong, Singapore, Korea and Taiwan – grew rapidly from the 1960s and are now perceived as high-income, developed economies. Their economic success was followed in the 1980s by the second-tier NIEs – Thailand, Malaysia and to a lesser extent Indonesia – and since the 1990s by China and Vietnam. These are very different countries but they share a location in East Asia and in all instances manufacturing industry and in particular manufactured exports both within the region and to the rest of the world played a critical role in their rapid growth. The story of their development over this period has been told many times and their success has been cited in support of various theories of development. This chapter focuses on the role of the state in terms of industrial policy, since there is a strong case that part of the economic success of at least some of these economies was due to active state intervention to change the structure of production and to boost manufactured exports.

Industrial policy can be defined broadly as measures to alter the allocation of resources within an economy in favour of manufacturing industry and within the sector to shift resources in line with a strategic view of where the greatest growth potential lies. In a sense, it is the policy response to the arguments in favour of industrialisation examined in Chapter 2. For many years, thinking about industrial policy was associated with the unsuccessful import substitution experiences in much of the developing world where trade barriers were used to encourage domestic production at the expense of imports. As noted in Chapter 3, much of this protected activity was high cost and inefficient by international standards. However, East Asian experience, whilst highly varied between countries, showed that when used flexibly, industrial policy could be associated with both a rapid growth of exports as well as successful import substitution.

More recently, there has been a revival of interest in aspects of industrial policy. This has been stimulated in part by globalisation and the perceived need to develop competitiveness strategies for economies. Governments have asked understandably what they can do to stimulate local production and maintain jobs in the context of an increasingly competitive world economy. An analysis of past industrial policy provides part of the answer to such a question. In addition, recent theorising about the behaviour of markets and the tendency towards *market failure* in the sense of externalities, imperfect information and monopolisation has created an intellectual case for greater policy activism.[1]

For example, a key failure of markets that in principle may be rectified by government intervention is that left to themselves they will generate insufficient innovation. Innovative firms create an external benefit for others, because they show other producers what can be produced profitably. The analysis illustrated in Chapter 5 (Figure 5.2) in the context of technical change holds here also. In this case, industrial policy will be the mechanism to intervene to shift allocation away from OQ (which is what the firm and the market would choose) to OQ* (which is what benefits society most). Box 7.1 summarises the different dimensions of industrial policy and sets out a taxonomy of possible interventions.

Box 7.1 Industrial policy

Industrial policy is used here in the sense of any measure used by a government to influence the allocation of resources to foster industrial development. As such, it has three dimensions:

- A vision or strategy that sets out what the government wants to achieve; this can be specified in general terms (e.g. increased international competitiveness or the development of higher-technology industry) or in very specific terms (e.g. a target share of exports taken by new manufactured goods or of manufacturing in total national income).
- A process through which the government interacts with the private sector to identify constraints to growth and solutions to overcome these.
- A set of instruments to implement the broad objectives of the vision or strategy.

Policy cannot be effective without a satisfactory interaction between all the three. Well-articulated strategies can be meaningless if the private sector is not induced to participate or if the application of the instruments is operated on a sectional basis favouring some groups over others. Similarly, well-executed instruments that address the wrong constraints or target the wrong priorities will not help very much.

Next, a taxonomy of possible industrial policy instruments is given, distinguishing between *market-based* and *promotional* measures, where broadly the former aim to correct for market failures as they affect existing activity and the latter to promote or create new activities with the potential for productivity growth and externalities (or to restructure activities with potential). *Functional* means widely available as opposed to *selective*, which refers to measures that favour particular sub-sectors or firms (although the distinction is never precise). Although the correspondence is not exact, many of the measures used in the East Asian NIEs at a relatively early stage if their development equate to promotional measures with the market-based measures closer to later interventions in the NIEs.

Industrial policy instruments

Market-based measures	*Coverage*	*Rationale*
R and D tax credits	Functional	Technology spillovers and risk-taking externalities
State industrial research and education	Functional	Creation of national technological capability
Labour training subsidy	Functional	Labour training externality
State venture capital funds	Selective	Risk taking externality
State export promotion agency	Functional	Lack of information and provision of a public good
Infrastructure provision for Special Economic Zones	Functional	Encouragement of clustering and agglomeration effects
Profits tax holidays	Functional	Encouragement of manufacturing investment
Undervaluation of exchange rate	Functional	Encouragement of internationally traded activities, including manufacturing
Promotional measures	*Coverage*	*Rationale*
Temporary financial assistance	Selective	Funding to allow restructuring of uncompetitive activities
Temporary import tariff protection	Selective	Protection of uncompetitive activities requiring restructuring
State procurement policy	Selective	Priority in access to public sector contracts
Export subsidy	Selective	Differential rates of subsidy based on productivity potential
Import tariffs	Selective	Differential rates of protection based on productivity potential
Directed credit	Selective	Priority allocation of credit based on productivity potential
Profits tax holidays	Selective	Favourable tax treatment for foreign investors
Incentive packages of tax, loans and infrastructure	Selective	Favourable treatment for foreign investors

As set out, the degree of controversy over these measures increases moving down the sequence. Thus, most governments subsidise private sector R and D, provide some state investment into research with commercial potential and fund labour training. The market-based measures have been described in many countries as *competitiveness policy* and most countries apply some or all of these. On the other hand, developing country governments are typically warned against selective promotional measures, particularly because of the risk of rent seeking, and WTO rules and those of regional trading agreements limit the scope for promotional measures. Selective as opposed to functional or general support is potentially actionable at WTO, where trading partners can show damage to their industries from such interventions, although in practice as yet very few such cases have been brought against low-income countries.

Whilst the theory is clear critics argue both that governments will often not know what is socially optimal and that the ways of intervening to achieve what is perceived as optimality may in turn create biases and distortions in the economy.[2] What is special about the East Asian experience with industrial policy is that unlike much experience elsewhere, governments appeared to judge correctly where and when to intervene and found ways of minimising any harmful side effect from this intervention. This chapter examines the role of industrial policy in the first- and second-tier NIEs in their formative growth periods, largely covering 1960 to the mid-1990s. At the end, it considers the relevance of this story for current policy given the present regulations of the WTO which rule out many of the measures used earlier in the region. The recent experience of China and India is considered separately in Chapter 8.

Export-led growth and the ladder of comparative advantage

There is no single policy model that can be described as the East Asian model; however, when generalisations are drawn about industrial policy in the region, they are usually based on the framework applied in Korea in the 1970s (at the high point of intervention there). Not only did this framework differ from that applied in other countries of the region, but policy in Korea itself has also undergone much change and the highly interventionist stance of the 1970s was replaced by a much more limited role for government in the following decades. Nonetheless, despite many differences of detail, there are some similarities in the patterns of development and in the policies used in the region.

There is no single factor that can explain the rapid economic growth of the first-tier (Hong Kong, Singapore, Korea and Taiwan) and second-tier (Malaysia, Thailand and to a lesser extent Indonesia) NIEs. However, it is a fact that in all cases, manufactured exports grew very rapidly and in most interpretations are seen as a critical factor in economic take-off around 1960 for the first-tier NIEs and in the early 1980s for the second tier. For example, the share of the first-tier countries in world manufactured exports rose from about 1.5 per cent in 1965 to over 5 per cent in 1980, whilst the share of the second tier although much smaller also rose, from less than 0.5 per cent in 1980 to 1.5 per cent in 1993.[3] The rapid growth of exports of manufactures was also found in China in the 1990s and has been continued into the present century.

There was broad similarity in the types of export industries in which the countries specialised at comparable stages of their development. This has been described as a *flying geese pattern* where, like geese, industries migrate between countries in response to changing market conditions (often driven by changes in wage rates). All countries started with a focus on technologically simple labour-intensive goods – such as clothing, sports goods, toys and processed foods. The speed at which countries graduated out of these into a range of more capital-intensive and technologically more sophisticated items varied, but there was clear tendency for this to occur with the second-tier countries emerging as exporters to fill the gaps in the export markets vacated by the first-tier economies. This common pattern of an initial specialisation on either labour intensive or natural resource intensive products, followed as resource endowments change by a move into more capital, skill and technology-intensive goods is precisely what is predicted by an analysis of the stages of comparative advantage (see Chapter 3). The changing export composition for Korea is a clear illustration of this shift up the ladder of comparative advantage. In 1961, the largest single export item was iron ore (13 per cent of the total); in 1980 the largest single item was textiles and clothing (at 29 per cent), whilst by1989 electronics had emerged as the single largest export category (also at 29 per cent).[4]

Over the period, there were several broad shifts in the composition of exports. For the first-tier NIEs (with the exception of Hong Kong), whilst in the mid-1960s primary product exports (principally food) were important, these declined rapidly as a share of total exports. Initially, textile, clothing and footwear exports dominated manufactured exports; however, a key trend in the first-tier NIEs was the emergence in the 1980s of substantial exports of capital-intensive and technologically more complex goods, like electrical machinery, chemicals and pharmaceuticals, computers and communication equipment with some of these goods embodying advanced best-practice technology. A broadly similar pattern was found in the second-tier NIEs with some differences of timing and content. Textile, clothing and footwear became the key exports approximately 20 years later than in the first-tier economies in the late 1980s rather than the 1960s. In the 1990s, in Malaysia and Thailand (again to a lesser extent in Indonesia) there was a major shift towards exports of higher-technology products as part of the process of global fragmentation of production (discussed in Chapter 4). This process was also in evidence in the Philippines, although the latter is not normally included as one of the second-tier NIEs due to its relatively slower economic growth. By the end of the 1990s, roughly, half of Malaysia-manufactured exports were in high-technology products and over one-third of Thailand's were in the same category. In the second-tier NIEs, these moves into the exports of high-technology products were driven by foreign direct investment as transnational firms (often but not exclusively from Japan) shifted the labour-intensive parts of their global production networks to lower-wage economies in the region.[5]

All countries, with the exception of Hong Kong, who has always been an open trading centre, started their industrialisation with varying degrees of trade protection by import tariffs and controls, with governments pursuing versions of import substitution. Whilst import tariffs raised barriers to imports and encouraged domestic sales, a variety of measures were also used to boost manufactured exports, including financial subsidies to export, the establishment of special export processing zones where exporters operated outside the normal tax regime of the country and could import all their production inputs duty-free, formal quantitative export targets and the avoidance of exchange rate over-valuation. As production experience and technological capability were built up, controls on imports were gradually dismantled initially in the first-tier and latterly in the second-tier economies.

In most interpretations of the story of high growth in East Asia, the NIEs are seen as taking advantage of the expansion of world trade by basing their economic strategy around a rapid growth of manufactured exports. This was quite distinct from other strategies at the time, where the export market was perceived as useful but largely unattainable for manufactures, necessitating the need to focus on sales in a sheltered domestic market. There has been debate about how important export demand was in the economies of Korea and Taiwan, since their exports were no more than 5 and 10 per cent of GDP, respectively, at the start of the high-growth periods in the early 1960s and arguably, this share would have been too small to create a substantial macro-economic stimulus. Nonetheless, even here, where domestic investment may have a played a greater role in growth, export markets could have provided the initial stimulus for investment.[6] Box 7.2 reports an empirical attempt to disentangle the relative importance of export growth, replacement of imports and growth of domestic demand in the first- and second-tier NIEs over part of this period.

Box 7.2 Export demand in the NIEs

Growth of manufactured exports has been very strong in East Asia and over the 1990s, the region increased its share of world manufactured exports by nearly 4 percentage points. In contrast, Latin America increased its share by less than 0.5 percentage points over the same period. Output as well as exports was growing rapidly and demand decomposition analysis is a means of disentangling the factors causing output growth. This can be done by breaking down increase in output over a given period into growth of domestic demand, holding the share of imports in demand constant, the growth of exports and import substitution, given by the change in the share of imports in domestic demand. This follows from the identity

$$P = d_1{}^*S + X + (d_2 - d_1){}^*S_2 \qquad (7.1)$$

where P is the change in domestic production between periods 1 and 2, S is the change in domestic supply (domestic production plus imports), S_2 is domestic supply in period 2, X is the change in exports and d_1 and d_2

are the shares of domestic production in domestic supply in periods 1 and 2, respectively. With division by *P* the contribution of the three sources output growth can be identified; the ratio $(d_1 * S)/P$ gives the contribution of domestic demand, *X/P* gives the contribution of export expansion and $((d_2 - d_1) * S_2)/P$ that of import substitution. A negative term for this latter effect means imports are rising as a share of domestic supply. A negative term for the export share (*X/P*) means an absolute fall in export value over the period.

This analysis was carried out for the 1980s and 1990s for the first- and second-tier NIEs and for contrast for a sample of Latin American economies. Some of the key results are summarised in the following section, distinguishing between manufactured goods on the basis of technology classification (resource-based, low-technology and medium–high technology). The results show the relative importance of export demand in the 1980s for the first-tier NIEs (taking 75 per cent of output expansion in the low technology category and 44 per cent in the medium- and high-technology category). These export shares are considerably higher than in Latin America. In the second-tier NIEs in the 1980s, export demand was proportionately even more important in the medium- and high-technology category (at over 80 per cent of output) representing the expansion of global production networks in these goods. By the 1990s, export demand had become proportionately more important in the second-tier than in the first-tier NIEs, as the domestic market in the latter had grown considerably. By the early 1990s, Latin American manufactured exports grew more slowly than manufactured exports in the East Asian NIEs (and the low technology category registered an absolute decline), although proportionately the share of export demand in the medium- and high-technology category exceeded that in the first-tier NIEs.

Region/time period	*Technology category*	*Domestic demand %*	*Export expansion %*	*Import substitution %*
First-tier NIEs 1985–89				
	Resource-based	91	15	–6
	Low technology	48	75	–23
	Medium–high technology	57	44	–2
1990–94				
	Resource-based	103	10	–13
	Low technology	60	40	0
	Medium–high technology	68	34	–2

(Cont'd)

Region/time period	*Technology category*	*Domestic demand %*	*Export expansion %*	*Import substitution %*
Second-tier NIEs 1985–89				
	Resource-based	99	–45	46
	Low technology	66	28	7
	Medium–high technology	39	81	–20
Second-tier NIEs 1990–94				
	Resource-based	77	31	–8
	Low technology	59	44	–3
	Medium–high technology	48	50	2
Latin America 1985–89				
	Resource-based	95	28	–23
	Low technology	83	25	–8
	Medium–high technology	129	–4	–24
1990–94				
	Resource-based	93	20	–13
	Low technology	136	–2	–34
	Medium–high technology	86	42	–28

Source: Weiss and Jalilian (2004).

Note
First-tier NIEs are Hong Kong, Singapore, Korea, Taiwan. Second-tier NIEs are Indonesia, Malaysia, Philippines, Thailand.

Export growth is claimed to have created significant benefits for the successful East Asian exporters. As discussed in Chapter 3, there are several possible mechanisms through which countries can benefit from rising exports:

- Export expansion allows producers to grow beyond the confines of the domestic market. There is likely to be an 'easy' stage of import substitution where demand originally served by imports can be satisfied. Beyond that, however, without exports demand, growth will be constrained by the growth of domestic incomes. In agrarian economies, domestic market growth will be driven by growth in agriculture which is likely to face physical limits due to land availability. Exporting overcomes a demand bottleneck and in activities where economies of scale are important, the declining unit costs as output expands will help to further stimulate output growth. The small economies of Hong Kong and Singapore in particular have small populations and firms operating there could not have attained economies of scale in production selling in the domestic market.

- Exporting exposes domestic producers to technologies and marketing links that would not have been available for domestic sales. As part of contract manufacturing in global production networks East Asian firms were exposed to foreign designs and technologies which allowed them to upgrade their production to international standards, thus raising productivity.
- Rapid growth of exports also generated the foreign exchange to fund the purchase of equipment imports embodying new technology as well as the purchase of technology under license. As discussed in Chapter 5, technology imports and their adaptation and modification is likely to have played a major role in the rapid industrialisation of the region.

Were there special preconditions for growth in East Asia?

In addition to the focus on manufactured exports, two features of the East Asian NIEs are often singled out as special and therefore as contributing to their high growth performance; these are their high education attainments and a high savings rates relative to countries with a similar income level. On its own, a highly educated population need not bring growth, but in combination with stimuli like high savings and the growth of exports, the availability of a skilled and educated workforce will be an important contributory factor. In regression models of the link between foreign investment and growth, for example, a common result is that the foreign investment variable is only significant where it is used in combination with a measure of education attainment. In other words, additional foreign investment raises growth more, the more educated the population is.[7]

There is evidence that in 1960 all the NIEs (with the exception of Indonesia) had an education level higher than, that would be expected for their income level. Even in Indonesia where literacy was low, it was not as low as expected for its low per capita income.[8] Government policy built on this initial advantage. Although in the region the share of education expenditure in GDP did not differ much from the developing country average, expenditure per pupil rose in line with rapid income growth and in the first-tier NIEs due to a shift in the population structure with a slower increase in school age children relative to other regions.

High domestic savings funding high rates of investment were found in the NIEs, although it is likely that rather than high savings causing high investment and hence high growth, savings rates (i.e. the share of income saved) were an outcome of the growth process itself. It is well established empirically that at low levels of income, domestic savings rates are low, with savings rates rising with income growth. For example, in the early 1960s, savings in Korea, Singapore and Taiwan were only around 10 per cent of GDP and rose substantially in later years. The savings rates in the second-tier NIEs were higher at the start of their export booms in the 1980s, but nonetheless still rose with the growth of incomes. It is no coincidence that historically savings have been lower in the Philippines, the slowest growing economy in East Asia, than in any other country in the region. Savings can also respond to demographic factors with, for example, a rising share of the working age group in the total population leading to a higher share of savings in national income. It has been argued that falling birth rates in the first-tier NIEs led to such a shift in population distribution, which also helped to raise savings rates.

High domestic savings allowed the financing of high rates of domestic investment and recent interpretations of the East Asian experience have stressed the interaction of high exports, high investment and high savings as the cumulative driver of the growth process.[9] Exports and domestic investment combined to provide the demand stimulus and the domestic savings out of the profits from investment provided the bulk of finance for further investment. Efficiency gains in terms of improved total factor productivity are now seen as a relatively modest source of growth as compared with higher investment. Furthermore, as discussed in Chapter 5, much of the new investment in manufacturing embodied foreign technology, which was subsequently adapted and modified for local conditions. The export market provided the key incentive to invest; however, experience in other parts of the world shows that a rising export share in national income is not inevitably followed by a sustained expansion of domestic investment. Hence, an explanation of why the initial growth spurt in the NIEs was followed by a sustained growth of investment becomes important, and it is here that one can turn to the role of government; see Box 7.3 for a discussion of Japanese experience that had a strong influence on policy thinking in Korea and Taiwan.

Box 7.3 Industrial policy in Japan post-1945

In many ways, the industrial policy pursued in Japan in the 1950s and 1960s provided a model for Korea and Taiwan to follow. The Japanese government, through the Ministry of International Trade and Industry (MITI), had a clear vision of how it wished to change the industrial structure, away from labour-intensive goods in which the country had a short-term comparative advantage towards goods that met the twin criteria of a high income elasticity of demand and a strong potential for productivity growth. Industrialisation in the 1950s and much of the 1960s was behind protective import tariffs and quota barriers; estimates of effective protection found rates as high as 66 per cent for automobiles and 49 per cent for clothing in the mid-1960s. Manufactured exports were not ignored, however, and profits tax incentives and the availability of subsidised credit provided export subsidies to offset, at least partially, the anti-export bias of the protective system. Foreign direct investment was also tightly controlled initially with a view to boosting the position of nationally owned firms, so that foreign firms switching to exploit their technology were forced to either set up joint ventures or to licence its use to domestic firms. Liberalisation of trade and foreign investment was ended in the period from the late 1960s to early 1970s, as part of Japan's re-emergence as a full partner in the global trading community and its membership of the General Agreement on Tariffs and Trade (GATT), but trade reform was introduced gradually and from a position of increasing competitiveness not weakness. Like China, currently it was running large trade surpluses with most countries and liberalisation allowed these to be reduced.

Although there has been a dispute as to how influential the MITI actually was in influencing the behaviour of the private sector over this period, there is no doubt that it introduced a series of measures aimed at improving industrial competitiveness which provided a model for other countries in the region to follow. Several features are particularly distinctive:

- Through licensing access to foreign technology the government was able to influence the pattern of industrial development; for example, in the 1950s access to licenses for consumer goods technology was restricted, with priority given to technology for capital and intermediate goods.
- The issue of licences to import foreign technology was also used to control entry into a sector to avoid small and therefore uneconomic scale of plants and what was deemed *excessive competition*.
- Informal suggestions by government (termed *administrative guidance*) combined with access to subsidised credit and tax incentives were used to encourage mergers and encourage specialisation between competing firms, plant modernisation and enterprise restructuring.
- Foreign direct investment was tightly controlled initially and in some cases firms formed by joint ventures with local partners were required to restrict production in their early years to allow local firms to improve their competitiveness and to licence their technology at 'reasonable rates' to local firms.

There were limits as to how far MITI was able to change private sector decisions, for example, the mergers it tried to encourage in the automobile sector did not go through, whilst others it had little involvement with went ahead because the firms involved wanted to merge. The general point is that government policy tried to influence private sector decisions, through a combination of suggestion and incentive, for the wider national good and the economic success of Japan in the 1960s and 1970s meant that this was a lesson picked up by other governments in the region.

Source: Weiss (1986).

The role of government in export growth

Precisely how the NIEs moved beyond their initial growth spurt to a period of sustained expansion is the key policy question of the East Asian experience.

The basic facts as outlined earlier indicate that all countries went through a period of export upgrading in a move up the ladder of comparative advantage into products with higher domestic value added and technological complexity. The first-tier NIEs were helped by the rapid expansion of world trade in the 1960s, but the increase in their shares in this trade was also impressive. Whilst, as noted earlier, no single common pattern exists, some generalisations about this experience are possible. Hong Kong remains the exception in this story.

In relation to the role of government the creation of a generally supportive environment for private investment, through support for the enforcement of contracts and property rights through the legal system, and the avoidance of serious macro-economic imbalances that could have created high rates of inflation and uncompetitive exchange rates (which would have seriously hindered exports) are widely acknowledged as having been important. In addition, however, a variety of specific interventions that affected manufacturing industry (i.e. the tools of industrial policy) created *rents* (i.e. higher than normal or competitive profits) for manufacturers, particularly exporters, which provided the incentive for re-investment and further expansion. The set of interventions used to generate rents varied between countries, as did the main beneficiary groups. However, in all of the NIEs, except Hong Kong, such policies were employed with the most extensive set of interventions in Korea and Taiwan. The outcome was that the profitability of the manufacturing sector was raised relative to that of other sectors. This in itself was far from unusual, since it is the result expected under an import-substitution trade strategy; however, what differed in the NIEs was the strong focus on manufactured exports with the beneficial result noted before.

In terms of stimulating exports, the NIEs introduced measures that (with the exception of export subsidies) broadly reflect the policy advice given currently to governments wishing to encourage manufactured exports. These covered:

- Adequate price incentives, based on a competitive exchange rate that at times was kept low specifically to encourage exports.
- Access to imported inputs required in the production of exports at world prices, either because they were not subject to import tariffs or if they were through the refunding or the waiving of these tariffs.
- A strong base of physical infrastructure (ports, roads, power supplies, and so forth) and of social infrastructure (through education and training facilities).
- The availability of finance to either support production (e.g. through export subsidies) or to fund sales through trade credits.

However, this general list does not reveal the full story and, with national variations, governments of the East Asian NIEs used a variety of much less conventional measures to raise the profitability of exporting and in particular to encourage industrialisation. These included:

- Selective import tariff protection for sales in the home market, which generated extra profits that firms used to fund the subsidisation of their exports (this was particularly important in Korea and to some extent in Taiwan, but less so elsewhere in the region).

- Access to finance for exporters at special low interest rates.
- Tax concessions to new investors in the form of periods during which they paid no tax (*tax holidays*) or in terms of the costs that could be used as an offset against tax liability (*accelerated depreciation allowances*).
- Preferential access to licenses to exporters for the import of capital goods or foreign technology.
- Priority lending to specific enterprises, where banks were set priorities by governments based on perceived export potential of different firms (*directed credit*).
- Creation of subsidised infrastructure and factory space for export-oriented firms locating in export processing zones.
- Encouragement of national commercial research and development both directly through government research institutes and universities and indirectly through tax credits to private firms, which treated investment in this area as tax deductible.
- Control of wage costs for firms through restrictions on labour bargaining or the subsidisation of wages through public housing programmes (really only in Singapore).
- Encouragement to foreign direct investment via tax and other incentives (principally in Singapore, Malaysia and Thailand, with foreign investment less significant in South Korea and Taiwan).

Sometimes these measures were generally available to all firms or to all firms in a particular line of production (*functional measures*), whilst in other cases, they were only available to favoured firms (*selective measures*). In some instances, these measures emerged in response to particular situations, such as a shortage of foreign currency or the need to create jobs, and developed ad hoc rather than as part of an overall strategy. Strategic use of these interventions was found most obviously in Korea, Taiwan and Singapore, and as noted earlier, it is normally the Korean experience that people have in mind when identifying an East Asian model of industrial policy.

It is also worth noting that a range of similar measures were common in today's rich countries at earlier stages of their development in the nineteenth and twentieth centuries as they supported their own then nascent industries.[10] However, in the second-tier NIEs of the region – Indonesia, Malaysia and Thailand (and including here the Philippines) – such interventions whilst present were often less clearly linked with the need for export growth and a transformation of the structure of the economy and more often with transferring income to particular beneficiaries, either on an ethnic, family or interest group basis.

In other developing economies, similar measures were tried in the past, but with much less success than in East Asia, with uncompetitive production sheltered from foreign competition but unable to break into export markets, typically the result. Even within East Asia, the effectiveness of these measures appears to have varied considerably between countries with the extremes being the successful cases of Korea and Taiwan and the largely failed case of Indonesia. Explanations for the success of these policies, where they worked well, usually single out two important aspects of their implementation.

- One is the time limited nature of the support offered to firms which was set for a given period to give firms an incentive to reduce costs and improve competitiveness to be ready for the point at which support would be withdrawn. This is clearest in cases where special protection through import tariffs was offered on infant industry grounds, but applied equally to incentives like preferential access to loans, subsidised power or factory space. This time-limited support is in direct contrast with the perceived blanket semi-permanent protection on offer in other parts of the developing world as part of import substitution strategies.
- The other explanation is that the higher profits or rents created by the special support offered to firms had to be competed for through contests between firms that created a form of competition. The clearest example here is the export targeting system used in Korea in the 1960s and 1970s where firms' access to concessional credit or licenses for investment or imports was determined by their success in meeting specific targets for export sales. Such contests, or *performance requirements*, were used widely in the region and elsewhere, but what is singular about the Korean, Taiwanese and to some degree the Singaporean cases, is the way in which the public bureaucracy was able to administer them effectively, in a way that met national economic objectives and did not degenerate into a struggle for personal gain on behalf of officials and the business sector. Precisely why this was possible in a few countries and not others remains a major puzzle.[11]

Economic analyses of this experience with export promotion have stressed the effect of price incentives. A common feature in countries of the region (up to the mid-1990s) was the avoidance of an exchange rate that overvalued national relative to foreign currency and which thus provided a boost to exports. In a few instances (such as Korea and Taiwan in the 1980s), governments deliberately managed the exchange rates to undervalue the national currency to boost new, principally manufactured exports (much as China has been accused of doing in the early years of the present century).

Considerable emphasis has been placed on how far these economies were able to avoid the bias against exports that is inherent in any system of trade protection. Such a bias arises since import tariff protection raises the prices at which imports can be sold domestically and thus boosts the profitability of domestic sales as compared with exports (see Chapter 3). The support measures outlined in the foregoing section worked to counteract this effect, because directly or indirectly they raised the profitability of exporting. In fact, empirical work for the 1960s identified a slight bias overall in favour of exports in Korea and Taiwan, although this average result does not rule out an anti-export bias in some sub-sectors of manufacturing.

In the first-tier NIEs in the 1960s and 1970s, a dual industrial structure operated with the same firms engaged in both import-competing and export production. Where a bias in favour of domestic sales existed, protected domestic firms were strongly encouraged through a combination of government pressure and financial incentives to break into export markets, even if in the short term such sales were less profitable. Financially this was feasible for such firms, because the profits from the protected domestic market could be used to cover any extra costs from exporting. In the second-tier NIEs, the dualistic structure in manufacturing was even more pronounced with one segment serving the protected domestic market and the other, largely driven by foreign investors and based in export processing zones, serving the international market. In this fragmented structure, switching of sales between the domestic and export markets was less common (particularly with the low domestic purchasing power in these economies) and hence the issue of anti-export bias was less significant. The important general point is that the government support measures raised the profitability of manufacturing relative to other sectors, with different instruments important in different economies at different times. Hence, whether the mechanism was tariff protection, export subsidies, subsidised credit and infrastructure or exchange rate undervaluation, the consequence was higher profitability for manufacturing and this combined with financial incentives and government pressure to export yielded a rapid growth in manufactured exports.

Country experiences

Country experiences varied in East Asia, both in terms of the interventions used at different times, and in terms of the major beneficiaries. For example, in Korea these were principally the large conglomerate firms (the *chaebol*), in Taiwan small- and medium-sized enterprises, in Malaysia Malay-owned (as opposed to Chinese-owned) firms and to some extent foreign investors, and in Singapore also foreign firms were key beneficiaries. In Indonesia, cronyism was particularly rife and political and family connections determined who gained most. Given this diversity, it is not surprising that the use to which these extra incomes or rents were put varied, as did their effectiveness in generating further exports and investment.

As noted in the foregoing section, Korea and Taiwan provide the clearest examples of a systematic and strategic application of industrial policy. However, in both these countries, this policy went through various phases from the 1960s and in both was gradually wound down in the 1990s once industries there had attained international competitiveness.[12]

Industrial policy in Korea

Initial efforts at industrialisation in the early 1960s focused on building up manufactured exports, principally in labour-intensive, low-technology goods, such as processed foods, clothing, footwear, sports goods and toys. During this period, there was import tariff protection of the domestic market at relatively high rates for some sectors and a system of licensing controls over who had access to foreign currency and imports. Government direction of the banking sector ensured that credit went to priority areas of which exports became the most important. Export promotion measures included subsidised credit for working capital, investment and trade finance, preferential access to licenses for foreign currency, direct cash payments and import tariff-free access to imported inputs used in the production of exports. This latter facility was also extended to indirect exporters, defined as local suppliers of inputs to exporters. From the mid-1960s onwards, firms were set specific export targets and receipt of long-term credit was linked directly with achievements in meeting these targets. This array of incentives was available for all manufacturers and the explicit or implicit subsidies to exporters largely offset the incentive to domestic sales granted by import protection and this largely avoided serious anti-export bias. At this stage, it was exports in general rather than particular sectors or firms that were supported, so interventions were largely functional rather than selective.

From the late 1960s, policy discussion in Korea shifted beyond a general export drive to the need to broaden the industrial base by moving into the production of industrial intermediate goods (like steel, plastics and chemicals) and heavy industry (like ships, and engineering equipment). This was formalised in a Presidential Decree on the Heavy and Chemical Industry Drive of 1973, which gave priority to six sectors – steel, petrochemicals, nonferrous metals, shipbuilding, electronics and machinery. These sectors were given short-term export targets and official statements made it clear that international competitiveness was to be achieved within a ten-year period. This focus on heavy capital-intensive activities was despite the fact that in the 1970s Korea's income per capita was still very low in comparison with developed economies.[13] At this stage, government support became more selective with individual large firms promoted on the grounds that large firms were needed to achieve economies of scale. It was at this stage that well-known firms like Samsung, Hyundai and Daewoo received more favourable treatment in comparison with their competitors. In particular, the government provided a guarantee for foreign borrowing that favoured firms engaged in exports. *Policy lending*, the channelling of funds to priority sectors and to favoured firms within these, was used extensively and at its peak in 1978 this directed credit accounted for over half of all credit in the economy. Short-term loans for working capital at subsidised interest rates were available to any exporter, but long-term funds at attractive interest rates were only available to priority sectors and firms. There was thus a deliberate strategy to create large firms, to direct them into particular sectors and to support them financially, should they run into difficulties.

This system reached it height in the late 1970s and was relaxed in the 1980s with change coming gradually. There was a staged process of import liberalisation, involving the phasing out of import licensing and the reduction of import tariffs. Export incentives were reduced, as was the bias in favour of priority activities and firms. Restrictions on foreign investment were eased at this time as a way of accessing new technology. Bank credit allocation was still influenced by the government, but the role of policy lending was scaled down. Loans were still channelled to priority areas and firms, but new priorities were identified, principally in high-technology activities, based around electronics and precision equipment. Government support for technological improvements became a key aspect of policy from the 1980s onwards with the share of R and D expenditure to GDP rising to a level comparable with that found in the United States and Japan by the 1990s (see Chapter 5). Public support was provided through tax credits for enterprises' own R and D, by the flow of knowledge and personnel between public sector research laboratories and firms and by public education investment in applied technical subjects. Over the period from the mid-1960s to the mid-1980s, as much as two-thirds of private sector R and D is said to have been financed by state support.

In addition, there was a new focus on small and medium enterprises and on firms in need restructuring. This change signalled a recognition that government support should not just be to expand output and exports, but should also allow firms to get smaller and to reorient their business. In the Industrial Development Law that became effective in 1986 shipping, foreign construction, textiles, ferro-alloys, dyes and fertilisers were designated for restructuring. Firms in these sectors could apply for subsidised credit to finance the upgrading of equipment and to fund reorganisation and merger, and restrictions on further entry by new firms into these sectors could be imposed by the government to avoid over-capacity. Table 7.1 summarises some of the key stages in the evolution of policy.

By the early 1990s, the application of a highly interventionist industrial policy began to be wound down. As the economy strengthening and Korea became a

Table 7.1 Stages of industrial policy in Korea

Period	*Priorities*	*Main instruments*
1960–73	Exports in general – key sectors labour-intensive manufactures	Import tariff protection, export subsidies, tariff-refunds, subsidised credit and export targeting
1973–80	Heavy and chemical industries – priority sectors steel, petrochemicals, nonferrous metals, shipbuilding, electronics and machinery; priority firms selected large enterprises	As above plus use of policy loans to fund priority sectors and firms, tax credits as investment incentives
1980–90	Manufactured exports in high-technology activities, small and medium enterprises, firms in need of restructuring	Phased import liberalisation, some directed lending, investment incentives for R and D, ending of restrictions on foreign investment
1990 onwards	Private sector-led development, restructuring of large firms, after 1997 Crisis, development of internationally competitive economy	Financial sector reform, open capital account, and support for R and D

highly competitive industrial economy, the need for the earlier government support was felt to be less although after the Asian Financial Crisis of 1997, the government did intervene again to break up some of the large groups that it had earlier encouraged. A key element of strategy in the 1990s was to reform the financial sector and in particular, to reduce the role of policy lending to ensure that credit flowed to private firms with good investment ideas.

Industrial policy in Taiwan

Experience in Taiwan was broadly similar to that in Korea, with some subtle differences. There was also a strong focus on exports combined with early protection of the domestic market and subsequent measures by government to upgrade the industrial structure. In Taiwan, however, which is a much smaller economy, in contrast with Korea, small and medium private enterprises and public-sector enterprises played a relatively more significant role as compared with large private sector *chaebol* firms, which the government helped to build up in Korea. Furthermore, whilst policy lending to direct the credit of the banking system to preferred areas was applied, its use was much less pervasive than in Korea, so the dominance of the government over the financial system was less strong.

Initially, Taiwan followed conventional import substitution policies applying a combination of import tariffs and licensing restrictions on what could be imported to protect the domestic market. The main import substitution activities in the 1950s were low-technology labour-intensive goods, like textiles, clothing, wood and leather products. A strategic decision was taken at the end of the 1950s to move to what has been called an *export substitution* phase, where the structure of exports shifted away from primary goods towards labour-intensive manufactures. The policy instruments used to encourage manufactured exports included a rebate system to refund duties paid on imported inputs used in production for export, subsidised loans available for exporters only, a deliberately undervalued exchange rate to maximise the profitability of export sales in national currency and for certain industries an export targeting system (although this was not as widespread or significant as in Korea). Measures were taken to encourage export-oriented foreign investment, including relatively lengthy holiday periods during which firms paid no profits tax and the freedom to repatriate all profits. However, more restrictively in some industries, local content requirements were imposed on foreign-owned firms to force them to develop linkages with domestic suppliers. In 1965, as part of the export promotion drive, the statute setting up export processing zones was passed and by 1970 these accounted for around 10 per cent of the total value of exports. Manufactured exports in this period were still largely in labour-intensive, low-technology goods, but the important items had widened beyond textiles, clothing and agro-processed goods to include simple consumer electronics, like radios and refrigerators, as well as watches, clocks and toys. Export promotion was partially selective with some sectors, and firms within these, receiving priority in the allocation of credits. However, in the 1960s, protection of the domestic market remained substantial and as in Korea, a dualistic structure of import-competing and exporting firms emerged, with some cross-subsidisation between domestic sales and exports.

As in Korea, the need to upgrade the industrial structure became a priority in the 1970s with a phase of industrial consolidation. This involved a shift in strategy to the domestic production of industrial intermediates and capital goods, such as iron and steel, machine tools, petrochemicals and electrical machinery. The aim was to diversify the domestic production base and to use these newly produced goods as inputs into export production. Given the capital-intensive nature of these activities, public enterprises initially had a major role in their establishment. In addition, there was heavy public investment in supportive physical infrastructure. Loans to exporters, with a high subsidy element, remained important and reached a peak of around 20 per cent of the value of all loans in the mid-1970s.

The 1980s saw a gradual trade liberalisation and with the emergence of low wage competition in the second-tier NIEs, as in Korea, the government targeted high-technology goods as new potential exports. Strategic areas for priority support were information technology, machinery, precision instruments, biotechnology, electro-optics and environmental technology industries. Their identification was justified by a list of criteria which included not only their high-technology intensity, but also their low energy use and low pollution impact, as well as their high value added and market potential. This shift in priorities was supported by subsidised loans available for broad categories of activity, rather than for individual firms, and in practice, one estimate suggests that the proportion of these that actually went to the strategic activities was no more than one-third. All exporters continued to receive credit at preferential rates, although the subsidy component in this finance declined substantially over the decade, and they continued to receive tax credits unavailable for domestic sales.

Support for firms' own R and D came from tax credits for this type of expenditure and the government's own technology initiatives. Public research institutes had an active role in both the diffusion and adaptation of imported technology and in some new activities publicly owned pilot plants played a significant catalytic role in the development of new national technologies, before these pilots were later sold to the private sector. For example, in the early years of the semi-conductor industry in Taiwan, it was public sector not private firms which entered into joint ventures with the big international players, like Motorola, Phillips and IBM. The government also adopted an active policy on science parks locating these close to universities and technical centres to encourage dissemination of information and interchange between firms in the park and the research community. Table 7.2 summarises these distinct phases.

Again, in parallel with developments in Korea, the 1990s saw the end of most elements of selectivity in policy, as between firms and sectors. Trade and foreign currency liberalisation was largely complete by the end of the decade, the financial sector was liberalised with the ending of interest rate controls and of the use of directed credit and tax incentives were made more neutral as between activities being available for general expenditure like R and D, pollution control and energy conservation, rather than for exporting or for investment in specific priority sectors.

Table 7.2 Stages of industrial policy in Taiwan

Period	*Priorities*	*Main instruments*
1953–57	Import substitution – key sectors textiles, clothing and other labour-intensive goods	Import tariff protection and import quotas
1958–72	Export substitution in labour intensive manufactures, including garments and consumer electronics	Competitive exchange rate, rebates of import duties, tax credits, subsidised loans, export processing zones, foreign direct investment, some export targeting; import tariff protection and import quotas
	Some import substitution in intermediates – basic metals and chemicals	
1973–80	Industrial consolidation through import substitution of intermediate and capital goods; priority sectors – petrochemicals, steel, shipbuilding, automobiles, machine tools, electrical machinery, consumer electronics	Public investment in state enterprises, tax credits, policy loans, rebates of import tariffs, selected import protection
	Continued focus on exports	As above
1981–90	High-technology activities – strategic sectors – information technology, machinery, precision instruments, bio-technology, electro-optics, environmental technology	Trade liberalisation, policy loans, tax credits, public investment in infrastructure and research, science parks, encouragement to foreign investment
	Continued focus on exports	As above
1991 onwards	Private sector-led development in high-technology and environmentally sustainable activity	Financial liberalisation, public investment for R and D, science parks, education, encouragement to foreign investment

Public support for high-technology activities though R and D expenditure, the creation of infrastructure for science parks and the expansion of higher education became the new focus of industrial policy.

Industrial policy elsewhere

Elsewhere in the region, Singapore has also been identified as an economy with a strategic view of industrial policy. As a small city state with no agricultural hinterland and an historic role as trading centre, Singapore has always been heavily dependent on foreign trade. It had a relatively short period of import substitution in the early 1960s but rapidly liberalised its trade shortly after that to become virtually a free-trade economy by the early 1970s. Changing the structure of exports was a key objective of policy and was pursued by encouraging foreign investment through a combination of tax incentives, infrastructure facilities and the creation of a skilled and well-educated workforce. Tax credits were differentiated by type of export activity and were used to encourage a shift to skill and knowledge-based activities.

Singapore offers a distinct model in terms of technology policy, since here foreign firms have been the key actors and the role of government has been to induce these firms to conduct R and D and various technological adaptations in Singapore rather than elsewhere in their global network. This has required a combination of heavy subsidies for R and D – with one estimate suggesting at its peak for every dollar of private sector R and D the government provided up to 30 cents – and heavy public investment in higher education and high-standard public research laboratories that provided support services to firms' own laboratories. Much of the locally conducted R and D by foreign firms has been production-based rather than pure research, but nonetheless the success of the government in stimulating local R and D clearly differentiates Singapore from other economies with a strong presence of international firms.[14]

In other countries of the region, whilst governments frequently intervened in industrial activity, these interventions often lacked a clear economic rationale and their impact was often unhelpful for economic growth. In Malaysia, after an initial period of import substitution in the 1960s policy shifted to export promotion based largely on foreign investors located in export processing zones. At one point from the early 1970s to the mid-1980s, interventions were linked closely with ethnic distributional issues rather than economic efficiency as the New Economic Policy introduced in 1970 sought to alter the balance of wealth and influence between Malays and Chinese to ensure that the indigenous Malay community owned a certain proportion of enterprises. In addition, in the early 1980s, Malaysia had its own equivalent of the Korean drive to establish heavy and chemical industries with an attempt to deepen the industrial structure though domestic production of such goods with a view to increasing the linkages between exporters and local input suppliers. This strategy involved chiefly government investment in iron and steel, cement, the Proton car project, motorcycle engines, petrochemicals and pulp and paper. However, the results were largely disappointing. The public sector enterprises concerned typically operated behind high tariff barriers, but still experienced financial losses and were slow to generate exports. Many of these were privatised in the 1990s. Since then, there has been a renewed focus on high-technology manufactured exports typically produced by international firms with efforts made to develop clusters of local suppliers to provide these with inputs (see Box 6.7). The issue of how far the export sector has been integrated into the industrial structure of the economy remains a concern.

Thailand also has relied heavily on foreign investors to drive its manufactured exports. Policy interventions here have been criticised for creating a system of patronage that has favoured large business groups and which did not establish clear performance criteria for the receipt of government financial support. Similarly, Indonesia in the 1980s and 1990s under the Suharto regime is seen as the clearest example where industrial policy interventions were subverted to favour the politically well-connected rather than those who could use the resources effectively for industrial transformation. Here, tax credits and R and D subsidies had a quantitatively modest impact, and whilst subsidised credit was available to specific enterprises, this had little to do with their economic potential.

How effective was industrial policy?

The story of East Asian industrial policy is confusing in that whilst broadly speaking experience in Korea, Taiwan and Singapore was largely positive, most observers feel the opposite was true in other countries of the region. However, it is actually very difficult to prove that a particular set of policies altered the structure, efficiency and long-run growth prospects of industry. Detailed empirical analyses that examine this question are really only available for Korea and Taiwan, which are clearly the most likely candidates to demonstrate the success of industrial policy and these reveal positive, but in some cases no more than modest, effects.

Initial tests assessed three things[15]:

- Whether priority industries actually received the bulk of financial assistance from the government.
- Whether the industrial structure in countries with an active industrial policy differed from what would be expected given the countries income and population.
- Whether productivity growth was higher in the industries receiving special treatment than that in others that did not.

None of these tests proved conclusive. Whilst Korea channelled substantial funds to its priority activities, in Taiwan, data for the 1980s show a majority of funds went to declining industries in need to restructuring rather than to the strategic industries.[16] Cross-country comparison of industrial structure are of limited use, since they inevitably compare specific countries (here Korea and Taiwan) with a very mixed set of comparator countries; further, they imply that without industrial policy, the countries would have reached their actual income level, which is the hypothesis that is being tested.[17] Assessments of productivity trends in supported firms or activities are of greater relevance, since without a productivity gain, there will be no benefit from industrial policy. The available evidence suggests greater positive infant industry effects in Korea than that in other countries, and this coupled with successful exports from the supported firms is probably the best evidence available to support a positive impact for industrial policy.[18] How far such success actually raised GDP growth is less clear. Analysis using an input–output framework suggests a positive but modest impact of an additional 0.5 percentage points to the annual growth rate of Korea in the 1970s and 1980s; for Taiwan, the result is similar but slightly lower.[19]

However, despite the ambiguity in empirical tests, the fact that Korea, Taiwan and Singapore had an active policy and also grew rapidly suggests an association. The ability of policy to stimulate high private investment in manufacturing, which subsequently led to productivity improvement and to exports is the key.

Industrial policy interventions were not optimal *first best* policies (in the theoretical sense of minimising any negative or distortionary side effects). Individual policies may have led to resource misuse and high-cost production and not all supported firms were profitable (e.g. not all of the investment in the Korean Heavy and Chemical Industry Drive was successful). However, collectively, these interventions raised the profitability of manufacturing and the export incentives on offer ensured that the bias against exporting found in many other countries was largely absent in East Asia. Probably in all of the NIEs industrial policy (even when it was not well targeted in efficiency terms) succeeded in stimulating industrial investment.

Successful industrial policy must be applied flexibly, so that it changes in response to the changing needs of the economy and the external environment. In Korea and Taiwan, both policy objectives and the policy instruments to achieve these were adapted over time to fit the new circumstances. The targeting of specific sectors or firms in the 1960s and 1970s, for example, when the industrial structure was relatively simple, was replaced in the 1980s and 1990s by a more functional, less directive approach, more supportive of the decisions of individual firms, reflecting the growing diversity and sophistication of manufacturing in these economies. At a relatively early stage in industrial development, it is possible to target broad industrial categories to create productive capacity; however, as an economy becomes more sophisticated in the face of rapid technical change, it is difficult to establish what a priority activity is. Similarly, when the financial system is not well developed and it is difficult for investors to obtain long-term finance at reasonable interest rates (because of the perceived risk of new activities) governments can intervene effectively to direct and sometime subsidise credit for new investors. Arguably, this arrangement should be transitional, since as an economy evolves a market-based commercial banking system has advantages over one based on directed credit. In both countries, liberalisation of the financial sector became a key aspect of policy in the 1990s.

What can we learn from the East Asian model?

The international economic environment has changed greatly since the heyday of industrial policy in East Asia between 1960 and 1990. An important shift has been the reduction in policy discretion created by WTO rules and those imposed by regional free arrangements (see Chapter 3). All member countries of WTO have agreed to give up a significant degree of freedom in trade policy for the right of equal access to the markets of other members under the most favoured nation principle. Measures used earlier by the NIEs like import licensing that set limits on what could be imported, export subsidies, credit directed at favoured enterprises, firm-level export targets and targets for the proportion of inputs sourced nationally are all ruled out by the WTO, although least developed countries can continue with export subsidies on a temporary transitional basis. In particular, the use of export sales as an indicator of how far firms are meeting government targets and as a simple guide to determine priority in the allocation of credit or other forms of government support, which played a key role in the East Asian model, is ruled out on the grounds that it is a form of trade distortion.

There is some modest scope for discretion in that tariff rates can be differentiated with higher than average rates set for sensitive products and temporary import restrictions can be imposed in the face of an unexpected surge in imports that threatens domestic producers. Some subsidies are still allowed, for example, to support R and D or skills training, provided they do not directly distort trade by favouring exports or domestic production that competes with imports. Retaliation in the face of dumping (defined as an export price either below cost of production or below the domestic selling price of the same product) through temporary tariff or quota barriers is also allowed and has arguably been used as a form of protection by some countries.

Nonetheless, even with this limited scope for discretion there are doubts about the feasibility of subtle and effective interventions being replicated in other countries with a less effective and dedicated bureaucracy than that possessed by the East Asian NIEs. In Korea, Taiwan and Singapore the public bureaucracy pursued a strategic vision of how manufacturing, with a focus on manufactured exports, could be supported through a combination of carrot and stick policies. The carrot came through the extra income accruing through protective and support measures like tariff protection or cheap credit, whilst the stick for non-performing firms came through the withdrawal of this support and a shift to support rivals. The precise combination of political and social conditions necessary to create the environment in which this type of policy could flourish is still not yet wholly understood and as we have seen, it worked much less well even in other parts of East Asia. It does not appear to be a simple case of an incorruptible bureaucracy, since in Korea and Taiwan there is ample evidence that there were serious cases of public corruption. However, in these environments with strong state direction, unofficial payments did not undermine the long-run goals of industrial transformation (see Box 7.4).

Broadly speaking, when we think of industrial policy, there are two alternative versions. The first corresponds closely to the East Asian model from its heyday in the 1960–90 period. This involves governments in identifying priorities (whether types of sales like exports, sectors with the greatest growth potential or favoured firms within these sectors). A variety of instruments can be used to create higher incomes for these priority activities with a view to stimulating their growth. Contacts between the public bureaucracy and firms will be close with governments taking a directive role. As we have seen, arguably versions of this policy were highly effective at a critical period in the recent history of some of the NIEs. It can be important at a relatively early stage of industrial development where a broadly based industrial structure and a well-integrated financial system are lacking and where government intervention to stimulate industrial transformation has a major role. However, it is difficult to do well and has been open to abuse and misuse in other countries. In addition, current trade regulations make it difficult to pursue in its original form.

The second version of industrial policy is closer to what has happened in the first-tier NIEs post-1990, and is likely to be more appropriate at a more advanced

Box 7.4 Corruption and growth in East Asia

There is a well-established literature on the links between corruption and economic growth. Whilst the misuse of state resources for private gain might be thought to be detrimental to growth, there is a body of theory that argues that much will depend on how corruption is organised. Corruption that is centralised (i.e. controlled in an organised way) as opposed to decentralised and carried out by many competing officials will be less harmful economically. Centralised corruption, where the groups involved take a long-term view of development prospects may even be helpful if the exchange of bribes for promotional privileges leads to rents that are reinvested productively. This provides a hypothesis for the East Asian model that has been tested empirically using cross-country data in a standard growth accounting framework. The model tested is of the general form

$$gi = \alpha + \beta_1 GPi + \beta_2 Xi + \beta_3 CIi + \varepsilon \quad (7.2)$$

where g is GDP growth over a given period for country i, GP is average GDP per capita at the start of the period, Xi is vector of control variables expected to influence growth (like the share of investment in GDP, population growth, the school enrolment ratio and the share of government consumption in GDP), CI is measure of corruption and ε is the error term. Several alternative indices of corruption are applied of which that developed by the World Bank, as an aggregation of other indices, is taken as the most rigorous.

When this model is run, it is found that the corruption index is negatively and significantly associated with growth for small developing countries (so β_3 is negative and significant). This it is suggested may help to explain why the small countries in East Asia with good anti-corruption records – Singapore and Malaysia – have grown faster than might be expected given some of their other characteristics. However, the corruption index for large East Asian NIEs (which includes here China, as well as Korea, Indonesia Thailand and Japan) shows a positive association with growth, implying that higher levels of corruption help growth. This *East Asian paradox* underlies the industrial policy interventions discussed in the foregoing section, since mutually beneficial deals were struck between officials and firms that traded state support for bribes. The key difference between this scenario and that in other parts of the developing world is that in East Asia, the rents that accrued were largely invested productively, rather than being taken out of the country, squandered in conspicuous consumption or put into white elephant projects.

Source: Rock and Bennett (2004).

industrial stage when a number of industries have reached the stage of international competitiveness and are operating using best-practice technologies. This sees industrial policy as supporting or facilitating rather than directing the private sector. The focus is no longer on government priorities (or attempts to *pick winners*) and more on understanding what are the key bottlenecks faced by the private sector and how governments can help relieve these. This requires an open dialogue with the private sector, for example, building on links between ministries and industry associations, and identifying what the private sector sees as the key obstacles to growth.[20] This may then involve government investment, for example, in skills training, standards agencies or physical infrastructure. The focus would be on the provision of generic services rather on support to particular sectors, firms or types of activity. Support for innovation and risk-taking is an important aspect of this process, and can be through public provision of finance for new and inherently risky initiatives (*venture capital*) and for support for R and D and applied research, either though public funding or tax concessions.

This version of industrial policy defines it more as a process of interaction between public and private sectors, than a series of direct interventions by governments. No specific types of policy instrument need to be specified, since intervention should evolve flexibly in response to perceived bottlenecks. This version is now often described as a *competitiveness policy*, since it is concerned with finding ways of strengthening the position of firms within the economy in the context of a global search for markets. In recent years, in many lower- and lower-middle-income countries encouragement of foreign investment, either through export processing zones or special incentive packages, has been at the forefront of this strategy as part of attempts to link with global production networks.

Conclusions

It is difficult to argue that experiences in a small number of countries 30 or 40 years ago (in a very different world economy) provide a model for others to follow. Nonetheless, the East Asian experience provides us with some general lessons, even where its details may not be directly applicable today. First, measures to raise the profitability of manufacturing and particularly manufacturing geared to the world market can have strongly positive effects in terms of growth of incomes and jobs. Second, governments can have a useful role in this process, provided they interact effectively with the private sector and provide support on the basis of transparent performance criteria. Third, and perhaps critically, any industrial policy measures must be used flexibly and be adapted to the circumstances of the economy. Hence, for example, as the technology base of an economy develops, it will be increasingly difficult to spot potential winners in terms of activities or firms and governments must let winners emerge from the existing set of firms in an industry rather than try to pick them from the outset.

Further reading

There is vast literature on the East Asian experience of industrialisation. Weiss (2005) surveys much of this. Key contributions are Amsden (1989) and (2001), Wade (1990), World Bank (1993), UNCTAD (1996), Kim and Leipziger (1997) and Stiglitz and Yusuf (2001). Chang (2002) gives an historical perspective and Chang (2009a) and Rodrik (2007) survey the arguments for and against industrial policy. Noland and Pack (2003) give a more critical assessment of its importance in East Asia. Chang (2009b) and Lin (2009) is an interesting exchange on the potential for industrial policy based largely around an assessment of the East Asian model.

8 Giants awakened

India and China

The recent rapid growth of China and India is a critical factor in current trends in globalisation and confirms that countries once seen as the epitome of poor developing countries can achieve growth and industrialisation. These two large and populous countries were important trading nations in the seventeenth and eighteen centuries well before the British Industrial Revolution, with India, for example, an important producer and exporter of cotton textile and silk products. Table 8.1 gives approximate estimates of their joint share in world GDP and population at three points over the last 200 years. More recent trends are thus a reflection of a revival in importance of once powerful trading nations. China accounted for around 8 per cent of world exports of manufactures and India around 1 per cent in 2004 and these shares are expected to increase significantly over the coming decades. This chapter reviews the historical experience of the two countries in terms of industrial development and stresses the distinct pattern each has taken. It commences with a discussion of India, before turning to China. It concludes with a discussion of the implications of these experiences for industrialisation elsewhere.

India: industrialisation strategy and the Licence Raj

After independence from Britain in 1947 and the accompanying partition of the country between India and Pakistan, India embarked on an ambitious industrialisation drive with a view to transforming the structure of the economy. Historically, there has been a tradition of manufacturing production, but growth in the colonial period was slow and, at the beginning of the twentieth century, only around 0.5 million workers were estimated to be engaged in some way in industry, with the majority of these in the railways, cotton and jute textiles and coal mining. In the 1914–39 period, domestic industry was supported by protective import tariffs, which shielded it from the worst impact of the Great Depression of that period. Further boosts during the Second World War came from war-time expenditure (which increased the demand for items like cement, paper and steel) and from the break in international trade during this period. However, by 1947, the labour force in total factory employment was no more than 2 million (or around 2 per cent of the workforce) with manufacturing still dominated by the textile sector, which accounted for over two-thirds of manufacturing employment.[1]

Table 8.1 Shares of world income and population

Region	*Share of world GDP*			*Share of world population*		
	1820	*1950*	*1998*	*1820*	*1950*	*1998*
China and India	49.0	8.7	16.5	56.7	35.9	37.5
Industrialised countries[a]	22.7	50.9	45.5	13.4	18.1	11.6
Rest of Asia	7.3	6.8	13.0	8.6	15.5	19.8
Latin America	2.0	7.9	8.7	2.0	6.6	8.6
Africa	4.5	3.6	3.1	7.1	9.0	12.9

Source: Maddison (2006), cited in World Bank (2009, Table 3.1).

Note
a G7 countries.

The year 1951 saw the onset of what has been characterised as a pattern of government-planned industrialisation based around regular Five Year plans in which the government tried to direct the development of the economy through a combination of public sector investment, controls over the activities of the private sector and tariff and non-tariff barriers to trade. This was not planning in the command economy sense, as practiced in the Soviet Union or in Communist China in its pre-reform period, where very precise quantitative targets were set for individual enterprises with rewards and sanctions related to the achievement of these targets. Equally it was very different from the flexible system of interventions used in Korea and Taiwan, as discussed in Chapter 7. However, it represented a highly influential experiment in economic management that influenced thinking in many developing countries and which led during the 1960s and 1970s to the application of Five Year planning as standard procedure for governments in the developing world.

The Indian strategy is perhaps the clearest example of import substitution industrialisation in any country. The focus was initially on production for the domestic market (export incentives were introduced in the 1960s, but as we discuss in the following section they never removed the bias against exporting inherent in the trade protection system) with a widely held view that exports would be difficult to increase. A strict licensing system restricted access to foreign currency and provided goods could be produced domestically; it was very difficult to obtain the licence needed to import a foreign alternative. This trade control system was coupled with a suspicion of the private sector (at least at some points in time) and a desire to create equitable distributional outcomes in terms of regions and firms, which influenced the allocation of investment licences. Import substitution was to be not just in consumer goods but was to extend further back in the production chain to intermediates and capital goods (what later came to be termed *secondary import substitution*). This latter stage was justified formally by a theoretical model developed by the distinguished Indian planner P.C. Mahanalobis, which showed that under the assumption of a fixed amount of export earnings the level of investment in an economy will be determined by the domestic capacity to supply the capital equipment required by investors (see Box 8.1).

Box 8.1 The Mahanalobis model and a capital goods constraint

The model was based on the simple idea that to raise growth a country needs to increase investment as a share of income (holding its productivity constant). Investment needs to be financed by savings but even if planned (or *ex ante*) savings are high enough to fund a target level of investment, for the investment to occur it will require a physical quantity of equipment (or capital goods). These capital goods can either be imported or made domestically. If beyond a certain point export revenue cannot be increased then (unless capital inflows like Aid are available) these capital goods must be produced domestically. The Mahanalobis model assumes this latter scenario of an export constraint. Its key parameters are the proportions of investment going to capital goods to make consumer goods (λc) and to capital goods to make other capital goods (machines to make more machines) (λk), as well as the productivity of investment in the consumer and capital goods sectors, respectively (βc and βk, which are the marginal output–capital ratios).

The increase in investment between years t and $t - 1$ is determined by the allocation of capital goods in the previous year and by the productivity of the capital goods sector, so that

$$I_t - I_{t-1} = \lambda k.\beta k.I_{t-1} \qquad (8.1)$$

where I refers to investment and t is time in years.

Similarly, the increase in consumption C is determined by the allocation of capital goods in the previous year and by the productivity of the consumer goods sector, so that

$$C_t - C_{t-1} = \lambda c.\beta c.I_{t-1} \qquad (8.2)$$

The complete solution for total income Y at time t shows that it depends on the initial share of investment in income (so that holding other things constant, an economy that starts with a higher investment level will have a higher subsequent income), the productivities of the two sectors and the investment allocation. A higher allocation to the capital goods sector (λk) increases the capacity to invest and always raises subsequent income. However, although later income will be higher, in the model if productivity is higher in the consumer goods sector (so $\beta c > \beta k$) then in the short-term consumption will be lower the higher is λk, so there will be a choice between consumption now and higher consumption later. The model assumes that savings adapt to the physical composition of goods in the economy and that once installed in a sector capital goods cannot be shifted to another sector, so their use is fixed. Because the economy is assumed closed to foreign trade only by producing more capital goods can investment take place.

The model is a major simplification of reality and India was in no sense an economy that was closed to foreign trade. However, foreign exchange was scarce at the time, and the model was used in policy circles to justify a shift in investment towards heavy industry (broadly representing the machines to make machines strategy). The model provided a rationale for this approach but the precise choice of investment allocations, it seems, was not based on parameters of this model.

Source: Bhagwati and Desai (1970).

A key feature of the strategy was an attempt to control the private sector through a complex licensing system whereby investors over a certain size were required to obtain a licence for new industrial investment, as well as for substantial expansion of existing capacity; in addition and arguably most restrictive of all, where firms wished to manufacture new products, not contained in the original licence application, a further licence was required, greatly limiting producer flexibility to adapt to changing demand. A reservation policy restricting output in some sectors to small firms was also employed. The share of output reserved for small firms was high in sectors like hosiery, wood products, leather goods and food processing. A degree of priority was also offered to small firms through directives to banks to lend to them on subsidised terms.

This bureaucratic control system (which came to be known facetiously as the *Licence Raj*) commenced in the early days of planning in the initial post-Independence period in the 1950s and continued with varying degrees of restrictions and exemptions until the major reforms of the early 1990s. Its key objectives were to control the private sector to ensure that private sector initiatives conformed to government priorities. These priorities related to both targets for specific industries, as contained in the Five Year plans, as well as broader social objectives relating to the control of large monopoly firms and equity in the regional devolution of industry within the country. In activities where the private sector appeared unwilling to invest or in what were perceived as strategic industries (particularly in relation to capital goods like engineering products and industrial intermediates like steel and petroleum) public sector enterprises were established under the central government.

However, both the concept of such a bureaucratic control system and the details of how it operated were the subject of a vast amount of criticism, with many observers arguing that rather than fostering industrialisation it held back development in India by decades. Observers pointed to the inability of the system to encourage the private sector to meet priorities, since licensing could deny the right to expand, but could not induce it. Particular aspects of the operation of controls were found to be counter-productive; for example, the common procedure of approving applications in sequence created a position of market power for the early successful applicant, since once the necessary capacity was installed, new entrants could not obtain a licence thus stifling competition. Since large firms had the resources to apply early for licenses despite the avowed intent to restrict their market power, they were favoured by the system. Even where large firms were not permitted to install new capacity, they were not stopped from take-overs of other firms as a means of boosting their market position. The need for approval of product changes restricted firms' ability to respond to shifts in market demand. Finally, the allocation of licenses across states and regions of the country was often based on political not economic criteria leading to fragmentation and to factories that were too small to be economically efficient.[2]

Public sector enterprises in turn were criticised for having low profitability. This was sometimes due to controls imposed by the government on the prices they could set, as well as other interventions, for example, in relation to job creation, but in other instances poor profitability reflected low productivity and operating efficiency, poor project design and capital cost over-runs. This perceived weak performance was a key factor in the wave of industrial privatisations that commenced in the 1990s and continued into the following decade.

The detailed licensing system was modified slightly in the late 1970s in response to concerns over the slow growth of manufacturing; however, major change only occurred in 1985 when 25 broad categories of industries were exempted from the need to obtain a licence. Even in 1985, only just over a quarter of total industrial output came from de-licensed branches and the major change only came in 1991 by which time roughly 95 per cent of output came from industries not requiring a licence. Further decontrol included relaxation of the restrictions on foreign investment; for example, in 2002, the new Auto Policy allowed 100 per cent foreign ownership in the sector and ended the policy of imposing minimum local content in production and other restrictions. In 2006–07, industrial licensing was required for only five branches, and only three (relating to atomic energy and railways) were restricted to public sector enterprises. The policy of reserving parts of a branch or sub-sector for small firms continued, but on a much reduced scale and foreign investment was allowed on a 100 per cent basis in most activities.

An area of controls that still remains and is the subject of continued controversy relates to regulations governing the hiring and dismissal of workers. The original post-Independence legislation was designed to protect the workers' rights, but allowed employers to lay off or retrench workers as financial conditions required, subject to minimum levels of protection through stipulated notice periods, severance payments and the sequence of dismissal (on a last-in-first-out basis). The legislation was tightened in the mid-1970s for large firms (over 300 workers) where employers were obliged to obtain state government permission to lay off or dismiss the regular workforce. This control was extended to all firms of over 100 workers a few years later and its application has varied across states. Whilst retrenchment is not ruled out, the charge against this legislation is that it made labour policy a political issue at the state level and reduced the freedom of firms to decide how to use their workforce. The argument is that if it is difficult to dismiss workers when market conditions change firms will be reluctant to take on new labour.

How far such legislation is actually a serious restraint on firms is a matter of dispute, since some argue that firms have found a way around the most restrictive aspects of the legislation by using non-regular contract labour and that surveys of firms that seek opinions on the problem they face have found that in many instances labour regulations come low down the list of concerns after aspects like infrastructure quality and reliability, taxes and corruption.[3]

India: trade policy

The other key aspect of industrial strategy in India has been trade policy. Initially a tight import substitution regime was applied. Import tariffs on foreign goods were very high by international standards; to take one example, in the early 1960s, imported bicycles had a nominal tariff of 75 per cent and as late as 1990 just prior to the major reforms of 1991 the average tariff rate was around 80 per cent. However, the main form of protection initially was not through tariffs, but through quantitative controls on what could be imported. This operated through a licensing system that required licenses to access foreign currency and to import specific commodities. Firms were entitled to *actual user* licenses for goods they needed for production; however, only commodities deemed to meet the twin criteria of being essential and unavailable from domestic suppliers could be imported and even here there were normally quota limits on the physical quantities of such goods that could be brought into the country. This system was designed to allow the government to control tightly the limited amounts of foreign currency available by screening potential uses and potential users, whilst at the same time enforcing rigorously the aim of replacing imports by domestic production, since the criteria of *indigenous non-availability* meant that where domestic supplies were available imports of the same good were ruled out, regardless of whether the domestic alternative was acceptable in terms of cost or quality.

As with investment licensing, this form of control was also highly criticised. The fundamental point was that there was no guarantee that the most efficient users received the scarce resource of foreign currency. In practice foreign currency allocations between firms were often related to historic shares of past allocations or to installed capacity in a sector, restricting competition between firms. In addition, since all imports competing with domestic products were ruled out, this restricted supply in the domestic market pushing up domestic prices of these goods above the world market level and creating a major incentive for an expansion of their domestic production.

The Effective Rate of Protection measure discussed in Chapter 3 was used to estimate the incentives created by the combined effects of the import tariff and control system. Effective rates of protection (ERP) give the increase in a producer's value-added created by protection. In India, at the peak of the import control system in the 1960s, ERP rates were found to be very high partly because import tariffs on final goods were very much higher than tariffs on capital equipment and industrial intermediates and partly because the import control system by limiting access to imports pushed up the price of domestic import-competing goods very

Table 8.2 India protection: selected products 1962

Product	*Nominal rate of protection %*	*Total ERP %*
Bicycles	75	−272
Sewing machines	45	274
Electric fans	55	329
Plastics	20	341
Rubber and rubber manufactures	50	125
Textile machinery	15	583
Ships	20	277

Source: Bhagwati and Desai (1970, Table 17.2).

substantially (creating a large *tariff equivalent* effect). Table 8.2 gives some ERP estimates from the early 1960s; overall, the protective effect of the quota control system was found to be between three and four times greater than that of nominal import tariffs.

The ERP estimates in Table 8.2 reveal both very high and varied levels of protection showing how domestic firms benefited from both controls and tariffs. A figure of 329 per cent, for example, means that value added is more than three times what it would be in the absence of controls and tariffs. A negative figure is either due to major inefficiency, so without controls and tariffs, it is cheaper to import all the inputs needed for production than to import the final good itself, or to quirks in the data valuing key items incorrectly. The main charge against trade policy therefore was that it sheltered inefficient producers, whose costs were often well above world market levels (since competing imports were normally not allowed whatever the cost difference). Unlike the more successful practice of import substitution in East Asia (as discussed in Chapter 7) in India sheltered producers were not given a strong signal that breaking into export markets was both desirable and feasible.

A form of export incentive scheme was applied from the early 1960s both in terms refunds on import tariffs paid on inputs essential for export production, modest concessional rates of tax on profits from export sales and most importantly preferential access for exporters to the foreign currency needed to import items necessary for export production under an *import entitlement* programme. Exporters could import goods up to a proportion of the value of their export sales, with the proportion varying between products. This form of decontrol was clearly necessary if export production was to expand in a situation of an overall scarcity of foreign exchange, but the boost to exporters from these measures was only modest relative to the much larger stimulus to sell at highly distorted prices in the domestic market. Hence, much larger profits could be made selling domestically than exporting creating a strong bias against exports, which in large part explains the relatively weak performance of India's manufactured exports over a long period from the 1960s. Even currently in a quite different policy environment India's manufactured exports are still much lower on a per capita basis than in the successful East Asian economies.

Dismantling of the trade control system only commenced seriously in 1991 in response to a major crisis in the balance of payments and the need for India to seek IMF financial assistance to meet international debt obligations. Licensing for the import of most capital and intermediate goods was removed and most goods saw their import tariffs (i.e. their *nominal protection*) lowered substantially. The share of imports subject to quantitative restrictions fell from nearly 85 per cent in the late 1980s to 54 per cent in 1992–93 and 46 per cent in 1997–98.[4] Average import tariffs fell from 80 per cent in 1990 to around 30 per cent in 1997–98. As part of the reform package, the Indian Rupee was made convertible against other currencies and devalued significantly against the dollar, whilst at roughly the same time restrictions on investment by foreign firms in Indian manufacturing were eased. Both import and export trade grew rapidly in the 1990s in response to these changes. Since then as part of its commitments as a member of the WTO India has removed remaining quota barriers to trade, set maximum bound tariff rates and lowered overall protection. It is now a much more open economy than in previous decades (total foreign trade was 45 per cent of GDP in 2007 as compared with only 16 per cent in 1990), although its average level of protection is still relatively high by current standards of WTO members.

Overall, in 2006–07, the average tariff on imports to India from other WTO countries was around 15 per cent (as compared with 32 per cent in 2001–02) although when additional specific taxes are taken into account the average rise to nearly 18 per cent. This average masks a number of significant differences. Agriculture receives far more protection than manufacturing and a wide range of exemptions are allowed which means taxes collected as a share of import revenue are often well below the published tariff rates. Within manufacturing two areas – automobiles and textiles and clothing – remain relatively highly protected. In 2006–07, in the former, the average applied tariff was around 33 per cent and in the latter 22 per cent, compared with a manufacturing average of around 15 per cent. As further protection, imports of second-hand motor vehicles over three years of age are subject to licensing restrictions as well as a 100 per cent import tariff. In other important sectors there has been a rapid reduction of protection; for example, in steel average applied tariffs fell from over 33 per cent in 2001 02 to 7 per cent in 2006–07, although a higher rate of 20 per cent applies to imports of cheaper, low-quality, defective steel products or 'seconds'.[5]

India: manufacturing performance

In the initial three decades after Independence in 1947 India's growth record and particularly its record in terms of manufacturing was relatively disappointing. For example, Table 8.3 gives comparative growth rates for national income and registered manufacturing from the early 1950s to the mid-1960s for India and a number of other economies with relatively large manufacturing sectors. India's average annual manufacturing growth of around 5 per cent is well below Taiwan and over the full period only Argentina had a lower growth.

Table 8.3 Comparative growth 1950–1952 to 1964–1966: annual growth (%)

Country	*GDP at constant market prices*	*Manufacturing at constant market prices*
Argentina	3.2	4.4
Brazil	5.2	7.8
Mexico	6.1	7.6
India	3.7	4.9
Pakistan	3.8	8.2
Philippines	5.6	9.5
Taiwan	8.3	13.5

Source: Little *et al.* (1970, Table 2.11).

The period from the later 1960s onwards did see an improvement in growth but not at the dramatic rates of increase recorded in the East Asian NIEs. For example, in the East Asian NIEs income per head increased by between 5 and 7 per cent annually 1965–95, whilst in India the increase was little more than 2 per cent.[6] Part of the reason for this slower income growth was the relatively modest increase in Indian manufacturing. Table 8.4 gives the trend rate of growth of the registered manufacturing sector (i.e. excluding small, unregistered firms who dominate in terms of employment) from 1971–2003 based on data from the Annual Survey of Industries. The bottom row of the table shows how this trend growth has changed since 1992 after the major liberalisation reform of 1991.

Over the full period, manufacturing grew by 6 per cent annually, which is historically a respectable rate for the country, but is not high by the standards set by the East Asian NIEs and China (China's manufacturing sector grew at double this annual rate for the period 1990–2005). It is significant that in India growth followed a relatively capital intensive path with employment creation little more than 1 per cent annually and capital stock growing by more than value added. The share of manufacturing in GDP has remained constant and relatively low at around 15 per cent over the whole period post-1991 (see Table 8.5). International comparisons suggest that allowing for India's income and population size its share of manufacturing in GDP is lower than what would be expected (in the same comparison that of China is much higher than expected).[7] What is particularly distinctive about the India growth experience is that the share of services in GDP is much higher than expected; reaching nearly 50 per cent in 2000, as compared with 38 per cent in 1980. It is for this reason that recent growth in India is often described as led by services rather than by manufacturing (in contrast to the theory examined in Chapter 2 and the current experience of China where as discussed in the following section manufacturing has played the leading role). At the level of individual states some of the fastest growing have seen a declining share of manufacturing, as dynamic, skill-intensive service activities like computing, software and telecommunications have grown rapidly.

Within manufacturing, international comparisons suggest that allowing again for its income level and size India has a distinctive focus on skill and capital-intensive industries. Thus, whilst countries at its income level might be expected to have a concentration on unskilled labour-intensive activity, this specialisation is not found for India. This is usually explained by the history of the economy with the early focus on public sector investment in heavy capital-intensive industry and the major investment in university, college and technical education. For example, on a per student basis India has spent considerably more on tertiary education than many other comparable countries, including China.[8]

Two periods are usually highlighted as turning points in recent economic history. The first is in the early 1980s as the newly re-elected Congress Party attempted to re-establish its credibility with the private sector with the removal of price controls, the lowering of corporate taxes and in 1985 the start of the dismantling of the licensing control system. This reform was only partial (approximately 40 per cent of manufacturing output was de-licensed and firms were given more flexibility in switching production within broad product lines) and trade protection remained high (the average tariff over the 1980s was around 150 per cent). These were not major reforms and they have been described as a *pro-business* rather than *pro-market* shift since essentially they granted greater freedom to existing firms, whilst keeping barriers to foreign trade and continuing to restrict new entrants into manufacturing. However, there is evidence that the protected manufacturing sector responded positively to the new freedom increasing the growth of both output and productivity. In the registered manufacturing sector, the growth of simple labour productivity was roughly three times higher in the 1980s than in the previous two decades and within the country, states with the highest share of manufacturing in total activity grew fastest.[9]

The other turning point is the major liberalisation of 1991, when the majority of manufacturing output was de-licensed and trade barriers were lowered. Although this is conventionally highlighted as the key turning point Table 8.4 shows that this can be exaggerated. The increase in trend growth in manufacturing whilst statistically significant is modest at half a percentage point. There was a slightly higher increase in investment with the growth of the capital stock 0.8 percentage points higher; however, the increase in the number of factories slowed and there was no statistically significant impact on employment growth, which was low. Furthermore, manufacturing growth in the post 1991 period has

Table 8.4 India: trend growth in manufacturing 1973–2003 (%)

	Manufacturing value-added	*Capital stock*	*Number of factories*	*Employment*
Trend growth 1973–2003	6.0	7.3	2.7	1.3
Post-1992 additional growth	0.5	0.8	−0.4	0

Source: Gupta *et al.* (2008, Table 1).

Note

Calculated from the equation $lnY = a + b_1T + b_2D$, where Y is the variable of interest, ln is natural log, T is time in years and D is a dummy for years post-1992. The time trend growth is b_1 and the post-1991 effect is b_2.

Table 8.5 India: manufacturing and GDP annual growth (%)

Year	*Growth of GDP*	*Growth of manufacturing*	*Growth of services*	*Manufacturing share in GDP*
1991	1.4	−2.5	4.6	14.4
1992	5.4	3.1	5.7	14.1
1993	5.7	8.6	7.2	14.5
1994	6.4	10.8	5.9	15.1
1995	7.3	15.5	10.1	16.2
1996	8.0	9.5	7.6	16.4
1997	4.3	0.04	8.8	15.8
1998	6.7	3.1	8.3	15.2
1999	6.4	3.2	9.5	14.8
2000	4.4	7.8	5.7	15.3
2001	5.8	2.5	7.2	14.8
2002	3.8	6.8	7.5	15.2
2003	8.5	6.6	8.5	15.0
2004	7.4	8.6	9.1	15.1
2005	9.4	9.0	10.3	15.1
2006	9.6	12.0	11.1	15.4
2007	8.7	9.4	10.7	15.5

Source: Calculated from national accounts data on the ADB India website; see www.adb.org.

been erratic. After the economic crisis of 1991 when manufacturing declined by about 2.5 per cent in that year, it rebounded strongly for the next three years with annual growth peaking at 16 per cent in 1995. However, growth decelerated in the next few years only starting to improve consistently after 2001 (see Table 8.5).

Productivity performance which improved significantly in the 1980s continued to improve after 1991 and there is evidence that the private sector firms exposed to the greatest reductions in protection experienced the greatest boost to productivity (although the same is not found for public sector firms). Overall, over the period 1989–96, for manufacturing in general, a decrease of 10 per cent in import tariffs is found to lead to an increase in trend total factor productivity growth of about 0.5 per cent.[10]

Indian manufacturing: what challenges remain?

The relatively capital and skill-intensive growth path that manufacturing is following has created relatively few jobs, but it has allowed the economy to upgrade its production structure and move into the export of relatively sophisticated manufactures, such as pharmaceuticals and specialist engineering products, although textiles and clothing are still by far the largest manufactured exports. However, despite its skill base, and the introduction of Special Economic Zones as part of a much more welcoming attitude towards foreign investors, India has been largely left out of the expansion of global production networks, particularly in the area of electronics. The contrast with China is stark; electrical equipment was 10 per cent of China's total exports in 2004 as compared with 2 per cent in India and whilst

China accounted for around 15 per cent of world exports of office machines and telecommunications equipment, India accounted for less than 1 per cent.

Nonetheless, Indian manufacturing has made considerable progress and with a large and growing domestic market confidence in Indian manufacturing is relatively high. Indian firms are also emerging as foreign investors in developed country markets (see Box 8.2). However, observers have pointed to a number of obstacles holding back manufacturing, of which most attention has been given to the labour laws, referred to earlier, and the quality of infrastructure, particularly in terms of road and rail links, ports and power supplies. A key argument is that more jobs would be created and the economy would be able to produce and export more labour-intensive products if the labour laws were amended to make it easier to both hire and dismiss workers. This would allow India to shift closer to the East Asian growth path where as we have discussed in Chapter 7 initially labour-intensive manufactured exports played a key role in industrialisation.

Recent formal analyses of these issues have utilised the fact that different states in the country have different quality of infrastructure and have amended and interpreted labour legislation in different ways. This allows an analysis across industries, states and time of how performance is affected by indicators that aim to capture the effect of labour legislation and infrastructure quality. In terms of the labour market the conclusion must be tentative because of measurement difficulties but the implication drawn by several researchers is that labour legislation has indeed held back manufacturing expansion, employment and productivity growth in the sense that in states where the legislation is interpreted in a less restrictive (i.e. *pro-employer*) manner the policy reforms of de-licensing and trade liberalisation have a stronger positive impact than in states where a restrictive (*pro-employee*) stance is taken. De-licensing in states with restrictive labour legislation can even reduce manufacturing output, relative to what it would have been without the reform. As noted before, there is an active debate on whether the labour laws are a real constraint on the freedom of firms in relation to employment (e.g. whether they can be evaded by using contract workers), and it is not always obvious how some states should be classified in terms of their interpretation of the laws, so the issue remains open.[11]

The infrastructure issue is less controversial. In terms of output and employment growth, infrastructure-intensive industries (where the share of infrastructure in total cost is higher than the average) are found to respond less to de-licensing, than the non-infrastructure intensive industries. The development expenditure of state governments also appears to have a positive role in improving performance (and in one analysis is the single biggest influence on performance). This includes not just spending on physical infrastructure, but also state government health and education expenditure.[12] This confirms not just the importance of infrastructure but also more general government support for industry. One of the key issues facing the government is therefore how best to provide a supportive environment, whether through further legislative labour market reform to introduce greater employer flexibility or through infrastructure and education expenditure.

Box 8.2 Changing industrial geography: buying into the heartland

India' s largest automobile company Tata Motors, which is part of the conglomerate Tata group, has made serious progress into the industrial heartland of developed economies and has become a global company. Tata Motors was established in 1945 and its first vehicle entered the domestic market in 1954. The Tata group has bought Corus steel in the United Kingdom (descendant of the once nationally owned and world-renowned British Steel Corporation) and in 2008, it entered the UK automobile market by purchasing the elite brands of Jaguar and Land Rover. In India, it has a joint venture with the Fiat group to both produce and market Fiat cars in India and has subsidiaries and associate companies in the United Kingdom, Korea, Thailand, Brazil and Spain. In 2005, it purchased Korea's largest truck maker Daewoo Commercial Vehicles, which has now become Tata Daewoo. In 2005, it acquired a 21 per cent equity stake in a Spanish bus and coach manufacturer, with an option to acquire the remaining shares. In 2006, it formed a joint venture with Marcopolo of Brazil to build buses and coaches for India and other markets and also with Thornburi Automotive Assembly Plant of Thailand to manufacture Tata pickup trucks in Thailand. The company has an active R and D programme with three centres in India and separate R and D centres in the United Kingdom, Korea and Spain. It developed both India's first indigenously designed Sports Utility Vehicle and passenger car (Tata Indica) in 1998 and in 2005, it launched the first indigenously developed mini truck (Tata Ace). In 2009, the Tata Nano, aimed to be the world's cheapest car for a mass, relatively low-income market was launched. It has a vast potential market in India and elsewhere, including China, and represents a product with developing country characteristics designed for other developing countries.

On a smaller scale, but highly symbolic, when General Motors of Detroit, once one of the world's Big Two automakers with Ford, filed for bankruptcy in 2009 it was able to sell a small part of its jeep operations – the production of the Hummer. The buyer was what the Financial Times described as a 'previously unknown Chinese firm' from Sichuan province, Sichuan Tengzhong Heavy Industrial Machinery. The Chinese firm purchased the designs for the vehicle, a network of dealerships and its brand name. It is not clear where the vehicle will be manufactured, whether in China or elsewhere, but significantly General Motors is seen as having changed from 'the most successful company in world history' in the 1950s to 'a failing giant … stumbling towards oblivion' (*Financial Times*, 2 June, 2009).

Re-emergence of China

China and India are often compared because of their large size in land area and population, and their very low incomes per capita when their development initiatives commenced in the post-1945 period; in India's case after independence from Britain in 1947, and in China's with the final success of the revolution that brought the Chinese Communist party to power in 1949. China in the mid-twentieth century was a particularly poor country. Although comparisons of income levels across countries and times are highly uncertain the available evidence suggests that China's income per capita was about 10 per cent less than that of India in the early post-1945 period and perhaps as much as 30 per cent below the African average (with all estimates in prices of the same base year). In terms of historical comparisons, it was also well below that of Japan in 1870 at the start of its modernisation and less than half that of Russia on the eve of the Bolshevik Revolution (see Table 8.6). It was also much poorer than the East Asian NIEs discussed in Chapter 7.

China was not always so poor in relation to other countries and in one sense what we are witnessing today is a re-emergence of the country in the world economy. A similar (although even more uncertain) comparison found that in 1500 China's income per capita was roughly on a par with that of the United Kingdom although 300 years later, by the beginning of the nineteenth century, Chinese income had stagnated and that of the United Kingdom had more than doubled (see also Table 8.1).[13]

However, in the post-1949 period, official statistics show that China's income growth has significantly outpaced that of India, so that currently China's income per capita is more than twice that of India using market exchange rates and almost twice using purchasing power parity exchange rates. Although there is some dispute about the accuracy of some of the Chinese data (e.g. some argue that physical measures like power usage have not changed as rapidly as would be expected from the income growth figures) the substantial achievements of the Chinese economy are widely recognised. Industry and particularly manufacturing has played a key role. Unlike in India, as noted in the preceding section, manufacturing as a

Table 8.6 Income per capita in 1990 US dollars

Country	*Year*	*GDP per capita US$ 1990*
China	1952	537
India	1952	629
Korea (South)	1953	1072
Taiwan	1953	1142
Japan	1970	737
England and Wales	1801	2,006
Russia	1913	1488
Africa (average)	1950	852

Source: Maddison (2001) and Maddison (2006).

share of national income is significantly higher than would be expected for a country of China's income level and population (and conversely the share of services is lower than expected). Manufactures now dominate China's exports and since the 1990s large amounts of foreign investment have flowed to the country predominantly into manufacturing with foreign firms accounting for over half of manufactured exports. Job creation in rural industry has been a particular feature of the industrialisation process in China in a pattern of rural-based industrialisation unmatched elsewhere.

China industrialisation strategy: the Maoist years (1949–76)

The decades prior to the Revolution had seen little in the way of development and the Chinese Communist Party (CCP) led by its Chairman Mao Zedong saw industrialisation as the key route to modernity, in what was then chiefly an agrarian economy. Critical to its thinking was both the experiences of the Soviet Union and the need to use industrialisation for defence purposes. In economic terms, the case for giving priority to heavy industry (producer goods), as opposed to light industry (consumer goods) followed the logic of the Mahanalobis model discussed in Box 8.1 earlier, and also matched Soviet experience. However, defence priorities, arising from a concern initially over an attack from the capitalist countries (and latterly from the Soviet Union), required that the country produce its own weaponry. They also influenced the location of much of the new heavy industry plants, which were sited away from the coastal regions, as the latter were perceived as more vulnerable to attack. Location priorities in the 1950s were initially in the central region (the so-called *Second Front*) and in the 1960s priority shifted to the western region (the *Third Front*).

Although a significant proportion of industry was confiscated from the Japanese occupying government in 1945 and taken into public ownership, private ownership and investment in industry was allowed up to the mid-1950s. The big shift to nationalisation of private firms occurred in 1955 and 1956, so that by the latter year the private industrial sector had all but disappeared. The years 1955–56 saw a dramatic acceleration of social change culminating in 1957 with the *Great Leap Forward* programme, which was aimed principally at establishing large-scale collective farms (later termed *communes*) as means of modernising agriculture. The industrial side of this plan was to divert rural labour from farming and use it to make producer goods, predominantly iron and steel products in 'backyard furnaces'. The overall programme is now widely recognised as a highly serious policy error with the rural reorganisation contributing to falling grain output, and subsequent famine, and the rural industrialisation producing only high-cost, low-quality products. The immediate reaction to this failure was to break up some of the larger communes into smaller production units, to allow small areas to be used as private plots and to reduce the scale of rural industrialisation.

Planning for industrialisation was characterised by the twin approach (*walking on two legs*) involving large-scale, predominately urban-based, state-owned enterprises alongside rural industrialisation based on relatively small-scale enterprises.

The former were subject to physical national plan targets and would sell their output at plan-determined prices. This central planning system was largely modelled on Soviet experience, with broadly similar results. It was a much tighter planning system than the Licence Raj in India, which could block initiatives, but was much less effective at stimulating them. In China, the investment rate was high, since the plan controlled the amount of consumer goods that were made available, and this allowed rapid growth in the sense of an increase in physical output at plan prices. Consumer choice was limited, since the plan determined what industrial goods were produced and technical change was very low, because there was very limited access to foreign technology and little incentive or scope for enterprises to experiment with new products or techniques.

On the other hand, in parallel in the 1960s and 1970s, there was a widespread programme of rural industrialisation based on relatively small-scale enterprises created and managed by county governments, and groups of producers (from communes and production brigades). This was designed to absorb rural surplus labour, without workers having to move to urban centres, and to provide inputs like farm machinery and fertiliser needed to raise the productivity of agriculture. By the end of the 1970s, it is estimated that about half of the industrial workforce were employed in these rural industries.[14] Although much of this rural industry was inefficient and high cost, arguably its development created a base of local skills in rural areas. When fiscal decentralisation was introduced in the early 1980s, local governments were allowed to keep a substantial share of the profits of rural enterprises and this incentive effect, combined with the existing skills base, provides a plausible explanation for the very rapid growth of rural industry in the 1980s and 1990s, with the enterprises renamed *Township and Village Enterprises* (TVEs).

China: industrialisation under market socialism (1978–96)

In the post-Mao era, when Deng Xiaoping became President a new strategy evolved gradually, shifting to a more economically decentralised and liberalised system, whilst initially retaining a large and dominant industrial public sector. The major reform came first in agriculture from 1978 onwards with the abandonment of the principles of collective farming and the move towards greater house hold cultivation for private sale (*the household responsibility system*). For industry restrictions on small private enterprise were lifted, so that from the early 1980s some TVEs and collectively owned enterprises were in practice owned by private individuals. Formal restrictions on private industrial ownership were lifted in 1984. Growth of employment and output in rural industry was very rapid, and it is estimated that for industrial TVEs output increased by as much as 24 per cent annually during 1978–2004, with over 100 million people employed in some sort of rural industry by the mid-1990s.[15]

For the large-scale state enterprise sector, some of the tight plan controls were lifted. Enterprises were allowed to retain a proportion of their profits and managers were given greater freedom in setting pay scales and bonuses and in taking strategic decisions on what to produce and how to produce it. Most critically, after a given production quota had been met enterprises were allowed to sell the remainder of their output at market-determined, not plan prices. This process was gradually extended so that by the mid-1990s the bulk of all sales (roughly 80 per cent for producer goods and 90 per cent for retail sales) were at market-determined prices.

In addition, steps were taken to attract foreign investors with the aim of both generating jobs and bringing in foreign technology and marketing links. The key move here was the establishment in 1979 and 1980 of four Special Economic Zones on the coast, close to Hong Kong, offering foreign investors access to imported inputs needed for production at prices free of import duties and holidays on profits taxes. At this stage, foreign investors were encouraged to establish joint ventures with state-owned firms, partly as a means of modernising the latter. These four zones were followed in 1984 by fourteen coastal cities, which were granted similar zones status. Several other zones followed, including in 1990 what is now the very large Pudong industrial zone outside Shanghai. This was significant since Shanghai was historically the centre of industry in China and the zone represented a conscious effort to widen the *opening-up* to the heartland of industry. Subsequent changes in the 1990s spread zone status to provincial capitals in non-coastal parts of the country in an effort to equalise benefits across the regions.

Although the definitions are hazy most estimates suggest that the state sector still dominated industry in the mid-1990s, despite the growth of small private companies and foreign investment (see Table 8.7). Hence, the transition away from a socialist development pattern was much more gradual in China than that in the Soviet Union and only really occurred post-1996. Deng Xiaopeng's use of the slogan, '*crossing the river by touching the stones*', is emblematic of this gradualism. However, by the mid-1990s, it appears that the limitations of much of the large-scale state industrial enterprises (manifested, for example, in declining recorded rates of profit and associated difficulties in making loan repayments) convinced the Communist Party leadership of the need for more radical change. This was to be based on a combination of more rapid opening-up to the world market and ownership reform and restructuring of the state sector and TVEs.

Table 8.7 Ownership structure of China's industrial output 1980–1996 (%)

	1980	*1989*	*1996*
Urban SOEs and COEs	89.0	72.2	40.2
Rural COEs	10.5	19.6	27.7
Private and household	0.5	4.8	15.5
Foreign	0	3.4	13.3
Shareholding enterprises	0	0	3.3

Source: Bramall (2009, Table 12.5).

Notes

SOE is state-owned enterprise; COE is collectively owned enterprise; Rural COEs are TVEs (some of whom were privately owned); Shareholding enterprises are state-owned.

The large-scale state enterprise sector was subject to mergers, closures and privatisation, in many cases to the enterprise managers (*insider privatisation*). The peripheral aspects of the enterprises' original activity (such as health clinics, schools, canteens and hotels that many large firms had owned and run previously) were either handed over to local governments or sold to private investors. Large numbers of workers no longer required by these enterprises were laid off and offered modest compensation payments. After 1998, the pace of change was rapid with the number of state-owned industrial enterprises halving between 1998 and 2004 from around 65,000 to below 32,000. There are various estimates of the numbers of workers laid off over this period with one as high as 27 million. Exactly how large this left the state industrial sector is difficult to establish due to definitional difficulties regarding what precisely constitutes a firm that remains in public as opposed to private ownership. However, most estimates suggest a figure of around one-third of formal industrial activity in 2005. Estimates of employment share are even lower at around 20 per cent.[16] For smaller, publicly owned enterprises, principally the TVEs and enterprises owned by local governments, experiments in privatisation started in some parts of the country in the early 1990s were allowed to spread nationally. The numbers employed in publicly owned TVEs fell by over 30 million between 1995 and 2003 with private investors taking over their business or absorbing their workers.

However, the state retained control over key aspects of industry, through a *national champion* policy of developing large state-owned industrial firms in what were perceived as critical technologically dynamic sectors subject to economies of scale, like electronics, pharmaceuticals and aerospace. These large firms were typically formed by mergers of existing state firms and received special financial support from the central government. Typically they were groups controlling a large number of subsidiary enterprises in a conglomerate structure. The number of such firms identified for this special treatment were 163 and whilst they have considerable managerial autonomy they are administered by the State Council, the key government technical body (broadly equivalent to the UK Cabinet Office). These national champions are distinct from the other large industrial groups which have been created from mergers of state-owned firms. Similarly, provincial governments have also sought to identify firms with dynamic potential for special treatment to develop provincially based firms as provincial champions. This policy of developing national or provincial champions clearly parallels some of the earlier industrial policy of the East Asian NIEs, discussed in Chapter 7 and the large groups have similarities with the *chaebol* of Korea. Hence, although public ownership of industry is now much less than in the mid-1990s, it is concentrated on large strategically important firms.[17]

China: opening up to trade and foreign investment

China in the Maoist period was never totally closed to foreign trade; however, it was not until well into the liberalisation introduced by Deng Xiaopeng that foreign trade started to become significant. Exports as a share of GDP were rarely more than 5 per cent over the period 1949–79. After that they rose steadily to about 12 per cent in 1991 and then accelerated rapidly during the 1990s as the outward looking strategy started to have an effect. At the time China joined the WTO in 2001 exports were around 20 per cent of GDP and they subsequently increased significantly to about 37 per cent in 2006. This latter export share is very high for a country of China's size and well above the comparable figures for other large, fast-growing economies like India (about 20 per cent), and Brazil (17 per cent). This disparity still holds when GDP data are recalculated at purchasing power parity exchange rates, although trade shares fall for all three countries.

The opening up to trade commenced in the early 1990s when the strategy was to promote manufactured exports, through the special zones around the coast with the import of capital equipment, raw materials and technology, but to keep the domestic market for consumer goods relatively protected. Table 8.8 gives estimates of average tariff rates (equivalent to nominal rates of protection) which show relatively high levels in the late 1980s and a gradual reduction in the 1990s leading up to WTO accession at the end of 2001. These estimates do not capture the effect of non-tariff controls, nor the impact of protection on value added, which would certainly have been very high for consumer goods (like automobiles, refrigerators and televisions). Nominal tariff protection on autos was over 120 per cent in the mid-1990s, for example, and effective protection would have been far higher.[18] In addition, during the 1990s local protection by provincial governments also became significant as a barrier to domestic trade within the country, as provincial governments tried to protect their local industries from the competition of producers based in other provinces.

The motives behind trade reform culminating in WTO accession were to both stimulate competition for domestic industry (and in this sense to reinforce the privatisation programme) and to make it easier to expand production for export. WTO membership offered the great attraction of guaranteeing Chinese exports entry to

Table 8.8 China: average import tariff rates (%) 1982–2003

Year	*Unweighted*	*Weighted*
1982	55.6	na
1988	43.7	na
1992	42.9	40.6
1994	36.3	35.5
1995	35.2	26.8
1996	23.6	22.6
1997	17.6	16.0
1998	17.5	15.7
2001	15.3	9.1
2002	12.3	6.4

Source: Prasad (2004).

Note
na is not available.

the markets of other members on the same terms as everyone else (*most-favoured nation status*). In practice because of the scale of Chinese exports they have been more subject to restrictions based on threats to domestic industry and the balance of payments than those of other countries. However, critically, prior to WTO membership, the most favoured nation status in the key US market was subject to annual approval by the US Congress and the Chinese government perceived this politically determined decision as a serious risk to the country's long-run export prospects. The great attraction of WTO membership was that it removed this risk.

As part of its negotiations on joining the WTO, China steadily reduced its import tariffs and quota controls so that by the time of accession these were already relatively low. At entry to the WTO, China committed to lowering import tariffs to an average of 9 per cent for industrial goods and 15 per cent for agricultural, as well as to removing import quota restrictions for all but exceptional circumstances. In addition to the standard membership terms (see Chapter 3), it also agreed to limit domestic subsidies to agriculture to 8.5 per cent of production value and to remove all agricultural export subsidies. Most of the modelling analyses done at the time predicted significant aggregate welfare gains for China from WTO accession (although potential losers amongst peasant farmers and laid off state enterprises workers were also identified) and broadly speaking this positive overall outcome has occurred.[19]

Export growth has been particularly noticeable. Not only have China's manufactured exports continued to grow very rapidly, but their composition has shifted away from labour-intensive simple technology items like clothing, footwear, textiles and toys (which were around 40 per cent of exports in the early 1990s) to more technologically sophisticated products, like computers, telecommunications equipment and electrical machinery. A majority of manufactured exports now come from foreign-owned firms based in the special economic zones. The net domestic value-added as a share of the export price of such goods is not always high, since much of the operations involve the processing or assembly of imported parts and components. This is a central part of the global production networks found in East Asia and as China typically exports the finished goods to the United States and Europe and imports the parts and components from other parts of East Asia, it has long-run trade surpluses with the former group and long-run trade deficits with the latter. Employment (and thus wage income) for large numbers of migrant workers has been the principal gain to the country from this activity.

China's rapid export growth has transformed its role in world trade from a peripheral exporter to a globally significant economy. Table 8.9 contrasts the shares of China and India in world manufactured exports. In 1980, overall China had a trade share in manufactures approximately 60 per cent greater than that of India, in 1990 its share was nearly four times that of India, whilst in 2004, it was roughly nine times; the gap for the more technologically sophisticated electronics category (office machines and telecommunications equipment) is particularly wide.

Table 8.9 China and India: shares in world exports (%)

	1980		*1990*		*2004*	
	China	*India*	*China*	*India*	*China*	*India*
Manufacturing	0.8	0.5	1.9	0.5	8.3	0.9
1. Iron and Steel	0.3	0.1	1.2	0.2	5.2	1.6
2. Chemicals	0.8	0.3	1.3	0.4	2.7	0.7
2.1 Pharmaceuticals	neg	neg	1.6	1.2	1.3	1.0
3. Office machines and telecommunications equipment	0.1	neg	1.0	0.8	15.2	0.6
4. Auto parts	neg	neg	0.1	0.1	0.7	0.1
5. Textiles	4.6	2.4	6.9	2.1	17.2	4.0
6. Clothing	4.0	1.7	8.9	2.3	24.0	2.9

Source: Yusuf *et al.* (2007, Table 2.1).

Note
Neg is negligible.

China: manufacturing performance

Comparable data to that in Table 8.5 on India are not available since Chinese national accounts do not distinguish clearly between industry and manufacturing (with the former including mining and utilities like electricity as well as manufactures). However, official statistics reported in Table 8.10 show a highly dynamic industry sector growing by around 12 per cent annually and taking an increasing share of national income. As noted already, cross-country comparisons suggest that both historically and currently China has a higher share of industry in GDP than that predicted by its income level and population size. Productivity data are problematic due to problems in the valuation of the capital stock and uncertainty over the labour force engaged in manufacturing. Although the data are uncertain, it appears that, as in India, employment growth in manufacturing did not increase to anything like the same extent as output. Official figures suggest only a very modest rise of 3.4 million extra workers employed in manufacturing between 1991 and 2003, which is no doubt to do with the restructuring and closure of many state-owned manufacturing enterprises.[20] Corrections to this data to account for the omission of workers from what was the TVE sector and migrant workers suggest total manufacturing employment in 2002 of 109 million (as compared with the official figures of 83 million), but still suggest the same trend of a slow overall growth with employment peaking at 130 million in 1996 and declining subsequently with the changes in ownership and restructuring.[21] However, in terms of the composition of manufacturing, the same study that found an unusually high share of value added from skill-intensive sectors in India found this to be much less the case in China. The share of unskilled labour activities has also declined in China over the 1990s (as reflected in the slow employment trends) but has done so from a much higher starting point than in India.[22]

Table 8.10 China: industry and GDP growth (%)

Year	*Growth of GDP*	*Growth of industry*	*Growth of services*	*Industry share in GDP*
1991	9.2	13.9	8.9	31.1
1992	14.2	21.2	12.4	33.0
1993	14.0	19.9	12.2	34.7
1994	13.1	18.4	11.1	36.5
1995	10.9	13.9	9.8	37.5
1996	10.0	12.1	9.4	38.4
1997	9.3	10.5	10.7	39.1
1998	7.8	8.9	8.4	35.3[a]
1999	7.6	8.1	9.3	39.8
2000	8.4	9.4	9.7	40.4
2001	8.3	8.4	10.3	40.5
2002	9.1	9.8	10.4	40.8
2003	10.0	12.7	9.5	41.9
2004	10.1	11.1	10.1	42.4
2005	10.4	11.7	10.5	42.9
2006	11.1	13.0	12.1	43.6
2007	11.9	13.4	12.6	44.2

Source: Calculated from national accounts data in ADB China website www.adb.org.

Note

a Date for 1998 seems entered incorrectly in original table.

With declining manufacturing employment from the mid-1990s and continued high growth of output, productivity must have been rising strongly, although there is uncertainty over the precise magnitude of the rise. Estimates by ownership category suggest that in the 1990s total factor productivity was growing considerably more slowly in state-owned enterprises than that in the foreign-owned sector or in the collectively owned sector, which provided a rationale for the privatisation of the late 1990s. However, estimates of overall productivity growth in industry suggest strong growth from the early 1990s onwards. One estimate puts this at as much as 6 per cent annually (1993–2004), which is high by historical standards and well above that of India, which is put at 1 per cent by the same study.[23]

The most tangible aspects of this performance has been the rapid expansion of China's trade share in the large and highly competitive markets of the United States and European Union, where a combination of productivity improvements, relatively low wages and a highly competitive (many argued undervalued) exchange rate with the US dollar saw China's share of trade increase substantially. Loss of market share in the United States, for example, has become a major factor for East Asian competitors in some of the higher-technology product ranges, particularly electronics, and for Mexico and the Central American economies in some of the more labour-intensive products. China is thus highly competitive in different product ranges (see Chapter 4).

In China, foreign direct investment is widely accepted as playing a leading role in both raising productivity and in breaking into export markets. Over half of manufactured exports now come from foreign-owned firms and estimates suggest foreign firms account for around 20 per cent of the employment in large industrial corporations.[24] Key concerns have been the extent to which these foreign firms have generated links with domestic suppliers to reduce their import content and the degree to which they influence the overall technological level of the economy either by their own research and development in China or through indirect spillovers, as local firms imitate and learn from their presence in the market. Much foreign investment activity remains import-intensive, particularly in the assembly-type operations (and this has been encouraged by the Special Economic Zones where inputs can be imported free of duty) and for China, as elsewhere, the evidence on significant positive technology spillovers from foreign investment is limited (see Chapter 5). This is partly due to its enclave nature being highly concentrated in the coastal regions and zones within these. The level of foreign investment per capita of population in the eastern coastal part of the country is many times higher than that in the central and western regions where levels of foreign investment remain very modest. However, some of the large transnational firms operating in China (like Alcatel, General Electric, Intel, Matsushita, Microsoft and Siemens) have established large research centres in China that work closely with their head office research institutes in part due to government pressure to raise their research effort in China.[25]

Chinese manufacturing and spatial imbalances

Given the dramatically high growth that has been achieved in the last two decades, it is perhaps surprising that the specialist literature on China has a lengthy list of economic challenges for the country. As noted in the foregoing sections, there is the need to integrate the large foreign-owned sector more fully into the economy through stronger domestic linkages and domestic R and D and the need to operate the remaining state-owned enterprises as internationally competitive firms. In addition, there is a key problem to be addressed in terms of the spatial balance of manufacturing within the country. In the Maoist-era, most industry was concentrated in the North East (in Manchuria) as the old industrial heartland of the economy, with a new wave of industrial activity introduced in the centre and west in the 1960s. The new foreign investment-driven export activity was set up in the eastern coastal regions thus creating a dichotomy between the old industrial bases dominated by state enterprises and new centres based around private ownership. Although this distinction has been reduced over recent years, it still remains a powerful factor and explains the large-scale migration of workers from the west and central regions to the new industrial centres in the east. The imbalance in regional incomes is in part due to this uneven spread of industry and has been a major pre-occupation of the government in recent years as part of the *develop the West* and *harmonious society* policies. Thus, whilst a significant part of the explanation for divergences in levels of manufacturing development across regions in China is historical, attention is being given to ways of improving the general business environment (*the investment climate*) in the more backward parts of the country.

Much empirical work has been conducted on regional growth. One strand of this literature uses the framework of a neoclassical growth model to test whether there has been income convergence across provinces; in other words whether there is evidence of catch-up with poorer provinces growing faster than richer provinces. The precise results vary between periods and the form of specification adopted with at least some studies finding evidence of convergence of income from the early reform in the late 1970s until the early 1990s, in particular as the relatively poorer eastern coastal provinces grew rapidly. In the more recent period since the early 1990s, with the opening up of trade and foreign investment, there has been clear divergence as a result of the rapid growth of the coastal provinces in the eastern region. Two possible factors to account for this more rapid growth in the eastern coastal region are the policy environment, based around the Special Economic Zones and other related incentives for foreign direct investment and the favoured geography of the coastal provinces with easy access to the coast and thus international trading networks and easy access to the overseas Chinese business communities in Hong Kong, and Taiwan.

The main attempt to disentangle these two effects finds both to have been important in explaining the growth of the coastal region with geographical factors, having a slower acting but slightly more important impact up to 1998. In this analysis, policy is captured by a crude scoring index determined by the type of zone in a province and the main geographical variable is the proportion of the population of a province living within 100 kilometres of the coast or a navigable river. Ownership of enterprises in a province also appears to have had an important impact on growth. The share of foreign-owned firms (what are termed *foreign invested enterprises*) in economic activity in a province appears to have had a positive growth effect either directly through its impact on efficiency or indirectly through externalities. Conversely, the share of state-owned enterprises (SOEs) in provincial activity appears to exert a negative effect, which may be in part due to their own inefficiencies, but in part also to the requirement over much of the period covered for banks to channel funds to SOEs at the expense of new forms of non-state enterprise. Foreign investment inflows are partly driven by the incentive system on offer to foreign investors and hence are correlated with the policy index referred to earlier.[26]

An important aspect of the investment climate that impacts on provincial growth has been shown to be the quality of provincial infrastructure, particularly roads and telecommunications. Infrastructure activities link provinces with the external sector and are a means of overcoming geographic barriers like distance to a port. In addition, they link provinces with each other and thus stimulate inter-province trade. It seems likely that foreign investment inflows across provinces will be influenced by a range of factors like geography, income, wage and education levels, as well as 'hard' (such as rail and road connections) and 'soft' (degree of government regulation, enforcement of legal rights, access to finance and corruption) infrastructure. These infrastructure dimensions form part of the overall investment climate that is now seen as a key factor in explaining investment levels (see Box 8.3). In summary, the consensus is that what matters for relative rates of provincial growth

Box 8.3 The investment climate across China: regional differences

A very detailed analysis of the investment climate across provinces is given in World Bank (2006). This analyses the results of a large survey of 12,000 firms across 100 cities in China (roughly looking at 100 firms per city). Data are collected on firm performance and aspects of the investment climate at the district level in terms of both the hard and soft infrastructure distinction. A range of different investment climate measures per city are constructed based on a combination of firms' responses and external sources. For example, an index of government efficiency is constructed based on four indicators obtained from firms – their effective tax burden (collected taxes over value-added), the share of entertainment and travel expenses in sales (used as proxy for payments for corruption), customs efficiency (days needed for goods to pass through customs) and time in days per year dealing with government bureaucracy, for example, in relation to tax administration, public security, and environmental, labour and social protection. Indicators of firm performance (total factor productivity growth in each firm or percentage of firms with foreign ownership) are explained in a regression model that includes a set of investment climate variables, as well as controls for firm and industry characteristics. An estimate of the quality of the investment climate across the 100 cities is found by identifying the gap between actual firm performance and what would be achieved in the hypothetical situation that for each individual investment climate variable, the city concerned achieved the investment climate standards of the city at the 90th percentile level. A ranking of cities can be obtained from the size of the predicted gains, with the larger the predicted gain the poorer the investment climate. The position of provinces can be derived from the data for cities within each province with considerable variation found across provinces by the two performance measures.

For example, the northeast and the northwest are areas that have been highlighted as having a poor investment climate that acts as a key disincentive for new manufacturing activity. This is illustrated with data from the World Bank survey. The northwest region is the place where the largest average number of days spent dealing with government officials is reported by firms (78 days). The average is lower in the northeast, but there the highest national figure of days spent with officials (86 days) is reported for high-value firms. The proxy indicator used to elicit information on corruption (the share travel and entertainment costs in sales) is higher in these two provinces than elsewhere, although the margin relative to other regions is not great. Very revealing in terms of the potential for private sector development are the results that these two regions have the lowest share of small private firms reporting that they have access to bank loans and the northwest has the highest share of small firms (10 per cent) reporting the expectation of having to make informal payments to access such loans. Finally, investor confidence in the future protection of their property rights was lowest of all regions in the northwest, followed by the northeast.

Source: World Bank (2006).

are openness to foreign investment and trade, ownership and by implication competition, the constraints imposed by provincial geography and various aspects of the investment climate covering both hard and soft infrastructure.

Conclusions: what can other countries learn from India and China?

China and India are very different countries although they share some similarities such as a very large population and land area, a large stock of well-educated people, and a successful and dynamic diaspora willing to invest in and generally retain links with their country of origin. They both started their economic development in the early 1950s with very low income levels and having undergone major political transformations; in India after a long period of colonial rule, and in China after occupation by a foreign power and a destructive civil war. Their size creates a much larger domestic market than in other low- and middle-income countries, and this allowed initial industrial development on the basis of import substitution with relatively high barriers to trade. However, size also creates its own problems in terms administering large geographical areas and in managing regional imbalances within the country.

A few of the stylised factors of this experience hint at possible lessons for others.

- The opening to the world market in both countries came in the 1990s after a long period of relatively inward looking industrial development commencing four decades earlier. During this time, production experience learnt in operating for the internal market was built up and could be applied effectively when market incentives changed.
- Part of the reason for this success, which was not found in Latin America for example, was the large education base of both economies which combined high skill and education levels with low wage and salary costs. In both countries, but particularly in China, the availability of scientists and engineers has encouraged international foreign-owned firms to undertake research and development within China rather than at sites in their home country.
- High growth of manufacturing was possible in what many see as still unsatisfactory institutional environments; in India this relates to restrictive labour market legislation and in China to the degree of bureaucratic interference and corruption. Hence, perceived ideal institutional environments are not necessarily required for rapid growth.
- Foreign direct investment has been an important catalyst for growth, although it remains a small part of total national investment. Both countries initially restricted inward foreign investment but shifted policy in the early 1990s. In China, most foreign direct investment has gone into manufacturing initially for export, but now also for domestic sales. In India, unlike China, a majority of foreign investment has been in financial markets as equity (*portfolio investment*) rather than as direct investment in physical assets of companies,

reflecting a more developed stock market in India. In addition, in India a higher proportion of direct foreign investment has been in services, rather than manufacturing. These trends largely explain India's much weaker links with global production networks.

- In both countries, job creation has lagged behind growth of manufacturing output reflecting a trend towards increased capital-intensity in production. This in part explains the fact that rapid manufacturing growth has been accompanied by rising inequality in national consumption in both countries, although more so in China than in India. Hence, rapid industrialisation has raised material wellbeing substantially, but in neither case has its pattern ensured an equitable distribution of the proceeds of growth.
- Finally, perhaps the main point is that two countries, which thirty years ago were seen as synonymous with underdevelopment, have undergone a major economic transformation, with manufacturing industry playing an important role. This banishes permanently the once prevalent notion that only a group of relatively small countries benefiting from favourable external conditions (the original four Tiger economies of Korea, Taiwan, Hong Kong and Singapore) have been able to sustain rapid rates of economic growth and undergo industrialisation.

Further reading

Bramall (2009) is a very useful recent work on the economy of China; similarly for recent work on India see McCartney (2009). On the impact of China and India on other countries, Winters and Yusuf (2007) give considerable detail, whilst Boardman (2007) focuses on the impact on sub-Saharan Africa. The special issue World Development (2008) reports detailed country and regional studies on the consequences of competition from China on trade and investment.

Notes

1 Industry and development

1 See UNIDO (2009, Table 10.4).
2 See UNIDO (2009, Figure 9.1).
3 See UNIDO (2009, Annex II, Table 4).
4 See UNCTAD (2000, Table 2 and Appendix III).
5 See Kaplinsky (2006).
6 See UNCTAD (2007a, Table 4.2.2); the data on East and Southeast Asia exclude China but include the first-tier NIEs (Korea, Taiwan, Hong Kong and Singapore). With the year 2000 set at 100 the commodity terms of trade for Africa rose from 99 in 1995 to 146 in 2006, whilst that for East and Southeast Asia fell from 107 to 89 over the same period.
7 Data come from WTO website; www.wto.org.
8 UNCTAD World Investment Report is the main source of data on foreign investment; see UNCTAD (2007b).
9 See Bramall (2009: 376).
10 Weiss (1990) discussed this approach in detail.
11 See Lin (2003).

2 Engine of growth

1 See, for example, Solow (1956).
2 See, for example, Chenery (1979). The S curve (technically a logistic curve) was initially demonstrated with data from the 1960s and early 1970s and was confirmed with more recent data in UNIDO (2005, Table 10.4).
3 See ADB (2007: 294–297). The equation used is

$$M = a + b_1 y + b_2 y^2 + b_3 T + b_4 P$$

where M is manufacturing share in GDP, y is income per capita, T is the share of export and imports in GDP, P is population, and all variables are in natural logarithms.

The expectation is that M will rise initially with income, but will turn down beyond a certain point and to capture this effect the square of income is also included with the expectation that its coefficient will be negative, which is confirmed by the data.
4 See ADB (2007: 293).
5 See UNCTAD (2003, Table 5.1).
6 For example, the preliminary results of Szirmai (2009) based on a large sample of countries with comparable data and looking at growth over five-year periods show

the coefficient on manufacturing share to be positive and significant. The coefficient on the service share is also positive but lower.

7 Rodrik (2006a) discusses the implications of the original work on growth and points to evidence that the manufacturing share in exports rises during such accelerations; ADB (2007: 297–303) finds that in Asia this result holds, if weakly, for its output share also.

8 Revealed comparative advantage is defined as the share of good j in the exports of country k, divided by the share of j in world trade. The higher is the ratio, the more specialised is country k in good j.

9 For example, in the OECD countries between 1971 and 1994, the growth of labour productivity in manufacturing (at 3 per cent annually) was nearly three times that of productivity growth in services (at 1.1 per cent); see Rowthorn and Ramaswamy (1997).

10 Manufacturing's share in GDP in the region fell by more than 10 percentage points from 28.2 to 17.8 per cent from 1980 to 2000 (UNCTAD 2003, Table 5.2).

11 See Pieper (2003).

12 This model comes from Thirlwall (1986).

13 See Bauer *et al.* (2008, Appendix 1).

14 The higher poverty figures are due to an upward revision of the cost of living in poor countries; see Chen and Ravallion (2008).

15 See Bauer *et al.* (2008: 8).

16 Dasgupta and Singh (2006: 14), for example, cite growth of informal manufacturing employment in India of nearly 3 per cent annually 1993–94 to 1999–2000 as compared with less than 1 per cent in the formal sector over the same period.

3 Trade and efficiency

1 Technically a non-traded activity is one where the domestic supply price is above the world market export price (so the goods cannot be exported competitively), but below the import price (so it can undercut imports).

2 This is in contrast with the increasing returns discussed in Chapter 2. When these are introduced, there will be full specialisation.

3 There is a large literature on testing for the impact of dynamic gains from trade; Rodriguez and Rodrik (2001) is the seminal work questioning the approach applied of linking trade openness and growth. Dollar and Kraay (2004) is one of the key examples on the other side of the debate.

4 Estimates come from Weiss (1988).

5 See Kim and Leipziger (1997, Table 3.1).

6 See Weiss (1984) for a discussion of the incentives in the early 1980s. Ten Kate (1992) covers the period of trade reform.

7 For example, the Mexican government is judged to have used export and local content targets effectively in its dealings with foreign investors in the automobile sector; see Ros (1994).

8 See Siphana (2005) cited in Weiss (2005).

9 See UNIDO (2009, Table 6.2).

10 Jayanthakumaran and Weiss (1997) conducted a cost–benefit comparison of zones in Sri Lanka comparing employment, tax and foreign exchange benefits with infrastructure costs and found modest returns to the national economy.

11 See Weiss (1999) for a survey of these and other studies on trade reform in Mexico.

12 See Hay (2001).

13 See Clerides *et al.* (1998); however, evidence from Africa suggests that learning by exporting stimulating productivity has been important, so there are regional variations between studies.

4 Globalisation and industrialisation

1 See Venables (2001).
2 Here, for simplicity, we treat non-traded inputs as traded inputs with a zero tariff and assume away the impact of tariffs, quotas and trade costs on their price. Similarly, this expression assumes no interaction between tariffs and trade costs, whereas in practice tariffs are typically imposed on *cif* values which will include trade costs; see Weiss (2007a) for further discussion.
3 Also, there is the issue of bias in estimating aggregate measures when using this approach, since the weights (*wi*) will reflect actual trade patterns that have been influenced by trade costs. Ideally, the weights should reflect the potential trade shares in the absence of trade costs (similar to the free trade input coefficients *aji* required in theory in Equation 3.5.
4 See Anderson and Wincoop (2004: 693) who argue that 'inferred border costs appear on average to dwarf the effect of tariff and non-tariff barriers'.
5 This example draws on Venables (2001); Weiss (2007b) expands the argument in the context of regional development.
6 Porter (1990) is the classic statement of this approach.
7 See World Bank (2005) for a general discussion; Boardman (2007) examines the investment climate in sub-Saharan Africa.
8 Lall *et al.* (2004) discuss the formation of networks in electronics and automobiles.
9 Again, this has been highlighted as a particular constraint in the African context; see Boardman (2007: 309)
10 The data are averages 2000–2006; see UNCTAD (2008a, Table 7).
11 These figures relate to 2005; see UNIDO (2009, Appendix B, Table 4).
12 See UNCTAD (2008b) Statistical annex, Table 5); in 2006, the respective shares are 8 and 14 per cent.
13 See Collier and Venables (2007) for an analysis of trade preferences for African economies under AGOA.
14 See Kaplinsky and Morris (2007).
15 The following discussion draws heavily on UNCTAD (2008a) and Bigsten and Soderbom (2006).
16 See Bigsten *et al.* (2004).
17 See Gereffi (2008).
18 Krugman (1994: 44) argues that 'competitiveness is a meaningless word when applied to national economies. Moreover, the obsession with competitiveness is both wrong and dangerous'; see also Krugman (1998).
19 See the discussion in Boardman (2007, Chapter 2).
20 Lall and Weiss (2005) discuss these adjustment issues in the context of Chinese competition for Latin American producers.
21 See Dimaran *et al.* (2007).
22 See Roland, Holst and Weiss (2004).
23 This result was found by Lall and Weiss (2005) and appears to have been broadly confirmed by more recent data; see the update for Mexico by Gallagher and Porzecanski (2007).
24 See Kaplinsky and Morris (2007).
25 The results of different studies testing for an effect of China in diverting foreign investment away from Latin America are reviewed in Jenkins *et al.* (2008).
26 This rise and then decline in emissions relative to GDP has been termed an *environmental Kuznets curve* in recognition of the same inverted U-shaped pattern identified by Simon Kuznets in relation to inequality and income. This interpretation has been challenged, however, with a consensus view emerging that whilst it may hold for some pollutants, it does not hold for all; see Perman *et al.* (2003: 38).

27 For example, Wheeler (2001) cites data on improvements in air quality in the 1990s in China, Brazil and Mexico.
28 These alternative explanations are discussed in depth in Copeland and Taylor (2004).
29 See Tol (2009) for a survey of approaches to the estimation of the social cost of carbon.
30 Stern (2007) discusses the options available for carbon pricing.
31 See Stern (2007).

5 Technology and industrialisation

1 An example of this redefinition in recent years is the innovation, introduced initially by Canon, of converting a camera into a computer with a lens.
2 This discussion draws heavily on UNCTAD (2006).
3 For a survey of alternatives see Archibugi and Coco (2004).
4 See Hobday (1995).
5 See Hobday (1995).
6 See Kaplinsky (1994).
7 Support to local auto part producers in Mexico from foreign firms is an example of this effect at work; see Ros (1994) for a discussion of industrial policy in the 1980s aimed at strengthening the auto sector in Mexico through controls over foreign investors.
8 See the surveys by Gorg and Greenaway (2004) and Saggi (2002).
9 Glass and Saggi (1998) argue that a wider gap leads to less spillover. Kokko *et al.* (1996) find evidence to support this for Uruguay, whilst for Indonesia Sjoholm (1999) finds the reverse, the larger the gap the greater the spillover.
10 For example, in 2002, the European Union set itself the target of reaching 3 per cent of GDP for R and D by 2010 as part of the Lisbon Treaty agenda.
11 Cited in Maloney and Rodriguez Clare (2007).
12 See Yusuf (2006).
13 See Amsden *et al.* (2001).
14 See Weiss (1986).
15 Weiss and Jalilian (2004) give comparative data on East Asia and Latin America in the 1980s and 1990s from the perspective of export growth.
16 See Pack (1987) who applies this choice of technology analysis to the textile sector.

6 Small-scale industry: sink or seedbed?

1 See Ayyagari *et al.* (2003) for the database and Beck *et al.* (2005) for a formal analysis of the link between SMEs and growth.
2 US Small Business Administration, cited in Fajnzylber *et al.* (2006).
3 The information from these surveys is summarised in Bigsten and Soderbom (2006).
4 Opportunity cost refers to the value of a resource in its alternative use (e.g. r is the return on investment elsewhere in the economy). Strictly for Equation 6.2 to hold there should be divisibility and constant product quality, so the same output could be produced by one large firm or a number of smaller firms.
5 See, for example, Little *et al.* (1987) who conduct this type of analysis for different firm sizes in several countries. They find that small firms are not always the least capital-intensive and that optimal firm size varies between countries.
6 See Tybout (2000).
7 However, what is small in the United States is defined in the statistics as any firm below 500 workers, and such firms are classed as large in most other countries. Large firms dominate in sectors with high R and D budgets such as pharmaceuticals and aircraft; see Audretsch (2002).
8 See Schmitz and Nadvi (1999).
9 See Berry *et al.* (2002).

7 Industrial policy and the East Asian miracle

1 See the theoretical models of Hausmann and Rodrik (2003) focusing on innovating externalities, and Murphy *et al.* (1989) focusing on demand co-ordination.
2 See Chang (2009a) and Rodrik (2007) for summaries of the case for and against industrial policy.
3 See World Bank (1993, Table 1.5).
4 See Kim and Leipziger (1997).
5 See the discussion in UNCTAD (1996), and Weiss (2005).
6 See Rodrik (1994).
7 See Borenzstein *et al.* (1998) for an analysis of foreign direct investment and growth; Jalilian and Weiss (2002) have an analysis of its role in growth in East Asia. In both analyses, the interaction of FDI and a measure of education attainment is a significant variable in explaining growth.
8 See Rodrik (1994).
9 See Alkuz (1999).
10 See Chang (2002).
11 In comparing Latin American and East Asian experience, Rodrik (2007) argues that whilst East Asian NIEs used both a 'carrot and stick' approach, in Latin America there was 'too much carrot and too few sticks'.
12 The following sections on country policies draw heavily on Weiss (2005).
13 At market exchange rates, Korea's income was little more than 5 per cent of that of the United States in the early 1970s; see Chang (2009b).
14 In relation to technological initiatives Hewlett Packard Singapore was given operational autonomy from its California headquarters and began modifying basic designs developed initially in the United States to develop a portable, relatively-low-cost printer suitable for the Asian market and subsequently exported from Singapore; see Amsden *et al.* (2001).
15 These were in the East Asian Miracle study, World Bank (1993).
16 See Smith (2000).
17 See Wade (1994).
18 See Kim and Lerpziger (1997).
19 See Noland and Pack (2003).
20 Hausmann *et al.* (2008) stress this process side of industrial policy.

8 Giants awakened: India and China

1 Data in this section come from Bhagwati and Desai (1970).
2 Key works setting out these critiques were Bhagwati and Desai (1970), Ahluwalia (1987) and Joshi and Little (1994).
3 The economic impact of this labour legislation across states has been tested empirically; see Besley and Burgess (2004).
4 See Topalova (2004, Table 1).
5 These data on import tariffs come from the India Country Review on the WTO website www.wto.org.
6 These figures come from ADB (1997).
7 Predicted shares are calculated from a cross-country regression, where manufacturing share is a function of GDP per capita, GDP per capita squared, foreign trade to GDP ratio and population: see ADB (2007: 294).
8 The specialisation on relatively capital-intensive activities is demonstrated in Kochar *et al.* (2006).
9 The information in this paragraph comes from Unel (2003) and Rodrik and Subramanian (2004).
10 See Topalova (2004).

11 Gupta *et al.* (2008) survey some of these results; see also Aghion *et al.* (2006).
12 See Gupta *et al.* (2008).
13 See Maddison (2006).
14 Bramall (2009) provides much of the data in this section.
15 See Bramall (2009: 406).
16 See Bramall (2009: 422–423).
17 See Nolan (2001) for a discussion of this national champion policy.
18 For more details see Prasad (2004) and Ianchovina and Martin (2003).
19 See Ianchovina and Martin (2003).
20 The official data series stops at 2003; see ADB Country website www.adb.org.
21 See Bramall (2009: 426).
22 See Kochar *et al.* (2006: 22).
23 Jefferson *et al.* (2003) give productivity estimates by ownership and institutional type. Bosworth and Collins (2007) give the aggregate estimates for industry.
24 See Bramall (2009: 426).
25 See Yusuf (2006: 152).
26 See Demurger *et al.* (2002).

Bibliography

ADB (2007) *Asian Development Outlook*, Asian Development Bank, Manila.

——— (1997) *Emerging Asia: Changes and Challenges*, Asian Development Bank, Manila.

Agarwala, R. (1983) 'Price distortions and growth in developing countries', *World Bank Staff Working Paper*, 575, World Bank, Washington D.C.

Aghion, P., R. Burgess, S. Redding and F. Zilibotti (2006) 'The unequal effects of liberalisation: evidence from dismantling the Licence Raj in India', *CEP Discussion Paper 728*, Centre for Economic Performance, LSE.

Ahluwalia, I. (1987) *Industrial Growth in India: Stagnation Since the Mid-Sixties*, Oxford University Press, Delhi.

Alkuz, Y. (1999) (editor) *East Asian Development: New Perspectives*, Frank Cass, London.

——— *Asia's Next Giant*, Oxford University Press, Oxford.

Amsden, A. (2001) *The Rise of the Rest: Challenges to the West from Late-Industrializing Economies*, Oxford University Press, New York.

Amsden, A., Tschang and A, Goto (2001) 'Do foreign companies conduct R and D in developing countries?' Asian Development Bank Institute, Working Paper 14, Tokyo, available at www.adti.org.

Anderson, J. and E. van Wincoop (2004) 'Trade costs', *Journal of Economic Literature*, 40, 11, 691–751.

Archibugi, D. and A. Coco (2004) 'A new indicator of technological capabilities for developed and developing countries', *World Development*, 32, 4, 629–654.

Audretsch, D. (1998) 'Agglomeration and the location of innovative activity', *Oxford Review of Economic Policy*, 14, 2, 18–29.

——— (2002) 'The dynamic role of small firms: evidence from the US', *Small Business Economics*, 18, 13–40.

Aw, Bee Yan (2002) 'Productivity dynamics of small and medium enterprises in Taiwan', *Small Business Economics*, 18, 69–84.

Ayyagari, M., T. Beck and A. Demirguc-Kunt (2003) 'Small and Medium Enterprises Across the Globe: a new database', *World Bank Policy Research Working Paper*, 3127, World Bank, Washington DC.

Balassa, B. (1982) *Industrial Strategies in Semi-Industrial Economies*, John Hopkins for the World Bank, Baltimore.

Bauer, A., R. Hasan, R. Magsombol and G. Wan (2008) 'The World Bank's new poverty data: implications for the Asian Development Bank', *ADB Sustainable Development Working Paper Series Number 2*, Asian Development Bank, Manila.

Beck, T., A. Demirguc-Kunt and R. Levine (2005) 'SMEs, growth and poverty: cross country evidence' *Journal of Economic Growth*, 10, 199–229.

Berry, A., E. Rodriguez and H. Sandee (2002) 'Firm and group dynamics in the small and medium enterprise sector in Indonesia', *Small Business Economics*, 18, 141–161.

Besley, T. and R. Burgess (2004) 'Can labour regulation hinder economic performance? Evidence from India', *Quarterly Journal of Economics*, 119, 1, 91–134.

Bhagwati, J. and P. Desai (1970) *India: Planning for Industrialisation*, OECD and Oxford University Press.

Bigsten, A. and M. Soderbom (2006) 'What have we learned from a decade of manufacturing enterprise surveys in Africa?', *World Bank Economic Review*, 21, 2, 241–265.

Bigsten, A., P. Collier, S. Dercon, M. Fafchamps, B. Gauthier, J. Gunning, A. Oduro, R. Oostendorp, C. Patillo, M. Soderbom, F. Teal and A. Zeufack (2004) 'Do African firms learn from exporting?' *Journal of Development Studies*, 40, 3, 115–141.

Blomstrom, M. and B. Hettne (1984) *Development Theory in Transition*, Zed Books, London

Boardman, H. (2007) *Africa's Silk Road: China and India's New Economic Frontier*, World Bank, Washington DC.

Borenzstein, E., J. de Gregorio and J. W. Lee (1998) 'How does foreign investment affect economic growth?', *Journal of International Economics*, 45, 115–135.

Bosworth, B. and S. Collins (2007) *Accounting for Growth: Comparing China and India*, Brookings Institute, mimeo www.brookings-edu.

Bramall, C. (2009) *Chinese Economic Development*, Routledge, London.

Chang, H-J. (2002) *Kicking Away the Ladder: Development Strategy in Historical Perspective*, Anthem Press.

——— (2009a) 'Industrial policy: can we go beyond an unproductive confrontation?', Plenary paper at World Bank ABCDE conference, Seoul, June.

——— (2009b) 'Should industrial policy in developing countries conform to comparative advantage or defy it?', *Development Policy Review*, 27, 5.

Chaudhuri, S. and M. Ravallion (2007) 'Partially awakened giants: uneven growth in China and India' in L. Winters and S. Yusuf (editors), *Dancing with Giants*, World Bank and Institute of Policy Studies, Singapore, Washington DC.

Chen, S. and M. Ravallion (2008) 'The developing world is poorer than we thought, but no less successful in the fight against poverty', *Policy Research Working Paper* 4703, World Bank, Washington DC.

Chenery, H. (1979) *Structural Change and Development Policy*, Oxford University Press for the World Bank, New York.

Clerides, S., S. Lach and J. Tybout (1998) 'Is learning by exporting important? Micro dynamic evidence from Colombia, Mexico and Morocco', *Quarterly Journal of Economics*, 113, 3, 903–947.

Collier, P. and A.Venables (2007) 'Rethinking trade preferences: how Africa can diversity its exports', *World Economy*, 30, 8.

Copeland, B. and M. S. Taylor (2004) 'Trade, growth and the environment', *Journal of Economic Literature*, 42, 1, 7–71.

Dasgupta, S. and A. Singh (2006) 'Manufacturing, services and premature de-industrialisation in developing countries: a Kaldorian empirical analysis', *Centre for Business Research, University of Cambridge Working Paper*, 32.

Dee, P., C. Findlay and R. Pomfret (2007) 'Trade facilitation: what, why, how, where and when?' in D. Brooks and J. Menon (editors) *Infrastructure and Trade in Asia*, Edward Elgar and the Asian Development Bank Institute, Cheltenham Brooks and Menon.

Deininger, K., S. Jin and M. Sur (2007) 'Sri Lanka's rural non-farm economy: removing the constraints to pro-poor growth', *World Development*, 35, 12, 2056–2078.

Demurger, S., J. Sachs, W. T. Woo, S. Bao and G. Chang (2002) 'The relative contributions of location and preferential policies in China's regional development: being in the right place and having the right incentives', *China Economic Review*, 13, 444–465.

Dimaran, B., E. Ianchovichina and W. Martin (2007) 'Competing With Giants: Who Wins and Who Loses?' in L. Alan Winters and S. Yusuf (editors) *Dancing With Giants: China, India and the Global Economy*, World Bank, Washington DC and Institute of Policy Studies, Singapore.

Dollar, D. and A. Kraay (2004) 'Trade, growth and poverty', *Economic Journal*, 114, F22–F49.

Fajnzylber, P., W. Maloney and G. Montes Rojas (2006) 'Micro-enterprise Dynamics in Developing Countries' *World Bank Economic Review*, 20, 3, 389–419.

Felipe, J., M. Leon-Ledesma, M. Lanzafame and G. Estrada (2007) 'Sectoral engines of growth in developing Asia: stylized facts and implications', *ERD Working Paper Series*, 107, Asian Development Bank, Manila.

Gallagher, K. and R. Porzecanski (2007) 'What a difference a few years makes: China and the competitiveness of Mexican exports', *Oxford Development Studies*, 35, 2, 219–223.

Gereffi, G. (2008) 'Development models and industrial upgrading in China and Mexico', *European Sociological Review*, 35, 1, 37–51.

Glass, A. and K. Saggi (1998) 'International technology transfer and the technology gap', *Journal of Development Economics*, 55, 2, 369–398.

Goldstein, A. (2002) 'The political economy of high-tech industries in developing countries: aerospace in Brazil, Indonesia and South Africa', *Cambridge Journal of Economics*, 26, 521–538.

Gorg, H. and D. Greenaway (2004) 'Much ado about nothing: do domestic firms really benefit from foreign direct investment?', *World Bank Research Observer*, 19, 2, 171–197.

Gupta, P., R. Hasan and U. Kumar (2008) 'What constrains Indian manufacturing?', *Asian Development Bank ERD Working Paper* 119, ADB, Manila.

Hausmann, R. and D. Rodrik (2003) 'Economic development as self-discovery', *Journal of Development Economics*, 72, December.

Hausmann, R. and B. Klinger (2006a) 'Structural transformation and patterns of comparative advantage in the product space', *CID Working Paper* 128, Centre for International Development, Harvard downloaded from www.cid.harvard.edu.

——— (2006b) 'South Africa's export predicament', *CID Working Paper* 129, Centre for International Development, Harvard downloaded from www.cid.harvard.edu.

Hausmann, R., J. Hwang and D. Rodrik (2007) 'What you export matters', *Journal of Economic Growth*, 12, 1, 1–25.

Hausmann, R., D. Rodrik and C. Sabel (2008) 'Reconfiguring industrial policy: a framework with an application to South Africa', *CID Working Paper* 168, Centre for International Development, Harvard downloaded from www.cid.harvard.edu/southafrica.

Hay, D. (2001) 'The post-1990 Brazilian trade liberalisation and the performance of large manufacturing firms: productivity, market share and profits', *Economic Journal*, 111, 620–641.

Hobday, M. (1995) 'East Asian late comer firms: learning the technology of electronics', *World Development*, 23, 7, 1171–1193.

Ianchovina, E. and W. Martin (2003) 'Economic impacts of China's accession to the World Trade Organisation', *World Bank Policy Research Working Paper*, 3053, World Bank, Washington DC.

Iqbal, F. and S. Urata (2002) 'Small firm dynamism in East Asia: an introductory overview', *Small Business Economics*, 18, 1–12.

Jalilian, H. and J. Weiss (2002) 'Foreign direct investment and poverty in the ASEAN region', *ASEAN Economic Bulletin*, 19, 3, 231–253.

Jayanthakumaran, K. and J. Weiss (1997) 'Export processing zones in Sri Lanka: a cost benefit appraisal', *Journal of International Development*, 9, 5, 727–737.

Jefferson, G., T. L., Rawksi, L. Wang and Y. Zheng (2003) 'Ownership, performance and innovation in China's large- and medium-sized industrial enterprise sector', *China Economic Review*, 14, 89–113.

Jenkins, R., E. Dussel Peters and M. Mequita (2008) 'The impact of China on Latin America and the Caribbean', *World Development*, 36, 2, 235–253.

Joshi, V. and I. Little (1994) *India: Macroeconomics and Political Economy 1964–1991*, World Bank, Washington DC.

Kaldor, N. (1966) *Causes of the Slow Rate of Economic Growth of the United Kingdom*, Inaugural Lecture, Cambridge.

——— (1967) *Strategic Factors in Economic Development*, Cornell University Press, Ithaca, New York.

Kaplinsky, R. (1994) *Easternization: the Spread of Japanese Management Techniques to Developing Countries*, Frank Cass, London.

——— (2006) 'Revisiting the revisited terms of trade: will China make a difference?', *World Development*, 34, 6, 981–995.

Kaplinsky, R. and M. Morris (2007) 'Do the Asian drivers undermine export-oriented industrialisation in SSA?', *World Development*, 36, 2, 254–273.

Kesidou, E. and H. Romjin (2008) 'Do local knowledge spillovers matter for development? An empirical study of Uruguay's software cluster', *World Development*, 36, 10, 2002–2028.

Kim, K. and D. Leipziger (1997) Korea: a case of government-led development' in D. Leipziger (editor) *Lessons from East Asia*, University of Maryland, Ann Arbor.

Kochar, K., U. Kumar and R. Rajan (2006) A. Subramanian and I. Tokatlidis 'India's pattern of development: what happened, what follows?', *IMF Working Paper* 2006, 22.

Kokko, A., R. Tansini and M. Zejan (1996) *Journal of Development Studies*, 32, 602–611.

Krueger, A. (1978) *Liberalisation Attempts and Consequences*, Ballinger for National Bureau of Economic Research, Cambridge, Mass.

Krugman, P. (1994) 'Competitiveness: a dangerous obsession', *Foreign Affairs*, 73, 2, 28–44.

——— (1998) 'What's new about economic geography?', *Oxford Review of Economic Policy*, 14, 2, 7–17.

Krugman, P. and M. Obstfeld (2003) *International Economics*, Addison Wesley, 6th edition.

Kuchiki, A. (2008) 'Industrial clustering and MNE mangement in East Asia: recent progress and prospects for the Asian Triangle' in M. Fujita, S. Kumagai and K. Nishikimi (editors) *Economic Integration in East Asia*, Edward Elgar and IDE-JETRO, Cheltenham.

Lall, S. (1992) 'Technological capabilities and industrialization', *World Development*, 20, 2, 165–186.

——— (2000) 'The technological structure and performance of developing country manufactured exports 1985–1998', *Oxford Development Studies*, 28, 337–369.

——— (2001) *Competiveness, Technology and Skills*, Edward Elgar, Cheltenham.

——— and M. Albaladejo (2004) 'China's Competitive Performance: a threat to East Asian manufactured exports', *World Development*, 32, 9, 1441–1486.

Lall, S., M. Albaladejo and J. Ziang (2004) 'Mapping fragmentation: electronics and automobiles in East Asia and Latin America', *Oxford Development Studies*, 32, 3, 407–432.

Lall, S. and J. Weiss (2005) China's competitive threat to Latin America: an analysis for 1990–2002, *Oxford Development Studies*, 33, 2, 163–194.

Lall, S., J. Weiss and J. Ziang (2006) 'The sophistication of exports: a new trade measure', *World Development*, 34, 2, 222–237.

Lewis, W. A. (1954) 'Economic development with unlimited supplies of labour', *Manchester School*, 22, 139–191.

Lin, J. (2003) 'Development strategy, viability and convergence', *Economic Development and Cultural Change*, 53, 2, 277–309.

——— (2009) 'Should industrial policy in developing countries conform to comparative advantage or defy it?', *Development Policy Review*, 27, 5, 483–502.

Little, I., D. Majumdar and J. Page (1987) *Small Manufacturing Enterprises: A Comparative Analysis of India and Other Economies*, Oxford University Press for the World Bank, New York.

Little, I., T. Scitovsky and M. Scott (1970) *Industry and Trade in Some Developing Countries*, Oxford University Press.

Maddison, A. (2001) *The World Economy: A Millenial Perspective*, OECD, Paris.

——— (2006) *World Population, GDP and per capita GDP 1–2003 AD*, at www.ggdc.net/Maddison.

Maloney, W. and A. Rodriguez Clare (2007) 'Innovation Shortfalls', *Policy Research Working Paper* 4283, World Bank, Washington DC.

McCartney, M. (2009) *India: the Political Economy of Growth, Stagnation and the State 1951–2007*, Routledge, London.

McCombie, J., N. Pugno and S. Bruno (2002) *Productivity Growth and Economic Performance: Essays on Verdoorn's Law*, Basingstoke, Palgrave.

Mensah, V., M. Tribe and J. Weiss (2007) 'The small-scale manufacturing sector in Ghana: a source of dynamism or of subsistence income?', *Journal of International Development*, 19, 253–273.

Montgomery, H. (2005) 'Meeting the double bottom line: the impact of the Khushhali Bank's microfinance lending in Pakistan', *Asian Development Bank Institute*, Tokyo.

Mulaga, G. and J. Weiss (1996) 'Trade reform and manufacturing performance in Malawi', *World Development*, 24, 7.

Murphy, K., A. Shleifer and R. Vishny (1989) 'Industrialization and the big push', *Journal of Political Economy*, 97, 5, 1003–1026.

Nelson, R. and H. Pack (1999) 'The Asian miracle and modern growth theory', *Economic Journal*, 109, 416–436.

Nolan, P. (2001) *China and the Global Economy*, Palgrave, London.

Noland, M. and H. Pack (2003) *Industrial Policy in an Era of Globalization*, Institute for International Economics, Washington DC.

Oyelaran-Oyeyinka, B. and R. Rasiah (2009) 'Rapid expansion with slow upgrading in Malaysia', Chapter 4 in *Uneven Paths to Development: innovation and learning in Asia and Africa*, Edward Elgar, Cheltenham.

Oxford Review of Economic Policy (1996) *Special Issue on competitiveness*, 12, 3.

Pack, H. (1987) *Productivity, Technology and Industrial Development: A Case Study in Textiles*, Oxford University Press for the World Bank, New York.

Perman, R. Ma. Yue, J. McGilvray and M. Common (2003) *Natural Resource and Environmental Economics*, Pearson-Addison Wesley, Harlow.

Pieper, U. (2003) 'Sectoral regularities of productivity growth in developing countries – a Kaldorian interpretation', *Cambridge Journal of Economics*, 27, 831–850.

Poncet, S. (2003) 'Measuring Chinese domestic and international integration', *China Economic Review*, 13, 444–465.

Porter, M. (1990) *The Competitive Advantage of Nations*, MacMillan, London.

Prasad, E. (2004) 'China's growth and integration into the world economy', *IMF Occasional Paper* 232, IMF, Washington DC.

Rock, M. and H. Bennett (2004) 'The comparative politics of corruption: accounting for the East Asian paradox in empirical studies of corruption, growth and investment', *World Development*, 32, 6.

Roda, J., M.P. Cadene, P. Guizol, L. Santoso, and A. Uzair Fauzan (2007) *Atlas of Wooden Furniture Industry in Jepara*, Indonesia, French Agricultural Research Centre for International Development, Montpellier, France and Centre for International Forestry Research, Bogor Barat, Indonesia; available at http://www.cifor.cgiar.org.

Rodriguez, F. and D. Rodrik (2001) 'Trade policy and economic growth: a skeptics guide to the cross-national evidence' in B. Bernanke and K. Rogoff (editors) *Macroeconomics Annual 2000*, MIT Press for National Bureau of Economic Research, Cambridge Mass; also available at www.ksg.harvard.edu/rodrik.

Rodrik, D. (1992) 'Closing the productivity gap: does trade liberalisation really help?' in G. Helleiner (editor) *Trade Policy, Industrialisation and Development: New Perspectives*, Clarendon Press, Oxford.

——— (1994) 'King Kong meets Godzilla: the World Bank and the East Asian Miracle' in *Lessons from the East Asian Experience*, Overseas Development Council, Washington DC.

——— (2006a) 'Industrial development: stylized facts and policies', mimeo Harvard www.ksg.harvard.edu/rodrik.

——— (2006b) 'What's so special about China's exports?', *China and the World Economy*, 14, 5.

——— (2007) 'Normalizing industrial policy', mimeo Harvard, www.ksg.harvard.edu/rodrik.

Rodrik, D. and A. Subramanian (2004) 'From Hindu growth to productivity surge: the mystery of the Indian growth transition', *IMF Staff Papers*, 52, 2, 193–228.

Roland Holst, D. and J. Weiss (2004) 'ASEAN and China: export rivals or partners in regional growth', *World Economy*, 27, 8.

Ros, J. (1994) 'Mexico's trade and industrialization experience since 1960' in G, Helleiner (editor) *Trade Policy and Industrialization in Turbulent Times*, Routledge, London.

Rowthorn, R. and R. Ramaswamy (1997) 'De-industrialisation: causes and implications', *IMF Working Paper*, 42, IMF, Washington DC.

Saggi, K. (2002) 'Trade, foreign direct investment and international technology transfer: a survey', *World Bank Research Observer*, 17, 2, 191–235.

Schmitz, H. and K. Nadvi (1999) 'Clustering and industrialization; introduction', *World Development*, 27, 9, 1503–1514.

Sjoholm, F. (1999) 'Technology gap, competition and spillovers from direct foreign investment: evidence from establishment data', *Journal of Development Studies*, 36, 1, 53–73.

Siphana (2005) 'Lessons from Cambodia's entry into the World Trade Organisation', *ADBI Policy Papers* 7, Asian Development Bank Institute, Tokyo.

Smith, H. (2000) *Industrial Policy in Taiwan and Korea in the 1980's*, Edward Elgar, Cheltenham

Solow, R. (1956) 'A contribution to the theory of economic growth', *Quarterly Journal of Economics*, 70, 65–94.

Stern, N. (2007) *The Economics of Climate Change: the Stern Review*, Cambridge University Press, Cambridge.

Stiglitz, J. (2002) *Globalization and its Discontents*, Norton, New York and London.

Stiglitz, J. and S. Yusuf (2001) (editors) *Rethinking the East Asian Miracle*, Oxford University Press, New York.

Szirmai, A. (2009) 'Industrialisation as an engine of growth in developing countries 1950–2005' paper presented at UNU-WIDER/UNU-MERIT/UNIDO Workshop Pathways to Industrialisation in the 21st Century: New Challenges and Emerging Paradigms, Maastricht, 22–23 October.

Ten Kate, A. (1992) 'Trade liberalization and economic stabilization in Mexico: lessons of experience', *World Development*, 20, 5.

Thirlwall, A. (1986) 'A general model of growth and development on Kaldorian lines', *Oxford Economic Papers*, 38, 2, 199–219.

Tol, R. (2009) 'The economic effects of climate change', *Journal of Economic Perspectives*, 23, 2.

Topalova, P. (2004) 'Trade liberalisation and firm productivity: the case of India', *IMF Working Paper* 04/28.

Tregenna, F. (2009) 'Characterising de-industrialisation: an analysis of changes in manufacturing employment and output internationally', *Cambridge Journal of Economics*, 33, 433–466.

Tybout, J. (1992) 'Linking trade and productivity: new research directions', *World Bank Economic Review*, 6, 2, 189–211.

——— (2000) 'Manufacturing firms in developing countries: how well do they do and why?', *Journal of Economic Literature*, 38, 1, 11–44.

UNCTAD (1996) *Trade and Development Report 1996*, United Nations Conference on Trade and Development, UN, New York and Geneva.

——— (2000a) *Trade and Development Report 2000*, United Nations Conference on Trade and Development UN, New York and Geneva.

——— (2000b) *World Investment Report 2000*, United Nations Conference on Trade and Development UN, New York and Geneva.

——— (2003) *Trade and Development Report 2003*, United Nations Conference on Trade and Development, UN, New York and Geneva.

——— (2005) *World Investment Report 2005*, United Nations Conference on Trade and Development UN, New York and Geneva.

——— (2006) *Least Developed Countries Report 2006: Developing Productive Capacities*, United Nations Conference on Trade and Development UN, New York and Geneva.

——— (2007a) *Handbook on Globalization UN*, United Nations Conference on Trade and Development UN New York and Geneva.

——— (2007b) *World Investment Report 2007*, United Nations Conference on Trade and Development UN, New York and Geneva.

——— (2008a) *Economic Development in Africa: Export Performance Following Trade Liberalisation: Some Patterns and Policy Perspectives*, United Nations Conference on Trade and Development, UN, New York and Geneva.

——— (2008b) *Least Developed Countries Report 2008*, United Nations Conference on Trade and Development, UN, New York and Geneva.

UNIDO (2005) *Industrial Development Report 2005*, United Nations Industrial Development Organisation, UN, New York.

——— (2009) *Industrial Development Report 2009*, United Nations Industrial Development Organisation UN, New York.

Unel, B. (2003) 'Productivity Trends in India's Manufacturing Sectors in the last Two Decades', *IMF Working Paper*, 22.

Venables, A. (2001) 'Trade, location and development: an overview of theory', paper prepared for the Patterns of Integration in the Global Economy Project, mimeo World Bank, Washington DC.

Wade, R. (1990) *Governing the Market*, Princetown University Press, Princetown.

——— (1994) 'Selective industrial policies in East Asia: is the East Asian Miracle right?' in *Lessons from the East Asian Experience*, Overseas Development Council, Washington DC.

Weiss, J. (1984) 'Alliance for Production: Mexico's incentives for private sector development', *World Development*, 12, 7, 723–742.

——— (1986) 'Japan's post-war protection policy: some implications for less developed countries', *Journal of Development Studies*, 22, 2, 385–406.

——— (1988) 'An application of the domestic resource cost ratio to Mexican manufacturing', *Industry and Development*, 29 UNIDO, Vienna.

——— (1990) *Industry in Developing Countries: Theory, Policy and Evidence*, Routledge, London.

——— (1999) 'Trade reform and manufacturing performance in Mexico: from import substitution to dramatic export growth', *Journal of Latin American Studies*, 31, 151–166.

——— (2002) *Industrialisation and Globalisation: Theory and Evidence from Developing Countries*, Routledge, London.

——— (2005) 'Export growth and industrial policy: lessons from the East Asian Miracle experience' mimeo Asian Development Institute, www.adbi.org.

——— (2007a) 'A framework for considering infrastructure in regional co-operation' in D. Brooks and J. Menon (editors) *Infrastructure and Trade in Asia*, Edward Elgar and the Asian Development Bank Institute, Cheltenham.

——— (2007b) 'Globalization, geography and regional policy' in H. Hill and A. Balisacan (editors) *The Dynamics of Regional Development: the Philippines in East Asia*, Ateneo de Manila University Press, Manila.

Weiss, J. and H. Jalilian (2004) 'Industrialisation in an age of globalisation: some comparisons between East and South East Asia and Latin America', *Oxford Development Studies*, 32, 2, 283–307.

Wheeler, D. (2001) 'Racing to the bottom: foreign investment and air pollution in developing countries', *Policy Research Working Paper* 2524, World Bank, Washington DC.

Winters, L. A. (2004) 'Trade liberalisation and economic performance: an overview', *Economic Journal*, 114, F4–F21.

Winters, L. A. and S. Yusuf (editors) (2007) *Dancing with Giants: China, India and the Global Economy*, World Bank and Institute of Policy Studies, Singapore, Washington DC.

Wolf, M. (2004) *Why Globalization Works*, Yale University press, New Haven Conn.

World Bank (1993) *The East Asian Miracle*, World Bank, Washington DC.

——— (2005) *World Development Report 2005*, World Bank, Washington DC.

——— (2006) *China: Governance, Investment Climate, and harmonious Society: competitiveness enhancement for 120 cities in China*, Report number 37759-CN, Poverty

Reduction and Economic Management, Financial and Private Sector Development Unit, East Asia and Pacific Region, October 8th.

——— (2007) *World Development Indicators 2007*, World Bank, Washington DC.

——— (2009) *World Development Report 2009*, World Bank, Washington, DC.

World Development (2008) *Special Issue on Competition from China*, 34, 6.

——— (1999) *Special Issue on Clusters*, 27, 9.

Yusuf, S. (2006) *Innovative East Asia: The Future of Growth*, World Bank, Washington DC.

Yusuf, S., K. Nabeshima and D. Perkins (2007) 'China and India reshape global industrial geography' in L. A.Winters and S. Yusuf (editors), *Dancing with Giants: China, India and the Global Economy*, World Bank and the Institute of Policy Studies, Singapore Washington DC.

Index

Bold page numbers indicate figures and tables.

For Product Safety Concerns and Information please contact our EU representative GPSR@taylorandfrancis.com Taylor & Francis Verlag GmbH, Kaufingerstraße 24, 80331 München, Germany

Batch number: 10725798

Printed by Printforce, the Netherlands